FROM RICE FIELDS TO KILLING FIELDS

Syracuse Studies in Geography
Don Mitchell, Tom Perreault, and Robert Wilson, *Series Advisers*

FROM RICE FIELDS

Nature, Life, and Labor under the Khmer Rouge

TO KILLING FIELDS

J A M E S   A .   T Y N E R

Syracuse University Press

∞ The paper used in this publication meets the minimum requirements
of the American National Standard for Information Sciences—Permanence
of Paper for Printed Library Materials, ANSI Z39.48-1992.

For a listing of books published and distributed by Syracuse University Press,
visit www.SyracuseUniversityPress.syr.edu.

ISBN: 978-0-8156-3556-7 (hardcover)
978-0-8156-3541-3 (paperback)
978-0-8156-5422-3 (e-book)

Library of Congress Cataloging-in-Publication Data

Names: Tyner, James A., 1966– author.
Title: From rice fields to killing fields : nature, life, and labor under the Khmer Rouge / James A. Tyner.
Description: First edition. | [Syracuse, New York] : Syracuse University Press, 2017. |
Series: Syracuse studies in geography | Includes bibliographical references and index.
Identifiers: LCCN 2017030992 (print) | LCCN 2017032597 (ebook) |
ISBN 9780815654223 (e-book) | ISBN 9780815635567 | ISBN 9780815635567 (hardcover : alk. paper) |
ISBN 9780815635413 (pbk. : alk. paper) | ISBN 9780815654223 (e-book)
Subjects: LCSH: Cambodia—Politics and government—1975-1979. | Parti communiste du
Kampuchea. | Communism—Cambodia. | Political violence—Cambodia—History—20th century.
Classification: LCC DS554.8 (ebook) | LCC DS554.8 .T95 2017 (print) | DDC 959.604/2—dc23
LC record available at https://lccn.loc.gov/2017030992

To the memory of those who died,
and to those who continue to endure
the legacy of war in Cambodia

Contents

List of Illustrations • *ix*

Preface • *xi*

Acknowledgments • *xxiii*

1. A Critique of Khmer Rouge Political Economy • *1*

2. Revolution • *20*

3. Reconstruction • *59*

4. Production • *98*

5. Manufacturing Indifference • *135*

6. Abolishment and Reproduction • *160*

7. Dead Labor • *187*

Notes • *199*

Bibliography • *223*

Index • *237*

Illustrations

1. President Richard Nixon   •   *52*

2. Map of American bombing of Cambodia   •   *54*

3. CPK leaders riding on a train   •   *81*

4. Provincial and zone-level boundaries   •   *87*

5. Forced laborers constructing irrigation canal   •   *109*

6. Khmer Rouge cadre harvesting rice   •   *115*

7. Khmer Rouge cadre threshing rice   •   *127*

8. Khmer Rouge women's unit collecting rice   •   *128*

9. Khmer Rouge children learning about harvesting   •   *133*

10. Ieng Thirith visiting forced-labor camp   •   *155*

11. A Khmer Rouge wedding   •   *163*

Preface

Between 1975 and 1979, the Communist Party of Kampuchea (CPK), also known as the Khmer Rouge, fundamentally transformed the social, economic, political, and natural landscape of Cambodia. During this time, as many as two million Cambodians died from exposure, disease, and starvation or were executed at the hands of the party.

The dominant interpretation, known as the Standard Total View, of Cambodian history during this period presents the CPK as a totalitarian, communist, and autarkic regime seeking to reorganize Cambodian society around a primitive, agrarian political economy.[1] Under the STV, the victims of the regime died as a result of misguided economic policies, a draconian security apparatus, and the central leadership's fanatical belief in the creation of a utopian, communist society. In short, according to the STV, Democratic Kampuchea, as Cambodia was renamed, constituted an isolated, completely self-reliant prison state. This present work disrupts the standard narrative and provides a documentary-based Marxist interpretation of the political economy of Democratic Kampuchea.

In *The German Ideology*, Marx and Engels famously write, "It is not consciousness that determines life, but life that determines consciousness." My reading of CPK policy suggests that Pol Pot and other high-ranking CPK officials most likely internalized this statement, for it is my argument that the CPK recognized that political consciousness was related to a particular production of nature and, specifically, of precise laboring activities that would transform nature into value. Indeed, party documents indicate that another famous Marxist maxim appears to have been internalized. In his *Theses on Feuerbach*, Marx declared that philosophers had only interpreted the world, while the point is to change it. Marx's statement was in part a critique of idealism, that concrete action is required as opposed to idealist thinking. In a report prepared by the CPK in December 1976, it was stated, "We have not relied on theory. We have acted clearly."[2]

The CPK is disingenuous, for they most assuredly did rely on theory. Indeed, a careful review of Khmer Rouge documents illustrates a sustained, although superficial, engagement with Marxist political philosophy. In September 1977, for example, Pol Pot, secretary-general of the CPK, delivered a long-winded speech that appears on the surface as an amateurish amalgamation of Marx's *The Class Struggle in France* and Stalin's *Dialectical and Historical Materialism*. Cambodia's history, according to Pol Pot, passed through a series of stages: primitive accumulation, slavery, feudalism, and capitalism. This sequence, of course, imitates Stalin's vulgar caricature of Marx and Engels's materialist approach to history articulated most clearly in *The German Ideology*.

Cambodia's communist revolution, according to Pol Pot, arose from the ashes of discontent, a pervasive socioeconomic malaise that included landlessness, usury, and rampant exploitation. Simultaneously a movement against imperialism and the tyranny of a weak monarchy, the Khmer Rouge, Pol Pot claimed, achieved victory single-handedly, that it was the perseverance and tenacity—the sheer will—of the revolutionaries that defeated the combined forces of the former republic and its imperial handlers, the French and the Americans.

As a historical record, the speech is pure propaganda. Indeed, previous scholarship has thoroughly and convincingly critiqued the "scientific" and "objective" analyses purportedly provided by Pol Pot, and I have no intention of replicating these studies.[3] My concern, rather, focuses on the theoretical foundation of Pol Pot's argument and, by extension, how it informs our understanding of CPK policy and practice. In other words, I am less concerned with assessing the validity of Pol Pot's conclusions than I am with his epistemology. I take as given that statements made by Pol Pot relating to extant structural conditions of Cambodia, such as landlessness and the indebtedness of the Khmer peasantry, are gross misrepresentations. Likewise, I give short shrift to Pol Pot's duplicitous claims that the CPK came to power without any foreign assistance—including the aid of the Vietnamese communists. Again, these are fields well plowed; readers are directed to the voluminous writings of, among others, David Chandler, Ben Kiernan, Steve Heder, Craig Etcheson, and Serge Thion.[4]

Pol Pot's speech is significant not for its accuracy but for the clues it provides in helping us understand better the philosophical foundations of the Khmer Rouge. Simply put, Pol Pot—and other high-ranking members of the CPK—attempted but failed to put into practice what French Marxist Henri Lefebvre put into words: "A revolution that does not produce a new space has not realized its full potential." Otherwise, as Lefebvre continues, such a revolution "has failed in that it has not changed life itself, but has merely changed ideological superstructures, institutions, or political apparatuses." According to Lefebvre, "A social transformation, to be truly revolutionary in character, must manifest a creative capacity in its effects on daily life, on language and on space."[5]

Communism, according to Marx, was necessary to overcome the alienated life that typified capitalism. This, I argue, was a central concern of the CPK. However, what the CPK actually brought about was anything but a socialist or communist society, but not for lack of trying. I do not doubt that many members of the CPK were committed to what they *believed* Marxism entails, that there was a concerted effort to bring about a socialist revolution in preparation for an eventual communist society. However, I also maintain that notwithstanding their attempts to establish and defend socialism and to move toward communism, they could not and did not install a communist structure as the prevailing social organization of production. Rather than erecting a nonexploitative system, the CPK merely replaced one form of exploitation with another. Indeed, the CPK reaffirmed a system of production for exchange, thereby negating its own philosophical premise. Quite simply, I will argue that the CPK—similar to the former Soviet Union and other so-called communist or socialist governments—installed a variant of *state capitalism*.

As employed throughout this book, the term *state capitalism* refers broadly to a mode of production whereby a ruling class controls the state apparatus and, through this control, manages the means of production and subsequently appropriates surplus value.[6] Such a usage may be traced back to the early writings of Marx and Engels. In *Anti-Dühring*, for example, Engels writes that "the transformation [of capitalist enterprises] . . .

into state ownership, does not do away with the capitalistic nature of the productive forces. . . . The workers remain wage-workers—proletarians. The capitalist relation is not done away with." Engels's statement builds on Marx's earlier observation that "state capital" exists whenever "governments employ productive wage-labor in mines, railways, etc., and function as industrial capitalists." In other words, as Stephen Resnick and Richard Wolff explain, a "change in ownership of productive assets, from private to state, does not necessarily entail a change in the capitalist, exploitative class structure of production. When it does not, state capital(ism) is just the substitution of state functionaries for private individuals in the roles of capitalist appropriators of surplus labor."[7]

State capitalism, I will argue, provides the theoretical foundation on which subsequent interpretations of Democratic Kampuchea must be built. Consequently, *From Rice Fields to Killing Fields* sits alongside previous scholarship that has reinterpreted other so-called socialist or communist forms of government. In the Soviet Union, for example, Resnick and Wolff find that a "discourse of 'socialism' settled in as the hegemonic self-description of the Soviet economy and society. This description functioned to secure a state capitalism by reconceptualizing it negatively as *not* capitalism and positively as a transitional stage to communism."[8] In Democratic Kampuchea, I find that a variant of state capitalism similarly emerged *in practice*, while rhetorically CPK cadre spoke incessantly of their own unique form of Marxism. Workers under the Khmer Rouge remained wageworkers—albeit with a twist. Likewise, the fundamental social relationship between those entities who owned the means of production (that is, the CPK as ruling elite) and those individuals denied access to the means of production (that is, the workers) remained intact.

Challenging the Standard Total View

According to Michael Vickery, the STV imparts a limiting framework from which to understand the policies and practices of the CPK. More problematic is that the STV has permeated public consciousness to such an extent that it has become conventional wisdom and may be forced on evidence that does not support it. It is commonly held, for example, that

Khmer Rouge policies were simply perverse and had no rational basis in either economic or political necessity, or that CPK policy was chaotic or simply nonexistent, or that policies were simply plucked from the sky.[9]

It is accurate that many policies were hastily conceived and that many are found wanting in detail. The CPK's Four-Year Plan, for example, identifies the "problem of energy" and concludes: "We must use electric-powered engines, and we can burn gas, charcoal, and use wood to make steam."[10] No mention is made of how gas, charcoal, or wood were to be obtained or how these resources would be converted into energy and distributed throughout the country. And while the plan implies that engines will be obtained from abroad, it is unclear as to how.

To simply identify the lack of details is to miss the larger picture. The plan also indicates that the "problem of energy" is internally related to the generation of agricultural surpluses—necessary, it should be noted, to purchase commodities such as engines. Consequently, according to this document, the generation of energy "is a matter of serving agriculture."[11] One must see the forest from the trees when examining CPK documents; it is not sufficient to highlight one or two poorly conceived or incomplete sections of the Four-Year Plan, for example, while neglecting to see it as a *comprehensive* planning document. What previous scholars have failed to address is the totality of the overall postrevolutionary development schemes pursued by the CPK. I maintain that it is necessary to consider specific policies and practices—regardless of implementation or success—to better understand the *intentions* of the CPK. If my argument holds, it was through the comprehensive strategies envisioned by the CPK, as manifested in policies and material practices, that the structures of violence leading to widespread death were generated.

My Approach

Marxist and neo-Marxist approaches are rarely the first choice among scholars of genocide, including the Cambodian genocide. Indeed, while identifying the Marxist roots of the Khmer Rouge, scholars have typically eschewed the use of Marxist theory as an interpretative framework. Ben Kiernan, for example, favors an approach that privileges racism and nationalism, while Alex Hinton adopts a more psychological framework based on constructed differences.[12] Similarly, genocide has been an infrequent subject of study for scholars of Marx. Some of this mismatch can be understood as definitional: neither "genocide" nor "Marxism" represents monolithic concepts. With ambiguity on both sides of the equation, it is not entirely clear how to link the two as broad concepts. Putting definitional issues aside, the lack of observed engagement between genocide and Marxism may be attributed to at least four additional factors.[13] First, Marxist approaches have been falling out of favor for some time, most notably since the 1989 breakup of the Soviet Union. Condemned to the shadows cast by free-market triumphalism, Marx's critique of capitalism still finds traction among the academic Left, but beyond this faction, its appeal to historical analysts has waned, a circumstance owing in part to a popular but misplaced association between Marxist theory and those regimes named "Marxist," "Leninist," "Maoist," or "communist." Given that these regimes have failed to live up to competitive expectations, the political theories on which they are thought to be based must contain essential flaws, or so the thinking goes. Here, the study of Marx is comparable to the study of Seneca or Epicurus: interesting, perhaps, but unsuitable and unnecessary to face the challenges of the twentieth and twenty-first centuries. As such, more recent historical analyses of genocide have favored the lenses of current economic and social theories. When Marxism is mentioned in the analysis—notable in the case of Cambodia—it is because the regime under examination has identified itself as communist, making the explanation of genocide a straightforward question of regime type. Thus, the organization of the state's economic and social relations need not be scrutinized when "communism" serves to explain the descent into chaos all by itself. To discount Marx in this way is to sacrifice the perceptual and analytical benefits of political economy to contemporary political biases.

Second, Marx has been neglected in genocide studies because the extraordinary immediacy of mass killing tends to draw attention away from the everyday political economy involved in its production. The tendency is to see genocide as an exception, an aberration in normal social functioning. The systems that govern society are intended to operate for the purpose of defending and reproducing the population: even when such systems produce forms of structural violence, such actions are often seen as supporting "the greater good." By contrast, the mass violence that has been conventionally labeled "genocide" is often seen as a collapse of the social system rather than its consequence. Genocide comes to be understood as a breakdown that occurs through the intervention of exogenous forces, or through the elevation of a dominant personality into the role of dictator. Both of these perceptions have been applied to the case of Cambodia. The interpretive reflex has been to see the CPK as outsiders who brought about the deaths of millions by forcing a wholesale transition to a unique form of despotism. In addition, Pol Pot and high-ranking members of the CPK have been identified as the dark visionaries behind the killings—a portrayal that draws attention toward the psychology of individuals and away from existing economic and political structures both inside and outside Cambodia. In this way, the Cambodian genocide is viewed not as an outcome of a functioning social system but as the consequence of a collapsed one, making political economy seem less relevant to an understanding of the genocide's emergence. To the contrary, as subsequent chapters illustrate, the genocide arose in the context of the CPK's attempt to build, in the aftermath of armed conflict and an indiscriminate American-led aerial campaign that unleashed five hundred thousand tons of bombs on Cambodia, a fully functioning state with infrastructure to support trade, education, health, and family in addition to the better-known apparatuses of rice production and security. Some of these attempts succeeded as planned, while others did not; either way, victims of the CPK died as a consequence of a new and all-encompassing system of social organization, not a lack thereof.

Third, in the case of the CPK, scholars have tended to highlight its Marxist origins, with debates centering around the particular type of Marxism embodied by the Khmer Rouge, variously "Marxist," "Marxist-Leninist," "Marxist-Leninist-Maoist," or "ultra-Maoist." David Chandler, for example, refers to the CPK as "the purest and most thoroughgoing Marxist-Leninist movement." Once identified as such, the CPK's "pure" communist credentials can be made to explain the ensuing horrors. In this way, the description of the state (as communist) comes to serve as a natural explanation for the mass killing, short-circuiting any incentive toward further analysis of the processes that motivate such violence. Indeed, it is de rigueur among many commentators on genocide and mass violence to cast the constellation of "Marxisms" as intrinsically violent. Benjamin Valentino, for example, asserts that the "communist utopias" of the Soviet Union, China, and Cambodia represent "history's greatest slaughterhouses." Valentino's ability to make such a claim is possible only through the omission of the Holocaust, Rwanda, and other incidents of mass violence conducted by noncommunist regimes. The accompanying implication of such a claim—namely, that noncommunist governments are less susceptible to mass violence—requires further examination. Valentino explains that "radical communist policies . . . have often had the effect of completely dispossessing vast numbers of people, stripping them of their personal belongings, the products of their labor, their land, their homes, and their livelihood."[14] It is hard to find a more apt description of the forms of dispossession visited upon Native Americans, the Aboriginal people of Australia and New Zealand, or myriad other populations that suffered under colonialism and continue to suffer today under the spread of capitalism. Indeed, when considered in the *longue durée*, the systematic displacement, dispossession, and slaughter of indigenous people seem a subject well suited for Marxist historical materialism.

Finally, at the same moment that a regime such as the CPK is established as communist within the standard narrative, Marxist analyses and approaches tend to fall out of favor, even when further analysis is deemed useful: after all, Marx's analyses critique capitalism, not communism. Principles of surplus labor, commoditization, and socially necessary labor time were deployed to explain systems of production for exchange, that is, capitalist systems. As such, it may not be immediately obvious that Marxist political economy would yield results in a system accepted as communist. To the contrary, I argue that the CPK's surplus production of rice for export, their efforts to construct ports and other infrastructures of trade, and their ongoing dialogue with China in particular to acquire fertilizer, tractors, and myriad forms of technical expertise dispute the narrative of a regime bent on autarky and self-imposed isolation. Instead, the rationing system designed to ensure rice surpluses, the transportation networks intended to speed distribution of agricultural inputs and outputs, and the extensive irrigation schemes developed to double or triple the number of harvests were all consistent with state capitalism, not communism. Certainly, the CPK claimed to be a communist party (after all, it is part of their name), and much communist rhetoric can be found in policy documents and propaganda, including the claims that they were launching a communist revolution and attempting to build socialism. Nevertheless, the production of rice and other agricultural commodities for trade on the international market, coupled with social policies like a ration designed to guarantee production surpluses, signals a deep-seated and pervasive profit motive on the part of the state. As such, a Marxist approach to the space-time economy of Cambodia under the Khmer Rouge seems both appropriate in this context and necessary for an understanding of the mass killing that took place.

In *From Rice Fields to Killing Fields*, I adopt a Marxist approach to understanding the Communist Party of Kampuchea. In so doing, I challenge both the accepted dogma surrounding the Khmer Rouge and our understanding of "actually existing" communist societies. To do so requires that we first discard the idea of any essentialist idea of Marxism, Leninism, Maoism, socialism, communism, or any other "ism" that has been and continues to be directed toward the Khmer Rouge. My purpose, following Marx and Engels, is not to look for a category in every period but to remain constantly on the real ground of history; the objective is not to explain practice from the idea but to explain the formation of ideas from material practice.[15] Consequently, we should be concerned less with applying the "idea" of Marxism (or communism and the like) to the CPK and more with interpreting actually existing Marxist philosophy as practiced by the CPK.

Toward a Critique of a Communist Party

There is a tendency for scholars and journalists—but especially those non-specialists of Democratic Kampuchea—to take at face value the propaganda disseminated by the CPK. Many slogans of the Khmer Rouge, for example, are widely known and widely repeated. Paramount is the saying "Spare them, no profit; remove them, no loss" (*Tuk min chamnenh, dah chenh ka min khat).* To build an argument around propaganda, however, is to begin on a weak foundation. Politicians routinely employ hyperbole in public announcements; their intent is to manipulate the discourse at an emotional, visceral level. Statements are intended, depending on the context and audience, to incite, mollify, inspire, embolden, or intimidate. Consequently, analysis of propaganda materials must be tempered by a systematic examination of policies and practices. Here, policies refer to the rules and regulations instantiated by the CPK, such as the Constitution of Democratic Kampuchea, promulgated on January 5, 1976, and the party's Four-Year Plan, articulated in the summer of 1976. These documents, and many others, indicate more clearly the intentions and purposes of the CPK. Of equal importance is documentary evidence of the CPK practice: the actual day-to-day doings of governance, including minute meetings, invoices, and shipping logs. These and other comparable materials provide a grounded understanding of how, or if, CPK policy was put into practice. Likewise, the mass graves, irrigation schemes, and remnants of prisons and warehouses testify materially to CPK policy.

Conceptually, therefore, my study centers on those policies and practices put forward by members of the highest echelon of the Communist Party of Kampuchea. My objective is to *critique* the political economy of Democratic Kampuchea as *planned* and *enacted* by the CPK. To this point, it is noteworthy that most of Marx's writings were subtitled as "critiques." His magisterial work *Capital*, for example, was a "critique of political economy," while *The German Ideology* (coauthored with Friedrich Engels) was a "critique of modern German philosophy." What precisely does "critique" mean within the corpus of Marx's writings? Marx was concerned less with capitalism as a historical object of study than he was in understanding the self-evident propositions put forward in support of capitalism.[16] This is, according to David Harvey, what Marx effectively does in *Capital*: he brings together divergent intellectual traditions to create a completely new and revolutionary framework for knowledge.[17] Accordingly, my objective is to apply a critique of the CPK's political economy and to challenge the categorical presuppositions put forward both by the CPK and by subsequent scholars who have interpreted—or, rather, framed—CPK policy as Marxist or Leninist or Stalinist or Maoist.

Ultimately, *From Rice Fields to Killing Fields* contributes in two principal ways. First, my hope is to contribute specifically to our understanding of the Cambodian genocide, to provide insight into the material practices that contributed to large-scale violence. It is my contention that Cambodia's mass violence was the consequence not of the deranged attitudes and paranoia of a few tyrannical leaders. Instead, the violence was structural, the direct result of a series of ill-fated political and economic reforms that were designed to accumulate capital rapidly: the dispossession of hundreds of thousands of people through forced evacuations, the imposition of starvation wages, the promotion of import-substitution policies, and the intensification of agricultural production through forced labor.

Second, I contribute to those literatures that have addressed forms of "actually existing" socialism. Here, my concerns extend beyond the specific study of Democratic Kampuchea to address more broadly the dialectics of political philosophy and state form. Employing a historical-materialist approach, my analysis of Khmer Rouge political economy speaks to deeper questions of "Third World" development, communist revolutions, social movements, and anticolonialism. It is a mistake, therefore, to view Democratic Kampuchea in isolation, as an aberration or something unique. Rather, the policies and practices initiated by the CPK must be seen in a larger historical-geographical context. Throughout the decades of the Cold War, numerous colonies achieved independence and attempted to remake their political economies. In turn, many of these embryonic countries would be typified by heavy-handed state intervention, state-led industrialization, the nationalization of resources, and anti-imperialist and nationalist fervor. As a former colony and newly independent state, Democratic Kampuchea embarked on a path that was well trod by its Asian and African colleagues, including the aforementioned policies of import substitution, dispossession, and agricultural-led industrialization. It is crucial, therefore, to consider why, in Democratic Kampuchea, these economic reforms led to widespread death, for satisfactory answers will remain elusive if we fail to position the Communist Party of Kampuchea within its proper historical and geographical context.

Acknowledgments

From Rice Fields to Killing Fields: Nature, Life, and Labor under the Khmer Rouge began with a basic question: How was rice produced under the Khmer Rouge? It is well known that many hundreds of thousands of men, women, and children died from starvation, disease, and exhaustion. These deaths were the direct result of specific policies enacted by the Khmer Rouge, namely, the production of rice for export. How, though, are we to interpret these policies? Various scholars have described these policies as the embodiment of extreme or pure forms of Marxism; others have interpreted these policies as irrational or as purposive attempts to deliberately starve the population into submission. Documentary evidence, however, would seem to belie these explanations. Required was an in-depth study that was grounded not in Khmer Rouge rhetoric but in Marxist political philosophy. What was needed was a reconstruction of the political economy of Democratic Kampuchea under the Khmer Rouge. This book marks an initial attempt at such a reconstruction.

This book would not have been possible without the support of the staff at Syracuse University Press, including Alison Maura Shay and Kelly Balenske. Alison has been exceptionally supportive in her time in seeing the book through to completion, from the initial review stage to the final acceptance; Kelly has been particularly helpful in walking the manuscript through to production. Special thanks are extended also to the editorial board at Syracuse University Press, for their critical feedback and pointed questions. The manuscript is considerably better because of their due diligence. At Kent State University, I express my appreciation to Jim Blank, Todd Diacon, Marcello Fantoni, Mandy Munro-Stasiuk, and Scott Sheridan. In Cambodia I am deeply grateful for the support and assistance of Youk Chhang and the staff at the Documentation Center of Cambodia. The center has been remarkably generous in providing documents for this project and others over the years. More specifically, I thank Terith Chy, Khamboly Dy, Kok-Thay Eng, Dany Long, Kok-Chhay Ly, Farina So, and Dara Vanthan. Special thanks are extended to Sokvisal Kimsroy and Savina Sirik for their assistance in the field and for their translations of several documents. This book would never have come to fruition without their help. Special thanks are also extended to Stian Rice, who ably drafted the maps.

Over the years I have benefited from the assistance and critical feedback of current and former students, including Gabriela Brindis Alvarez, Alex Colucci, Gordon Cromley, Christabel Devadoss, Kathryn Hannum, Sam Henkin, Josh Inwood, Sokvisal Kimsroy, Mark Rhodes, Stian Rice, Savina Sirik, Dave Stasiuk, Rachel Will, and Chris Willer. I have also benefited from the support, advice, and criticism of Caroline Bennet, Daniel Bultmann, Noel Castree, Craig Etcheson, Jeffrey Himel, Rachel Hughes, Helen Jarvis, Ben Kiernan, Don Mitchell, and Simon Springer. I am particularly indebted to Jim Glassman, who read the entire manuscript and provided invaluable feedback. Thanks are also extended to the anonymous reviewers who provided necessary criticism on the initial proposal and subsequent drafts.

This research has been supported over the years by grants from the National Science Foundation and the Association of American Geographers; funding has also been provided by the Department of Geography, the Office of Global Education, and the College of Arts and Sciences at Kent State University.

Portions of this book have appeared in previous publications, and I am thankful for the opportunity to use and expand upon this material. Chapter 4 is based on "Violence, Surplus Production, and the Transformation of Nature during the Cambodian Genocide," *Rethinking Marxism* 26, no. 4 (2014): 490–506; parts of chapter 5 appeared as "State Sovereignty, Bioethics, and Political Geographies: The Practice of Medicine under the Khmer Rouge," *Environment and Planning D: Society and Space* 30, no. 5 (2012): 842–60; and portions of chapter 7 appeared in "Dead Labor,

Landscapes, and Mass Graves: Administrative Violence during the Cambodian Genocide," *Geoforum* 52 (2014): 70–77.

Throughout the writing of this manuscript, I have been fortunate to provide preliminary results and interpretations at the following venues: the Department of Geography, California State University at Long Beach; Department of Geography, Ohio State University; Department of Geography, Pennsylvania State University; Department of Geography, San Diego State University; Center for Humanities and Department of Geography, Temple University; and Center for Southeast Asian Studies and the Department of Geography, University of Wisconsin at Madison. I thank the audiences for their comments and suggestions.

Closer to home I thank my parents, Dr. Gerald Tyner and Dr. Judith Tyner, for their continued support and encouragement. Throughout my career, my mother has been a generous sounding board on all things writing; my father has accompanied me on numerous trips throughout Southeast Asia. He is a remarkable traveling companion, and I hope to return with him to the region. As always, I thank my late-night companions: Bond, my now seventeen-year-old puppy, and Jamaica, my eighteen-year-old cat. My daughters, Jessica and Anica, have in their own unique way continued to provide inspiration. My greatest debt, of course, is to my wife, Belinda, who continually keeps me in line. Without her steadfast support, I would not be where I am today.

Finally, I dedicate this book to the memory of those individuals who died and to those who continue to endure the legacy of war in Cambodia. It is my hope that this manuscript, in some small way, might provide an element of understanding into the madness that encompassed Cambodia, not only at the hands of the Khmer Rouge but also from the geopolitical actions that failed to heed the warning "Never again."

FROM RICE FIELDS TO KILLING FIELDS

1

A Critique of Khmer Rouge Political Economy

The Communist Party of Kampuchea constitutes one of the most violent and inhumane apparatuses of organized terror in the twentieth century. Between April 1975 and January 1979, members of the CPK carried out a program of mass violence that is, in many respects, unparalleled in modern history. In just under four years, approximately two million people died from starvation, disease, exhaustion, inadequate medical care, torture, murder, and execution. The total number of deaths translates into one-fifth to one-quarter of Cambodia's pre-1975 population.[1] What accounts for such widespread violence?

To date, scholars of the Cambodian "genocide" have searched far and wide for causal explanations.[2] And, for the most part, scholars have underscored the apparent Marxist roots of the Khmer Rouge.[3] Why not? How could the *Communist* Party of Kampuchea be anything other than communist? One need only cite the words of Nuon Chea, deputy secretary of the CPK, who, in a statement made to the Communist Workers' Party of Denmark in July 1978, declared, "It is written in our party program that we shall continue our socialist revolution and advance towards communism after the national democratic revolution." And indeed, we see this point in the literature, as Scott Straus writes: "The Khmer Rouge were Communist. Pol Pot was the secretary of the Central Committee of the Communist Party of Kampuchea (CPK). In official documents the Khmer Rouge referred to itself as The Party; its stated goal was to bring about a 'socialist revolution' in the name of the 'worker-peasant.' Numerous Khmer Rouge idioms and practices directly resonated with other Marxist-Leninist movements, especially Maoism."[4]

Given the apparent "obviousness" of the CPK's Marxist credentials, it next becomes a matter of establishing what "type" of Marxists they were. To this end, the ideology of the Khmer Rouge has long been debated.[5] Indeed, what has emerged has become something of a Rorschach test. The CPK has been styled, variously, as "Marxist," "Marxist-Leninist," "Marxist-Leninist-Maoist," and even "ultra-Maoist." Thus, for example, Leo Cherne argues that the establishment of Democratic Kampuchea marks "the creation of the first pure Communist society anywhere in the world."[6] Boraden Nhem echoes this sentiment, explaining that "the Khmer Rouge was determined to reorganize society into a pure communist society." And in full transparency, I too have made similar statements in earlier works.[7]

I have come to realize that "purity" arguments provide little in the way of understanding. "Marxism" has always existed in the form of various (Marxist) trends and schools of thought; indeed, before Marx was dead, it had become apparent that Marxist theory and Marxist analysis would accommodate more than one interpretation and would not evolve on the basis of a single unique theoretical direction. Marxism was never a single monolithic theory, and all those scholars who declare that Marxism is reducible to economic determinism, technological determinism, blind obedience to authority, or any other caricature have either understood nothing or are simply exercising cheap propaganda.[8] A similar pronouncement can be made with reference to Lenin, Stalin, and Mao. One need only to think of the many debates engaged by Marxists over the generations, of the competing interpretations provided by, but certainly not limited to, Rosa Luxemburg, Georg Lukács, Karl Kautsky, Leon Trotsky, Georgii Plekhanov, and Eduard Bernstein. It is ironic indeed that contemporary scholars of the Khmer Rouge can entertain the idea that Pol Pot and other high-ranking cadre were so fluent in their understanding of "Marxism" that they alone could erect a pure communist society.

For other commentators, the CPK was less an example of "pure" communism as it was an amalgamation of disparate and contradictory Marxist influences. Matthew Edwards avows that "in addition to Maoist policies . . . Pol Pot and some of the Khmer Rouge leadership gathered a wide range of ideas from their time in France, including European Marxism and Stalinism." In a series of articles, Stewart Clegg, Miguel Cunha, and Arménio Rego describe the CPK through a combination of Marxist-related intellects. Thus, for example, they explain that the objective of the CPK was "to construct a radical Marxist-Leninist state of Democratic Kampuchea, inspired in part by Maoist thinking," whereby the vision was "one of pure socialism, the creation of a society with no traces of feudalism, capitalism or any other exploitative forms of social organization."[9] Elsewhere, they indicate that the CPK was "a Maoist-inspired political and military movement." Finally, Karl Jackson also states that "the Cambodian revolutionaries were communists." But, he explains, "they were communists of a peculiar sort, however, a post-Leninist amalgam of nostrums of the Left, a union derived from sources previously sought to be incompatible, namely Mao and Stalin, Frantz Fanon and Samir Amin, as well as indigenous Cambodian sources."[10]

These interpretations and explanations cannot all be correct. If you accept that the CPK was influenced by a wide range of intellects, including Marx, Engels, Lenin, Stalin, Mao, Amin, and Fanon, it is illogical to describe Democratic Kampuchea as a "pure" form of anything. Equally problematic, however, is that the literature is now saturated with contradictory, misleading, or simply erroneous statements, most stemming from questionable readings of Marx, Engels, and Lenin, as well as numerous CPK documents. Charles Twining, for example, explains that the leaders of Democratic Kampuchea "wanted genuinely to create a country totally independent from every point of view. To achieve this state, Cambodia must be self-contained and self-reliant to the point of autarky." Stewart Clegg and coauthors write that "the Khmer Rouge embarked on creating an agrarian, egalitarian, anti-professional, anti-technology and self-sufficient society—a primitive communist utopia." They continue that the "idea" of Democratic Kampuchea was "utopia founded upon an ideology of purity." Greg Procknow likewise states that "Democratic Kampuchean policies converted the bourgeoning capitalist economy into a communistic, rural-centric, independent, self-sustainable nation, with an emphasis on self-mastery. Money was abolished, foreign trade collapsed."[11]

This jumble of terms and phrases provides more confusion than it does clarity. Equally grievous is that these banal statements are not supported by empirical evidence. Consider, first, the assertion that the CPK sought to create an agrarian society. This notion is, in fact, countered by the CPK, as numerous documents testify that agriculture was to be promoted in an attempt to develop industry. This flawed claim is often married to the charge that the CPK eschewed technology in their promotion of a "primitive" communism. Nhem, for example, explains that the Khmer Rouge's bias for independence "precluded machinery from the planning (since they could not produce those machineries)."[12] Again, in numerous planning documents, the CPK acknowledged the need to acquire machinery. Moreover, various factories were in operation throughout Democratic Kampuchea, including tractor-repair facilities and shipbuilding operations.[13]

Consider, also, the oft-repeated charge that the CPK sought to establish a completely autonomous, self-reliant, and self-sufficient society. It is commonplace that scholars and other commentators interpret these "objectives" as part and parcel of an attempt to construct a communist utopia. In fact, much has been made of the CPK's rhetoric of "self-reliance" and "self-mastery." For some scholars, this language is evidence of a deeply entrenched attitude of isolationism bordering on autarky. Jackson, for example, explains that "the Khmer revolutionaries were trying to establish total sovereignty and self-reliance in the cultural, economic, and political realms" and that their "application of the doctrine of self-reliance led the revolutionaries to seal Cambodia off from all but a very few close allies." Randle DeFalco also concludes that "once firmly in control, the CPK government set about implementing its planned radical overhaul of Cambodia's agricultural sector and its extreme version of socialism throughout Cambodia." He continues that the promotion of a "utopian agrarian-socialist state . . . was to be achieved independent of any foreign aid according to the strict policy of extreme violence, referred to as 'independence self-mastery.'"[14]

How do these interpretations conform to material reality? On March 13, 1976, members of the Standing Committee of the CPK met to discuss commerce issues.[15] The occasion of the meeting warrants attention.

Since their ascension to power, the CPK had received a not insignificant amount of foreign aid. Within a week of capturing Phnom Penh, for example, China dispatched the first of many shipments of goods to Cambodia. Indeed, in July alone, aid shipments included, among other items, nearly twenty metric tons of rice, two thousand tons of unspecified cloth, two hundred tons of raw cotton, and eleven thousand tons of train-related components.[16] Foreign aid was promised by other governments as well, including the disbursement of US$3 million in aid from Yugoslavia and another US$5 million from Sweden.[17]

Consider also a meeting between representatives of the CPK and Chinese officials from the Chinese Ministry of Communications, held on June 16, 1977. For the Khmer Rouge, it had become apparent that the existing transportation infrastructure in Democratic Kampuchea was unable to meet the demands of their expanding *international* trade. This structural condition posed a significant limitation to the CPK's "currency issue."[18] Consequently, members of the CPK pondered the possibility of purchasing or leasing their own container ship, which would, in principle, afford the CPK a degree of independence within the global economy. Indeed, for the CPK, the advantages were palpable: with their own ship, it would be easier to export their goods; they would have greater control over scheduling and could thus dock the ship at the port of Kampong Som as long as they needed. However, when they met with the Chinese officials to discuss the feasibility of leasing the container vessel *Yong Kang*, a number of obstacles were raised. As Andrew Mertha details, the Chinese "went into excruciating detail over the myriad technicalities involved," including "certification, pricing structures, shipping fees, insurance, crew member salaries, and documentation."[19] Mertha summarizes the discussion:

> The two sides declared that the *Yong Kang* was "a production tool" and that "every single minute is profit." Since the vessel accrued daily costs of US$1,552 when idle, the *Yong Kang* had to operate, fully loaded, on a constant basis and avoid docking at too many ports in order to minimize or spread out docking fees. For instance, it cost the *Yong Kang* US$18,624 to dock at Huangpu for twelve days and US$20,176 to dock at Kobe for thirteen days. The Chinese delegation stressed the importance

of making financial calculations that balanced docking costs with potential profits from loading and unloading goods, emphasizing that it was critical to consider the amount of goods before loading them at port, especially Japanese ports. As for payment, the Chinese charged 3 percent of its profits, on the low end of China's typical 3 to 5 percent scale.[20]

From this alone we begin to sense that calls of "extreme" and "radical" self-reliance, isolationism, and autarky border on hyperbole and reflect a misreading both of sovereignty in general and of CPK policy specifically. At the most general level, all governments strive for sovereignty, that is, the ability to be free from foreign domination or undue influence. At this level, therefore, the desire of the CPK to avoid becoming entangled in foreign alliances should not be considered exceptional and certainly not radical. Indeed, this refrain was common among many leaders of anticolonial movements from the 1940s onward—most notably those states associated with the Non-Aligned Movement. Simply put, developing countries had to devise foreign policy concepts that would, on the one hand, ensure their separation from the evolving superpower military-political alliances (for example, the United States and the Soviet Union) and, on the other, help create the conditions most favorable for the defense of newly gained sovereignty, the raising of living standards, and the promotion of general socioeconomic progress.[21] But in their pursuit of sovereignty, could it be argued, following Jackson, that the Khmer Rouge went to extremes? Certainly, many embassies were initially closed, and most diplomatic relations were severed. However, surviving documents reveal much discussion related to the gradual—and selective—reopening of the country to foreign governments. For the CPK, a monastic isolation was not the intended goal; rather, international participation was to be determined on its own terms. So while welcomed for the possibilities that foreign aid offered— "We can buy anything we want or materials for repairing the hydro-electricity power station in Kirirum"[22]—the offer of aid was viewed skeptically.

The philosophical basis of Democratic Kampuchea's political economy was forcefully put forward by Pol Pot in a speech delivered in 1977. On this occasion, Pol Pot explained that Cambodia—in the 1950s—was increasingly becoming a "satellite of imperialism, in particular, U.S.

imperialism." This status meant, according to Pol Pot, that Cambodia "was neither independent nor free," that the country was "a semi-colony, in a situation of dependency on imperialism in general and, in particular, on American imperialism." Based on CPK analysis, Pol Pot stated that a fundamental "contradiction" existed between Cambodia's so-called independence (granted by the French in 1954) and its political and economic relations with foreign governments. A communist revolution was required to achieve internal, or domestic, independence. At the international level, however, it was necessary to eliminate any presence of foreign domination. Consequently, following their seizure of power, according to Pol Pot, the revolutionary task was transformed. National liberation and independence had been achieved; necessary now was the defense of the country, of its "sovereignty" and "territorial integrity," against the (perceived) continued threat of imperialism and foreign domination. Pol Pot concluded that in the two years following their victory in 1975, the CPK had "successfully protected, strengthened and expanded the fruits of the revolution, the state power of the revolution, and totally safeguarded the independence, sovereignty, territorial integrity and borders of [Democratic Kampuchea] by relying on principles of complete independence, initiative and self-reliance."[23] Autarky, in other words, was neither the goal nor the outcome of CPK policy and practice. As documented in subsequent chapters, independence for the Khmer Rouge meant a situation free from foreign interference (that is, unequal trade relations and conditions), and self-reliance reflected an economic strategy based on import substitution.

For many postcolonial governments, a crucial problem following independence was the ability to promote economic growth through the expansion of productive capacity.[24] This often required substantial investments not only in basic industries but also in the development of infrastructure. This problem was magnified when the government in question achieved independence following armed conflict. Such were the conditions confronting the Khmer Rouge in 1975. The leadership of the CPK understood that foreign aid would be insufficient and undesirable to obtain the necessary materials required for the economic growth and defense of Democratic Kampuchea. Therefore, the CPK considered, and pursued, various options to reestablish foreign trade. In a meeting of the Standing

Committee on December 2, 1975, for example, it was reported that the Thai government placed a request to purchase fish and timber.[25] Ongoing negotiations with Chinese officials also convinced the CPK that a more formalized, institutional approach to foreign trade was necessary. Thus, in June 1976 an arrangement was made between the Chinese Ministry of Foreign Trade and the CPK Ministry of Commerce to establish the Ren Fung Company. Based in Hong Kong, this company was to facilitate imports and exports between Democratic Kampuchea and selected other countries.[26] In time, the Ren Fung Company facilitated the international exchange of commodities with a number of foreign countries, including China, North Korea, Japan, Singapore, and Yugoslavia. Other arrangements were made that permitted direct or indirect trade with France, Madagascar, Bangladesh, and even the United States.

When the CPK met to discuss the offers of aid forthcoming from Sweden and Yugoslavia, the concern was how it would impact their overall objective of economic independence. According to Ieng Sary, deputy prime minister for foreign affairs, Sweden was prepared to extend about US$5 million in aid to Cambodia. However, Ieng Sary also noted that while the aid was portrayed as being unconditional, the Swedish authorities *also* requested that its airline be allowed access to Kampuchean airspace for its Bangkok–Hong Kong route. To this request, an unnamed spokesperson—presumably Pol Pot—cautioned that "any aid is conditional." He explained that "in order to receive the aids, we need to select the independent countries, namely countries that are satellite to neither the United States nor Soviet [Union]." Pol Pot then identified Sweden, Mexico, and Cuba as potential allies. In the end, Pol Pot determined that foreign aid would be accepted as long as it served the broader goals of improving people's livelihoods, agricultural production, transportation, and national defense.[27]

The aforementioned account should give any serious scholar of the Cambodian genocide pause. The voluminous materials now archived at the Documentation Center of Cambodia raise serious doubts as to the political and economic disposition of the CPK and, by extension, to our understanding of the policies and practices that led to such a massive loss of life. To ask, following Michael Vickery, "Were they Marxist Communists at all?" is not to deny culpability or to solicit immunity for their actions; it is an effort to provide much-needed clarity to a murky field and thereby facilitate efforts to bring about truth and reconciliation.[28]

A Marxist Critique of the Communist Party of Kampuchea

My thesis is straightforward. The dominant mode of production in Democratic Kampuchea was one of a system of production for exchange, in short a variant of state capitalism, with the CPK, by extension, assuming the role of ruling-state capitalist class. The political and economic transformations that followed revolution in Democratic Kampuchea, therefore, place the CPK in line with other anticolonial movements that imposed state-led programs from the 1940s onward. In general, state capitalist governments attempted to restructure agroexport societies through national industrialization, create internal markets through agrarian reform that limited or eliminated the political power of landlord classes, nationalize the control of natural resources, and harness labor to national development projects.[29] As detailed in subsequent chapters, the CPK planned or carried out (or both) myriad programs that resonated with political-economic practices throughout Africa and Asia.

My conclusion is based on a class analysis of the CPK, situated within a framework of historical materialism. In other words, through an examination of primary documents of the CPK, I provide a Marxist critique of a so-called Marxist social movement. Such an approach has one major advantage over previous attempts to disentangle the ideology of the Khmer Rouge, namely, it is more in line with the dialectic method employed by members of the CPK. Dialectics opens a space for a deeper and more profound analysis than a simple recanting of events. History as dialect consists not simply of disparate "things" or "events" but rather processes and relations. In other words, reality is more than the epiphenomenon that can be counted, classified, and mapped; it is more than the "observation" that strikes us immediately and directly, which masks the underlying structures and social relations.

When, on April 17, 1975, the Khmer Rouge assumed power in Cambodia, party members were confronted with the stark reality of governing a society in the aftermath of wholesale destruction wrought by years of uneven colonial development and armed conflict. Marx, of course, had very little to say about what might lie beyond capitalism, a limitation that posed and continues to pose problems for those individuals who have followed in his wake. Throughout the remainder of the nineteenth century following Marx's death, and well into the twentieth century, generation upon generation of scholars—far beyond the famous triumvirate of Lenin, Stalin, and Mao—have modified and amended, altered and adapted, the writings of Marx to fit their own local conditions and objectives. Members of the CPK were no different; they also had the advantage, or disadvantage more likely, of having to work through not only Marx but also the countless interpretations that followed.

As followers of Marx, but more generally as witnesses to myriad anti-colonial movements throughout the "Third World," members of the CPK would have understood the immediate necessity of reestablishing a functioning economy, for if there is a commonality to the various Marxisms that flourished when the Khmer Rouge was active, it was the need to provide for the basic material conditions of life itself: water, food, and shelter. This is clear from the discussions of the CPK in the early months of their regime. Between August 20 and 24, 1975, for example, top officials of the CPK reported on the conditions of various parts of the country; apart from a concern with the "enemy situation," considerable conversation centered on the provision of food and shelter.[30] And while one may question both the sincerity of these officials as well as the accuracy of their assessments, it remains clear that the CPK adhered to a materialist framework. To approach the political philosophy of the CPK, therefore, it is necessary to determine the overall social organization of production.

Marx focused his attention chiefly on the surplus generated within the capitalist organization of production. He did so through an examination of the particular class structure that defined any given society. Marxist class relationships, at a basic level, are determined by people's control over production and distribution. As Richard Wolff explains, "What defines an economic system . . . is not primarily how productive resources are owned nor how resources and products are distributed. Rather, the key definitional dimension is the organization of production. More precisely, the definitional priority concerns how the production and distribution of the surplus are organized." As Resnick and Wolff elaborate, the aspect common to all forms of communism is the class structure: a collective of surplus producers that also appropriates and distributes that surplus collectively. Conversely, forms of capitalism all display a different class structure: those who appropriate and distribute the surplus are different people from the collective of surplus producers.[31] A class analysis indicates that the political economy of Democratic Kampuchea—similar to the Soviet Union—was, contra Jackson, a peculiar form of capitalism and not communism.[32] Heretofore, if there is consensus among scholars of the Cambodian genocide, it is that the masses of forced laborers did not own their means of production and did not determine the distribution of the foodstuffs and other goods produced. Such a relationship is more indicative of capitalism than it is communism.

A Marxist critique of the Khmer Rouge, therefore, must begin with consideration of how the CPK proposed that collectives of individuals, rooted in time and place, were to obtain the basic necessities of life: food, water, shelter. It is notable that the first objective identified in the CPK's Four-Year Plan was to "serve the people's livelihood, and to raise the people's standard of living quickly, both in terms of supplies and in terms of other material goods." To be sure, for the CPK, livelihood translated into a litany of disparate "items": hygienic toilets, sheds for fertilizers, carpentry workshops, medical clinics, kitchens, vegetable gardens, bed supplies, water pitchers, teapots, raincoats, scissors, rice, fish sauce, and so on. Nor was there any detailed discussion as to how these various material necessities were to be obtained and distributed. However, and this is the key point, for the CPK it was compulsory "to pay attention to the improvement of social action, health, and raising the people's living standards, every year and in every plan, in order to nurture, strengthen, and increase our people's physical force." Following the provision of the people's material goods, therefore, everything else follows, for as Marx and Engels explain, "By producing their means of subsistence men are indirectly producing their material life." As explained by the CPK, the raising of the people's living standards "leads to an improvement in political forces and consciousness."[33]

To this end, both Marx and Engels forward the proposition that cultural practices and social institutions emanate from the satisfaction of the basic necessities of life. Religion, marriage, and inheritance rights, for example: they do not precede survivability, nor do they emerge separate from the attainment of the conditions of existence. As Marx explains, "Neither legal relations nor political forms could be comprehended whether by themselves or on the basis of a so-called general development of the human mind." Instead, "they originate in the material conditions of life."[34] This is not to suggest that "production" *determines* all facets of social reality; this myth is forwarded primarily by postmodernists and other critics who fail to appreciate (or understand) Marx's usage of the term *determinant*. For Marx, determinism is neither teleological inevitability nor a variant of fatalism.[35]

Marx did argue that the primary contingency was how any given society satisfied its attainment of the basic conditions of existence. Over time, as societies transform, specific institutional practices—such as marriage, but also divisions of labor, property rights, and criminal justice—emerge vis-à-vis the necessities of life: some of these practices become entrenched and "assume" an existence beyond the immediate production process; others may fall into disfavor or are replaced by other practices. As Marx and Engels explain, "Each new productive force, insofar as it is not merely a quantitative extension of productive forces already known (for instance, the bringing into cultivation of fresh land), causes a further development of the division of labor."[36] As the conditions of existence are transformed, for example, by the extension of trade or the development of tributary systems, other social relations and social institutions will (most likely) be transformed.

Consider the concept "division of labor," whereby different tasks are allocated to different individuals to satisfy the basic necessities of life. Women, for example, may assume responsibility for the gathering of fruits and vegetables; men may assume the task of hunting; children may be assigned the task of collecting water. Note that these divisions of labor are not inevitable; women do not naturally have to gather while men hunt. Nor, for that matter, is the division of labor a seamless, conflictless process. My point is, divisions of labor are social relations that emerge to satisfy the provision (production) of food, water, shelter, and clothing. Consequently, as we will see in later chapters, the CPK initiated various age and gendered divisions of labor in order to provide (in principle) the material needs of life.

Throughout his writings, Marx employs the concept *mode of production* in an attempt to capture something of the complex social organizations observed throughout history. Marx's clearest definition of the "mode of production" appears in his *Contribution to the Critique of Political Economy*, where he states: "In the social production of their existence, men [*sic*] inevitably enter into definite relations, which are independent of their will, namely *relations of production* appropriate to a given stage in the development of their material *forces of production*. The totality of these relations of production constitutes the *economic structure* of society, the real foundation, on which arises a legal and political *superstructure* and to which correspond definite forms of social consciousness. The mode of production of material life conditions the general process of social, political and intellectual life."[37]

As this passage indicates, the mode of production, on the one hand, is composed of two interrelated components: the relations of production and the forces of production. This latter component, however, is itself composed of the *means of production* (that is, raw materials, tools, technology) and the direct "producers," whether they are peasants, serfs, slaves, or wageworkers. The *relations of production* consequently encompass the direct producers plus nonproducers (for example, chieftains, lords, owners). The entire *mode of production* (or "base") is thus the combination of the means, forces, and relations of production. The *superstructure*, on the other hand, is composed of those institutions, relations, and practices that encompass, say, politics, law, education, and religion. These are not mere reflections of the mode of production—but they are interrelated.[38] In sum, "The totality of human society is thus represented by the preceding elements and relations. These comprise, for Marxist scientists, tools with which we can begin to isolate a part of the social whole for analysis without having to sever it from its defining place within the complete system."[39] Subsequently, our analysis of the political economy of Democratic Kampuchea will highlight the interconnectivity of disparate institutions, of the fundamental social relations of production, between those who owned the means of production and those who were denied ownership.

Common to both the relations of production and the forces of production is human labor; indeed, as discussed in subsequent chapters, labor (broadly conceived as those conscious activities that transform nature into use values, that is, *things* that may be used for consumption, such as food, or for trade and exchange) is a central concept of historical materialism. Originally, according to Marx, *human labor* was not unlike that of other animals: humans scavenged, gathered food, and hunted. The first transformative moment, however, occurred when humans put consciousness and deliberation into effect. In other words, they made tools; they *made instruments of production*.[40] Marx explains that "the use and construction of instruments of labor, although present in germ among certain species of animals, is characteristic of the specifically human labor process." Consequently, as Richard Peet summarizes, "Shaping natural materials into tools and instruments which shorten necessary labor time ('necessary' in terms of providing the essentials of life) is the economic key to social evolution."[41]

This is a point that bears repeating. In Marx's account, the labor process is *purposeful* activity aimed at the production of use values, that is, those *things* necessary for life itself.[42] For Marx, a second transformative moment occurs when the means of production come to be controlled by a ruling elite, thereby creating a fundamental cleavage between those who control the productive forces and those who perform the work.[43] How these social relations are arranged, between those who labor (the "non"-producers) and those who own the means of production (the "indirect" producers) can and do assume many different forms. Marx clarifies:

> It is in each case the direct relationship of the owners of the conditions of production to the immediate producers—a relationship whose particular form naturally corresponds always to a certain level of development of the type and manner of labor, and hence to its social productive power—in which we find the innermost secret, the hidden basis of the entire social edifice, and hence also the political form of the relationship and dependence, in short, the specific form of state in each case.

This does not prevent the same economic basis—the same in its major conditions—from displaying endless variations and gradations in its appearance, as the result of innumerable different empirical circumstances, natural conditions, racial relations, historical influences acting from outside, etc., and these can only be understood by analyzing these empirically given conditions.[44]

The specific arrangements of the social relations of production are the pivot to understanding any given mode of production, including that of Democratic Kampuchea. These arrangements, moreover, exhibit tremendous variation—albeit variability within limits. Similar conditions thus may give rise to very different political-economic structures. Capitalism in the United States, for example, is different from (but similar to) capitalism in Japan or capitalism in Germany. Accordingly, those practices that are characteristic but not determinant of capitalism, such as private property, manifest differently (but similarly) in the United States, Japan, and Germany. And by extension, criminal and civil law—as they relate to property relations—will also exhibit differences and similarities. In all three locations, however, it would be possible to empirically document the interrelations of the capitalist mode of production.

This returns us to the superstructure, those elements of the social formation that include, for example, legal systems, politics, religion, and so on. The relations between any given mode of production (or "base") and its superstructure have often been oversimplified into a fixed, deterministic hierarchy.[45] Such a myopic, reductionist interpretation not only does a disservice to Marx's own complex understanding of the relations, but also muddies our own understanding of the nonessentialism of any given social institution or cultural practice. Marx, for example, writes that "social relations are closely bound up with productive forces. In acquiring new productive forces men change their mode of production; and in changing their mode of production, in changing the way of earning their living, they change all their social relations. The hand-mill gives you society with the feudal lord; the steam-mill, society with the industrial capitalist."[46]

Broadly then, we surmise that the earliest humans most likely gathered foods, foraged, and scavenged—we may designate these activities as forming a particular mode of production. At some point, our ancestors began to hunt and fish. Particular social systems emerged, accounting for, say, religion and other rules and responsibilities among members of society that emanated from the specific mode of production. It would be quite nonsensical to argue the obverse—that religion precedes the ability to gather food and find shelter. Over time, alterations of the rules (located within the superstructure) might lead to transformations of the mode of production; likewise, alterations of the mode of production may lead to transformations of the superstructure. Throughout human history, therefore, a dialectic transformation of social formations is evident—although *not* predictable in any vulgar deterministic manner. Academics have, of course, since abstracted (at very high, universal levels) particular epochal social formations (for example, feudalism, capitalism) and have often presented these as static, linear stages of development—both approaches that actually run counter to Marx's ontology.

There are no clear breaks or necessarily identifiable irruptions between one mode of production and another.[47] Accordingly, certain elements exhibit continuity; marriage, for example, assumes different concrete forms in different social formations, although the concept "marriage" continues. Historians have documented, for example, how dominant conceptions of marriage as an institution defined by monogamous, heterosexual relations have transcended different social formations (for example, from feudalism to capitalism) and within variants of dominant social formations (from industrial capitalism to advanced capitalism).

Once established, any institution (criminal law, marriage, government) will develop a "life" of its own—albeit a "life" contingent upon the totality of the social formation. Paul Paolucci explains that superstructural elements may survive over time, especially if they are compatible with a transformed mode of production. Consequently, "if they survive, they are likely to take on the normative and metaphysical appearance of tradition, especially as knowledge of their origins recedes into the past (e.g., religion)."[48] To this end, we will understand that throughout Democratic Kampuchea, many policies exhibit more so a continuation of past practice than they do a radical break.

Finally, to argue that the superstructure emanates (rises) from the base is not to unduly privilege the latter over the former. It does not follow that "emanation" equates with "domination." Consider, for example, the statement that steam emanates from boiling water. Here, energy combines with water to produce steam; steam emanates from water. This does not privilege water over steam or steam over water. It is, however, recognition that absent energy or water, steam is not possible. As corollary, is it possible to have law or education, for example, without an underlying mode of production? I would argue no, because the mode of production accounts for the processes by which the materiality of day-to-day life is experienced. Does law or education influence how the materiality of social reproduction takes place? Yes, and this brings home the point that the *relation* between base and superstructure is dialectic, that the base and superstructure constitute a totality. Hence, health or educational systems in Democratic Kampuchea should be viewed not as distinct from economic practices, but instead as part of a complex, integrated social formation. In short, I argue against the tendency to view Democratic Kampuchea as an aberration—as a break or rupture—in the history of Cambodia. Too often scholars compartmentalize Cambodia's past into a series of discrete epochs: the precolonial era, the colonial era, the Sihanouk era, the Democratic Kampuchea era, the People's Republic of Kampuchea, and so on. While heuristically appealing, such epochal framing serves to hide the significant continuities that thread through Cambodia's past and continue to the present day.

The Path Forward

The ideology of the Khmer Rouge has been interminably discussed, yet any frank discussion of the forces and relations of production has been stubbornly lacking. *From the Rice Fields to the Killing Fields* provides the first explicit engagement with the social organization of production in Democratic Kampuchea. It therefore marks a clear break from previous scholarship in that I attempt to establish the political economy of the Khmer Rouge through a dialectic reading of the Marxist canon and CPK policy and practice. As such, this is a book that is not only about the Communist Party of Kampuchea and its material manifestation as Democratic Kampuchea; it is also a book on Marxist political philosophy and an exploration of an "actually existing" self-described Marxist party and its attempt to promote development in the aftermath of armed conflict.

Chapter 2 provides a historical background to the Khmer Rouge revolution. Although chronological in its outlay, emphasis is placed first on the "nature" of revolutions as expounded upon by Marx, Engels, and Lenin and, second, on the interpretation of these writings by the CPK. The CPK fashioned themselves as a vanguard of the peasantry; this would have a profound impact on the subsequent postconflict reconstruction efforts after April 17, 1975. Indeed, as detailed in chapter 3, the CPK paid little attention to the formation of "permanent" governmental structures, in part because of an adherence to Lenin's claim following a socialist revolution, that the state—as an instrument of the ruling, capitalist class—would "wither away." Thus, when scholars critique the ephemeral nature of CPK institutions, they fail to recognize that this is actually very much in line with Engels and Lenin.

The argument that the space-economy of Democratic Kampuchea was predicated on a system of production for exchange is made in chapter 4. Moreover, as a member of the Non-Aligned Movement, the CPK adopted many economic strategies that were commonplace throughout the developing world, including import-substitution policies. Here, I further document that the CPK envisioned labor not merely as a means of generating surplus value but, equally important, as a materially grounded process whereby political consciousness was to be built. By extension, as Democratic Kampuchea was subsumed to the logics of production for exchange, I argue in chapter 5 that a pervasive "indifference" to life began to typify Khmer Rouge policy and practice. Consequently, the CPK established a society based not on "equality" but rather on "equivalencies" among laborers, whereby productive workers were vitally preferred over so-called unproductive workers. This is seen most clearly in chapter 6, where I reconfigure the widely held presumption that the CPK sought to abolish the household in its promotion of blind loyalty to the party. I argue instead that CPK policies and practices as they relate to the household in general, and to gender relations in particular, must be understood in direct association with processes of social reproduction and the contradictions of production and consumption. By way of conclusion, in chapter 7 I call attention to the production of mass graves, for it is in the transformation of rice fields to killing fields that the social relations of production are revealed most clearly. Emphasizing the class dimensions of CPK production, I conclude that Democratic Kampuchea constituted a variant of state capitalism. In so doing, Democratic Kampuchea provides a case study of "actually existing socialism," namely, a government that attempted to promote a socialist revolution, only to replace the very same structures of exploitation it sought to eliminate.

2

Revolution

Keo Meas devoted his entire life to the Cambodian communist movement. And like many revolutionaries, his initial foray into communism
came from a desire to liberate his homeland from colonial domination.
Soon after the Second World War, at the age of fifteen, Keo Meas dropped
out of his courses at the Phnom Penh Teacher Training College to join
a Khmer Vietminh group in Svay Rieng Province. In 1950 he was one of
only twenty-one Khmer members of the Indochinese Communist Party.
Having proven himself, he was appointed commissar of the Action Committee for Phnom Penh. In 1952 he traveled to Beijing, becoming the
first Khmer revolutionary to meet Chairman Mao Zedong.[1] Keo Meas
began to see himself as the future leader of the embryonic communist
movement in Cambodia. He was diligent in his efforts, disseminating propaganda over the "Voice of Free Cambodia" radio station, often reciting
commentaries written by Saloth Sar, a soft-spoken yet charismatic young
man who would later be known as Pol Pot.

The political fortunes of Keo Meas continued to rise. In 1954 he
assumed the position of secretary of the Phnom Penh Committee of the
Khmer People's Revolutionary Party (KPRP) that had been established
in 1951. Keo Meas participated in national elections as a member of the
Pracheachon (People's Group), a political party that he in fact helped to
establish.[2] And in 1960 he was elected to the Central Committee of the
newly formed Workers' Party of Kampuchea (WPK). Three years later,
Keo Meas lost this coveted position—but he remained in good standing
with the party. Indeed, as the communist movement neared victory in
the early 1970s, Keo Meas served as ambassador to China on behalf of
the Gouvernement Royal d'Union Nationale du Kampuchéa (GRUNK),

a coalition government formed by the deposed prince Norodom Sihanouk and the Khmer communists. By April 17, 1975, as victorious communist forces entered the capital of Phnom Penh, the veteran revolutionary Keo Meas could take pride in knowing that his place in history was ensured.

But his confidence and his life were to be short-lived. Seventeen months later, on September 20, 1976, Keo Meas was arrested and sent to S-21, a security center located in Phnom Penh. For more than one month, Keo Meas was interrogated and tortured before his eventual execution. Transcripts of his handwritten confession total ninety-six pages and contain countless details of his alleged "traitorous" activities, including a discrepancy on the founding date of Cambodia's communist party.[3]

The ordeal of Keo Meas is particularly salient for any account of the Communist Party of Kampuchea, for the Orwellian nature of his captivity and execution personifies the administrative violence typical of the Khmer Rouge. When Keo Meas was arrested, there had been no public announcement of the party's existence. However, two contradictory magazine stories appeared around the time of his arrest. In 1976 the September issue of the CPK's youth magazine, *Yuvechon Nung Yuvanearei Padevat* (Youth of the Revolution), opened with a sixteen-page article celebrating the twenty-fifth anniversary of the party's founding. The article began: "From the moment of its creation on September 30, 1951, the Communist Party of Kampuchea led everyone, including the revolutionary Cambodian youths, in the struggle against French imperialism." The following month, however, the CPK's official journal, *Tung Padevat* (Revolutionary Flag), opened with a thirty-two-page article, commemorating the party's sixteenth anniversary. Most likely written by Pol Pot, the article explained: "Last year we informed people . . . that our Party was 24 years-old. . . . But now we celebrate the 16th anniversary of the party, because we are making a new numeration. What rationale is there for this? The revolutionary organization had decided that from now on we must arrange the history of the party into something clean and perfect, in line with our policies of independence and self-mastery."[4] It is likely that Pol Pot wrote both articles in an attempt to draw "1951" factions, including long-term revolutionaries such as Keo Meas, into the open. It was a move seemingly straight out of Stalin's notebook and provides our entry point into the political philosophy of the CPK and, by corollary, the political economy of Democratic Kampuchea.

The "Nature" of Revolutions

Every mode of production, Marx proposed, contains its own potential transformation. Following Hegelian logic, historical change—revolution—occurs when the forces of production are impeded by the relations of production. As class antagonisms harden, a revolutionary transformation is initiated that ultimately results in the establishment of a new mode of production—a new society, a new way of life. It was at this point that Marx, based on his reading of European history, offered four broad epochs: primitive communism, slavery, feudalism, and capitalism. For Marx, the designation of these epochs was not to develop a unified, linear metahistory, but rather to call attention to the dialectics of societal change. Consider, for example, capitalism, an economic system in which the material conditions of existence are to be obtained primarily on the "free" market. Wage labor is a defining characteristic, as is private ownership of the means of production. Furthermore, capitalism is driven by certain systemic imperatives, namely, competition and profit accumulation. Marx observed in England, France, and a handful of other European countries that capitalism had increased to the point that all basic material needs could be satisfied, yet throngs of men, women, and children lived in conditions of extreme poverty. Capitalists had enslaved the working class through their appropriation of the means of production and unfairly usurped the surplus value generated by the workers. Moreover, this form of exploitation was legal—but only from the standpoint that those who owned the means of production also had the means to determine law itself.

Contradictions—manifest in the material conditions of society—provided, for Marx, the catalyst for societal change.[5] For Marx, the fundamental contradiction, of abject poverty amid obscene plenty, was brought about by exploitation—the systemic and systematic theft of the fruits of workers' labors. Capitalism, according to Marx, had enslaved and alienated the proletariat through the appropriation of the means of production.

The resolution of this contradiction, Marx argues, is found within capitalism itself, for within every mode of production are found the seeds of its own destruction. In a series of articles written between January and October 1850, Marx proposed that revolutions are the locomotives of history.[6] Marx explains, "At a certain stage of development, the material productive forces of society come into conflict with the existing relations of production. . . . From forms of development of the productive forces these relations turn into their fetters. Then begins an era of social revolution. The changes in the economic foundation lead sooner or later to the transformation of the whole immense superstructure." Stated differently, as workers recognize the origins of their suffering—that poverty is not a natural human condition but instead results from exploitative and oppressive labor practices associated with the capitalist mode of production—a revolutionary transformation will spontaneously arise. Thus, while materially grounded, revolutions result from a changed *consciousness* among the exploited masses. It is here that Marx famously concludes: "It is not the consciousness of men that determines their existence, but their social existence that determines their consciousness."[7]

Throughout his lifetime there were many ill-fated attempts throughout Europe—but especially in France—to bring about a socialist revolution. In all cases, however, these efforts failed, leading those who followed Marx to ascertain why. On the one hand, it was thought that the conditions for revolution had not been appropriate, for Marx himself warned, "No social order is ever destroyed before all the productive forces for which it is sufficient have been developed, and new superior relations of production never replace older ones before the material conditions for their existence have matured within the framework of the old society."[8] Failed revolutions, simply stated, illustrated that an appropriate level of economic development had not been reached and that the proletariat had not sufficiently realized its exploitation.

On the other hand, some Marxists premised that the failure to develop a revolutionary consciousness was contingent upon other factors. In the early twentieth century, Vladimir Lenin provided an important addendum to the corpus of Marx's writings. Lenin deduced that European imperialism had delayed the proletarian revolution. For Lenin, capitalists were able to "buy" off their workers while still garnering substantial profits. Motivated to increase profits, capitalists were hindered by diminishing domestic markets and an increasingly agitated and potentially revolutionary proletariat. Consequently, through military-enforced imperial ventures, both states and private corporations were able to establish overseas colonies. Apart from providing new markets and sources of raw materials, colonies served to diffuse class animosity in the home country. Consequently, colonies fueled racist and nationalist discourse, and, in the process, capitalists were able to share some of their profits with the proletariat. In effect, profits were redirected to the workers in the home country and accounted for a marginal improvement in the lives of the workers. These improvements served to temper the contradictions inherent in capitalism.

It is not difficult to imagine the salience of these arguments for Pol Pot and other Cambodian revolutionaries. For the better part of a century, Cambodia constituted part of French Indochina, a political entity that included Tonkin, Annam, Cochin China, and Laos. Illustrating well the arguments of Lenin, French authorities exploited Indochina in an apparent effort to stave off revolution at home. Indeed, it would not have gone unnoticed to the Cambodians that the abortive class struggles in France that Marx described went hand in hand with France's imperial ventures in Southeast Asia.

France's colonization of present-day Vietnam, Laos, and Cambodia began in August 1858, when a French naval force bombarded the Vietnamese port city of Danang, ostensibly to obtain religious liberty for Catholics. A more pressing concern, though, was to force the acceptance of French trade and diplomatic representatives. In 1862, after three years of military conflict, France exacted a treaty from the Vietnamese emperor. As part of this agreement, Vietnamese ceded three southern provinces to the French, as well as assurances that no other part of Vietnam would be transferred to any other power. Furthermore, the emperor agreed to pay an indemnity of four million piasters in ten annual installments and to open three ports in central Vietnam to French trade. France was also given permission to freely navigate the Mekong River. Over the subsequent two decades, a French colonial presence spread to encompass the entirety of Vietnam, as French officials directed their attention northward, toward the Red River, and declared a protectorate over northern Vietnam (Tonkin), followed by the establishment of a protectorate in central Vietnam (Annam).

French expansion led to conflicts with neighboring kingdoms and, consequently, further territorial gains. In 1867 the Siamese king relinquished claims to Cambodia in exchange for two Khmer provinces. During the 1870s and 1880s, France likewise claimed the territories of present-day Laos. Laos, at the time, did not exist as a sovereign state but instead was composed of various principalities. The northern Laotian kingdom of Luang Prabang, for example, existed as a peripheral entity controlled by the Thai monarchy. In the 1880s France claimed the lands east of the Mekong River, arguing that these areas were once part of Vietnam and therefore now belonged to the French. In the 1890s French warships attacked the Siamese forces at Pakam, located at the mouth of the Chao Phraya, and gradually worked their way north to the capital at Bangkok. The Siamese court capitulated, ceding all control of Laos to the French.

For the neighboring kingdom of Cambodia, French colonialism was a double-edged sword. On the one hand, the French provided a level of security to an embattled Khmer king. On the other hand, this security came with a steep price, namely, a loss of sovereignty. By the nineteenth century, the Khmer kingdom was but a shadow of its former self. Between the ninth and fourteenth centuries, Khmer kings had reigned over vast territories that included all of present-day Cambodia and much of Thailand, Burma, Laos, and Vietnam. The reign of Suryavarman II (r. 1113–50), for example, stretched from central Vietnam in the East to the Irrawaddy River in the West. From the fifteenth century onward, however, internal decay, economic collapse, and foreign encroachment threatened the very survival of the Khmer polity. Various Khmer kings made ill-fated and largely unsuccessful attempts to secure the sovereignty of their kingdom. In 1593, for example, King Sattha (r. 1576–94) asked the Spanish governor of the Philippines for help in halting Siamese advances. This arrangement failed, and in 1594 Siamese forces captured the Khmer capital, then located at Lovek, north of Phnom Penh. A new capital was established at Oudong, and all subsequent Khmer monarchs were required to enter into vassal relationships with Siam. Similar political arrangements were demanded by Vietnamese emperors.[9]

In 1853 the Khmer king Ang Duang (r. 1848–60) dispatched a letter to the French emperor, Napoleon III, requesting assistance. It is unknown if Napoleon responded. However, three years later, a French diplomatic mission arrived to negotiate a commercial treaty with the Khmer king. This arrangement never materialized, but French officials became enamored with the economic possibilities offered by the Khmer kingdom. Interests were further whetted by the much-publicized travels of French naturalist Henri Mouhot, who had journeyed up the Mekong River between 1859 and 1861. It was Mouhot who had "discovered" the ruins of Angkor and raised the possibility that vast riches were to be found in the Khmer kingdom. Accordingly, following the death of Ang Duang in 1860, French officials secured a treaty with the king's successor and eldest son, Norodom (r. 1860–1904). In 1863, in exchange for timber concessions and mineral exploration rights, Cambodia was declared a French protectorate.[10]

In 1893 the Union Indochinoise was formed by French authorities, consisting of Tonkin, Annam, Cochin China, Laos, and Cambodia. It was hoped, for the French, that Indochina would provide needed raw materials for France. Colonies, however, are expensive propositions, and many French officials expressed concern that overseas ventures would result in a heavy domestic tax burden. Consequently, arrangements were made so that these costs would be transferred directly to the colonies. Throughout the region as a whole, a new tax system was imposed.[11] Local budgets were formed, based on direct taxation of residents, and used to defray the costs of developing the entire colonial structure. Additional revenue was generated by placing high tariffs on goods imported into the colonies and by organizing state-controlled monopolies that sold licenses for the production and distribution of opium, alcohol, and salt. Most of the funds were directed toward the construction of bridges, railroads, and harbors—necessary ingredients to fully exploit the raw materials offered by the colonies.[12] In addition, the French colonial government raised agricultural taxes and imposed a head tax that had to be paid in cash. This policy forced many peasant families—mostly throughout parts of Vietnam—to send their husbands, fathers, and sons to the cities, mines, and plantations in search of wage labor. Through the process, France created its own supply of surplus labor, one that was exploited for work in coal mines and rice and rubber plantations.[13]

The French emphasis on making Indochina self-sufficient and self-supporting contributed to wide-reaching and uneven transformations in local communities. On the one hand, Indochina as a whole would provide a source of raw materials for France. Rubber was promoted, and large quantities of latex were exported to France, where it was converted into tires and other finished products. In turn, these commodities were exported back to Indochina, generating profits for domestic industries in France. Consequently, throughout Indochina, manufacturing was largely neglected, and the region was further isolated as France prevented other European competitors from exporting manufactured goods to the region. On the other hand, French authorities approached the regional components of Indochina quite differently. French penetration in Tonkin, for example, was rather minimal. In the South, however, the Vietnamese society and economy were dramatically altered. From the outset, French colonial administration in Cochin China adopted a narrow fiscal objective of balancing the colonial budget, paying the ever-expanding French administration personnel, and, if possible, creating a profitable economy that would justify the costs of colonization. A major vehicle was the cultivation of rice for export.[14] This was made possible, in part, through the introduction of private ownership and the establishment of large landholdings. Here, conditions for a communist-inspired revolution were decidedly more palpable, in that absentee landlords had gained control of most cultivable land, leading to the emergence of a dispossessed, landless population. Peasants were further exploited through heavy taxes and high rates of usury. Rents, for example, usually represented 50 percent or more of the primary rice crop; in some cases, loans extended by the landlord for seeds, equipment, and draft animals could raise the landlord's share to 70 or 80 percent.[15]

By 1920 new social classes had emerged in Vietnamese society. On the one hand, there appeared an upper and a lower middle class. The former was composed of affluent members of the commercial and professional sectors and included bankers, land speculators, absentee landlords, engineers, agronomists, doctors, and merchants. Most of these individuals adopted a French cultural veneer: they sent their children to French schools, drank French wine, ate French cuisine, and lived in colonial villas in the suburbs of Saigon. The lower middle class, conversely, consisted of the noncommercial urban intelligentsia, composed of teachers, journalists, clerks, and students. These families, for the most part, obtained fewer advances from French authorities and so were less supportive of colonial rule. This petty bourgeoisie would, in time, form a primary source of revolutionary discontent against French colonial rule in Vietnam. On the other hand, a growing proletariat appeared. These workers were largely employed in enterprises associated with the colonial regime, as factory workers in Saigon and Hanoi, coal miners in Tonkin, plantation workers in Cochin China, or dockworkers in Saigon and Haiphong.[16]

Following the defeat of Japan, and pursuant to the Potsdam agreements of July 1945, British troops occupied Vietnam south of the sixteenth parallel, while Chinese nationalist forces occupied territories north of the partition. Initially denied access to their former colony, French officials maneuvered so as to reestablish a dominant presence on the Southeast Asian mainland. On February 8, 1946, the French secured, through the Franco-Chinese Accords, a Chinese withdrawal from the North; a subsequent agreement with the United Kingdom shored up France's position in the South. Ho Chi Minh, for his part, declared the Democratic Republic of Vietnam (DRV) independent on September 2, 1945.

On March 6, 1946, a Preliminary Convention was signed in Hanoi, whereby France promised to recognize the government of the DRV as a free state within the French Union. This would in effect grant Vietnam its own parliament, army, and finances; it would also be part of an Indochinese Federation that included Cambodia and Laos. A referendum was also to be scheduled throughout Tonkin, Annam, and Cochin China to determine, ostensibly, the final political status of Vietnam. This arrangement proved undesirable to the Vietnamese, however, in that it left unclear the question of whether Vietnam would remain a single unified country or possibly three republics.[17]

Ho Chi Minh sought a Vietnam that reunited Cochin China, Annam, and Tonkin. French officials, however, were adamant in their objective to tie their former colonies—in whatever political form—to France, both economically and politically. More precisely, the French viewed Cochin China in particular, but Indochina broadly, as pivotal to their postwar reconstruction plans. Given this political reality, Ho Chi Minh sought assistance from the international community; his efforts, however, went for naught. In the United States, the Truman administration was more concerned with the reconstruction of Europe; consequently, any interest directed toward Southeast Asia was in support of the French. The Soviet Union likewise failed to provide any substantial assistance. Similar to their American counterparts, Soviet officials balanced European objectives against those of Asia, with the former taking priority.

Failing to achieve success on the diplomatic front, the DRV turned to armed conflict, and on December 19, 1946, the Franco-Vietminh War began. Lasting eight years, the conflict would result in more than 170,000 casualties for the French, while upwards of 1 million Vietnamese would perish.

French Colonialism in Cambodia

In Cambodia similar but less drastic economic transformations were occurring. Throughout the early twentieth century, French colonial authorities implemented a dual economic development policy based on the export of agricultural products, notably rice. First, large-scale rice plantations based on modern farming methods and irrigation were established on land concessions, located primarily in Battambang Province. To facilitate the distribution of rice, a rail line was constructed from Battambang City to Phnom Penh; from there, barges would carry rice to Saigon via the Mekong River. A second system consisted of almost the entire Khmer peasantry, who continued to grow rice using traditional methods on small farm holdings throughout the country. Here, the French acquired needed surpluses of rice through taxation; this became the largest source of governmental revenue.[18]

Taken together, rice exports were to boost supply for the French agro-processing facilities and international export trade system centered in Saigon.[19] In effect, Cambodia became a colony within a colony. Moreover,

for reasons couched in colonial racist discourse, the French also facilitated the large-scale introduction of Vietnamese workers into the Khmer
economy. On the one hand, Vietnamese labor was preferentially hired to
work on the newly established rice and rubber plantations, and, on the
other hand, more skilled Vietnamese workers were hired as administrative
staff, in that the French, collectively, viewed Khmer workers as inherently
indolent.

Despite these conditions, as a whole, the Khmer peasantry was not
exceptionally interested in revolution.[20] Even during the Second World
War, as Cambodia was occupied by Japanese forces and governed by representatives of the collaborationist Vichy government, active resistance
by "liberation" groups, known as Issaraks, was minimal and concentrated
mostly in the provinces of Battambang and Siem Reap. Apart from forming the core of Cambodia's rice-growing regions—Battambang alone was
exporting upwards of thirty thousand tons of rice annually—these territories had recently been ceded by the French to the pro-Japanese government of Thailand, thus providing a nationalist argument for resistance.[21]

The impetus for revolution in Cambodia, consequently, was foreign
in origin.[22] Unlike Cambodia, Vietnam was witness to a host of revolutionary groups formed to liberate the country from French rule. Some of
these were nationalist in outlook, such as the Viet Nam Quoc Dan Dang
(Vietnamese Nationalist Party), modeled after the Kuomintang, Sun Yat-
Sen's Chinese Nationalist Party. Others were inspired by Marxist-Leninist
doctrine, such as the Vietnamese Revolutionary Youth League, or Viet
Nam Thanh Nien Cach Mang Dong Chi Hoi, formed in 1925 by the
thirty-five-year-old Ho Chi Minh. Even this latter organization, however,
was more nationalist in scope than it was communist.

During the 1920s and 1930s, Soviet influence over events in Indochina, but primarily in Vietnam, was substantial. From the perspective
of the Comintern, French colonial rule had imposed a framework of
unity among Indochina, and this, rather than nationalism, should serve
as the foundation for revolution.[23] Having witnessed the violent sunder-
ing of nationalist-communist alliances in both China and the Dutch East
Indies, Soviet officials pressured the Vietnamese to form a united front
against French imperialism. As a result, efforts were made to transform

Ho's Revolutionary Youth League into a communist, as opposed to nationalist, party. This proved unsuccessful, however, leading to the formation of the Indochinese Communist Party (ICP, or Dong Duong Cong San Dang). In turn, the Revolutionary Youth League renamed itself the Annam Communist Party (Annam Cong San Dang). To this was added a third competing communist party, the Indochinese Communist League (Dong Duong Con San Lien Doan).[24]

The existence of three competing communist parties was neither practical nor desirable for anyone involved. In response, at the urging of Ho Chi Minh, a united party was proposed. Ho proposed that the party, known as the Vietnamese Communist Party (VCP), be open to all Vietnamese who opposed the French. This suggests, at one level, Ho's commitment to a nationalist-based revolution. Under the instigation of the Soviet Union, however, the VCP was in 1930 transformed into the Indochinese Communist Party—not to be confused with the earlier party of the same name. This was not welcome news to many Vietnamese nationalists, although many came to accept the argument that liberation in Vietnam was contingent upon liberation in Cambodia and Laos.

In early 1951 the ICP was formally dissolved and renamed the Vietnamese Workers' Party (VWP, Dang Lao don Viet Nam), a move designed to coincide with Vietnamese efforts to facilitate the formation of separate revolutionary parties in Indochina. Consequently, Cambodia's first "authentic" communist party was established, the Khmer People's Revolutionary Party. Prominent members included Son Ngoc Minh, Tou Samouth, Sieu Heng, Keo Moni, So Phim, and Keo Meas, all veteran revolutionaries who, according to Dmitry Mosyakov, acted hand in hand with the Vietnamese in the anticolonial war and were truly valued allies and strict executors of all the plans drafted by the ICP.[25]

Within communist parties, titles are both significant and symbolic. Steve Heder explains that the "Vietnamese choice of the formulation Revolutionary People's Party . . . was derived from Soviet Communist terminology of the 1920s, according to which a Revolutionary People's Party was led and dominated by an external proletarian vanguard." Such nomenclature reflects a deep-seated chauvinism existing within the international communist bloc. The Comintern, for example, put forward the notion of a revolutionary people's party to apply to "backward," "primitive," or "tribal" areas; this reflected, in turn, "Stalin's conviction that the right of nations to self-determination should be understood in terms or proletarian self-determination, suggesting that those without proletariats had, at best, a qualified right to self-determination."[26]

The KPRP was heavily influenced, if not dominated, by their Vietnamese compatriots. Indeed, according to Heder, the "Vietnamese definition of revolutionary people meant it was to comprise 'the best elements in the mass organizations led and educated by the Party.'"[27] The final draft of the party's statutes, based on a simplified version of the VWP statutes, was first written in Vietnamese and then translated into Khmer. Equally telling was that the party's mandate was to fight imperialism and not to wage a socialist revolution. In retrospect, this is not at all surprising, and the explicit omission to any reference to communism actually conformed to Leninist doctrine—a point I develop in greater detail later. Here, suffice it to say that for both Khmer and Vietnamese cadre, it was essential to represent the revolution to the peasantry as a quest for independence from French rule.[28] In terms of organization, the KPRP "would be covertly led by the ICP, and, according to its Vietnamese-drafted statutes, function as 'vanguard of the Cambodian people incorporating those sincere patriots and democrats most noted for their loyalty, their enthusiasm and their spirit of sacrifice within the ranks of the resistance.'"[29]

A Vanguard in Search of a Revolution

For many people living in Cambodia in 1954, the future looked promising. In the previous year, the Khmer monarch, Norodom Sihanouk, had embarked on a "Royal Crusade" for independence. Making appearances in Paris, Washington, and even Tokyo, Sihanouk argued that he alone could keep his country free from communism. And while his direct efforts largely went for naught, French authorities were compelled to grant Cambodia its independence on November 9, 1953, mainly because they were preoccupied with deteriorating conditions in Vietnam. Indeed, by this point it was becoming all too clear that the French were destined to lose the first Indochina War.

For most Khmer revolutionaries, however, the year brought uncertainty in purpose. Simply put, the immediate goals of the revolution were accomplished: Cambodia was free from foreign rule, and both French and Vietnamese forces were departing. As Chandler explains, most Khmer "were reluctant to become involved in rebellious politics after Cambodia's independence had been won."[30]

Vietnam was a different story. Despite military victory at Dien Bien Phu, Vietnamese communists were compelled to accept a shattering diplomatic defeat. Between May 8 and July 21, 1954, an international convention was held in Geneva, Switzerland, to negotiate the end of the eight-year Franco-Vietminh War. The Vietnamese proposed a temporary division at the thirteenth parallel, just north of Saigon, with elections to determine national unity to be held in six months' time. The French countered with a boundary along the eighteenth parallel, south of Hanoi, with no elections. This in effect would create two sovereign states: the Democratic Republic of Vietnam in the North and the State of Vietnam in the South. As a compromise, Soviet foreign minister Vyacheslav Molotov proposed a partition along the seventeenth parallel, just north of Hue; elections would be held in two years. Vietnamese leaders were dismayed by this turn of events; anything short of a unified Vietnam was viewed as a failure. Representatives of the People's Republic of China (PRC), however, pressured the Vietnamese to accept the terms; from their vantage point, any stability on the Indochinese peninsula was preferable to the specter of possible American military intervention.[31]

Representatives of the Vietnamese Communist Party were also thwarted in their attempt to include members of the KPRP. Sihanouk had appointed a small delegation of representatives, including Nong Kimny, Sam Sary, and Tep Phan, none of whom were communists. In turn, Pham Van Dong, representative of the DRV, proposed that members of the communist-dominated "resistance movements" in Laos and Cambodia also be present, a proposition initially supported by both the Soviet Union and the PRC. However, the Sihanouk-backed representatives strongly voiced their objections, and both the PRC and the Soviet Union backed down, persuading Pham Van Dong to drop his request. Crucially, the Vietnamese did make private arrangements that, in principle, would facilitate their

Khmer counterparts, namely, that approximately one thousand Khmer communists would be permitted to stay in the DRV to receive military and political training. Included among these members was Son Ngoc Minh, the highest-ranking member of the KPRP, and most of the experienced and time-tested veterans of the anticolonial movement: Sieu Heng (who would return in ten months), So Phim, and Keo Moni.[32] At an appropriate time, these "Khmer Vietminh" would be expected to return to Cambodia to lead an armed revolution.

The acquiescence of China, Vietnam, and the Soviet Union to Sihanouk was a devastating affront for many Khmer revolutionaries, for it signaled more than anything the willingness of foreign powers to sacrifice Cambodia in pursuit of their own nationalist objectives. This was, however, consistent with the understanding of the communist movement in Cambodia put forward by the Vietnamese. Within Cambodia, the Vietnamese deduced that there was no viable proletariat; consequently, the country was viewed by the Vietnamese communists as "backward" and needing external guidance. Tactically, this meant that dual revolutions were proposed: The Vietnamese considered their revolution a people's democratic revolution, one that would sweep away feudalism and help build a foundation for socialism. The Cambodian revolution, conversely, was perceived by the Vietnamese as a simple national revolution, one that was not yet ready to build the foundation for socialism.[33] Consequently, the leadership in Hanoi determined that the Khmer revolution would be postponed until conditions in Vietnam warranted it. This meant, practically, that not only must the Khmer communists forestall armed insurrection, but they would also be required to support the neutralist and anticommunist monarch, Sihanouk. For the Vietnamese, the intensifying struggle against the United States was all-consuming, as it was imperative that Cambodia remain neutral—at least in the short term—so as to prevent the United States from establishing a base of operations on Vietnam's western border. It was for this *military* reason that the Vietnamese pressured the Khmer communists to support Sihanouk.[34] Consequently, a dual strategy was proposed, whereby, on the one hand, a legitimate political party, the Pracheachon, was formed to participate in upcoming elections and, on the other hand, more clandestine strategies were pursued. For this second approach, Khmer cadre would assume public positions as, for example, teachers or journalists while clandestinely recruiting new members. Organizationally, the KRPR was divided into two groups. Sieu Heng oversaw political activities in the rural areas, and Tou Samouth was responsible for party affairs in the capital and other provincial towns.

Disagreements within the Cambodian communist movement were apparent. Members of a growing Pol Pot faction, for example, participated, to a degree, with these tactics. However, their basic objectives and hence methods differed strongly from other Khmer revolutionaries. According to Ben Kiernan, "The Pol Pot group tended to be implacably opposed to [the Sihanouk regime], as a backward, dictatorial monarchy; as younger militants they wanted to strike back against repression, and being more middle-class in background they were particularly infuriated by Sihanouk's 'feudal' characteristics, his personalized autocracy, and the fawning praise of him that was required of everyone in public life. The veterans, on the other hand, were much more inclined to see Sihanouk's neutrality and his increasingly anti-imperialist stance as positive factors in an Indo-China-wide struggle for socialism."[35]

A quarter century later, Pol Pot would explain:

After preparing and building the revolutionary forces to defeat the enemy, what forms of struggle did we have to use? The First Congress of our Party[36] specified the following forms of revolutionary struggle: The first form of struggle was to use revolutionary violence and revolutionary armed violence. We resorted to revolutionary violence in both political and armed struggle to oppose and attack the enemy. The second form was legal, semi-legal and illegal struggle, taking illegal struggle as the basic form. We took the illegal form as the basis because, normally, making revolution is "illegal." There is no law of the exploiting classes authorizing revolution. To mobilize the people for struggle is "illegal," but don't we dare to struggle anyway? If you make revolution, you must dare to struggle, because revolution is "illegal." Revolution overthrows the old power and installs a new power. It is for this reason that our line specified illegal forms as the basis.[37]

The correct line, for the Pol Pot faction, closely mirrored Lenin's elaboration of the dictatorship of the proletariat. Marx used the phrase in reference to the political system adopted immediately after the French proletariat briefly seized political power in 1848. For Marx, all forms of rule were considered "dictatorships." This did not suggest, however, an opposition to democracy; indeed, it was through such dictatorships that authentic democracy could emerge. In the mid-nineteenth century, "dictatorship" was normally associated with the politics of ancient Rome, whereby a ruler would be granted or assume supreme power for a temporary period in order to defend the republic. In other words, a dictatorship formed a "state of exception," whereby law was not abolished but instead suspended. As Giorgio Agamben elaborates, drawing on German jurist Carl Schmitt, a state of exception exists whereby the sovereign (that is, the dictator) stands both inside and outside law itself. Agamben writes, "As a figure of necessity, the state of exception . . . appears as an 'illegal' but perfectly 'juridical and constitutional' measure that is realized in the production of new norms."[38] This has tremendous purchase in understanding both Lenin's conception of the dictatorship of the proletariat and the subsequent adoption of the concept by Pol Pot.

In 1903 Lenin reformulated Marxist doctrine to align with the material conditions of Russia. At the dawn of the twentieth century, Russia was still largely a feudal society and lacked a sizable proletariat. From an orthodox Marxist standpoint, the conditions for revolution were premature. Russian society had not developed to a point whereby class contradictions were readily apparent; the infinitesimal proletariat lacked an adequate political consciousness. However, Lenin read in Marx and Engels's *Communist Manifesto* a possible way forward, whereby an industrial stage could be bypassed on the path to communism. In the fourth and final section of the *Manifesto*, Marx and Engels write, "The communists everywhere support every revolutionary movement against the existing social and political order of things. In all these movements they bring to the front, as the leading question in each, the property question, *no matter what its degree of development at the time*."[39] In other words, optimal conditions for revolution were *not* necessary. Years later, this same passage would prove foundational for China's communist movement. In the 1920s and 1930s, China had an even smaller proletariat, as the country was predominantly agrarian. Was it possible, early Chinese Marxists wondered, to transition directly from a precapitalist society to a communal society? Stated differently, was a "great leap forward" possible?

For Lenin, the answer lay in the development of a political organization composed of professional revolutionaries—a dictatorship of the proletariat.[40] Required was an organization that was both *outside* and *inside* the revolution, an organization that established the limits of law itself.

According to one reading of Marxist doctrine, the political nation-state was a manifestation of bourgeoisie rule. In support of this position, one could point to the suggestion put forward by Marx and Engels that the superstructure reflected the interests of the dominant, or ruling, class, that is, those members who controlled the means of production. In slave societies, for example, it was the slave owners who determined and enforced the legal system; likewise, under feudalism it was the landed elite. As Marx and Engels maintain, "The ideas of the ruling class are in every epoch the ruling ideas: i.e. the class which is the ruling material force of society is at the same time its ruling intellectual force." They continue, "The class which has the means of material production at its disposal, consequently also controls the means of mental production, so that the ideas of those who lack the means of mental production on are the whole subject to it. The ruling ideas are nothing more than the ideal expression of the dominant material relations."[41]

The capitalist state, moreover, was a *repressive* state. Law, for example, was written by the ruling class, and violent state apparatuses, such as the police and the military, were deployed in support of law. For Lenin, therefore, the capitalist state was synonymous with a "dictatorship of the bourgeoisie," and the ruling class inhabited a state of exception. It was only through this political structure that the *legal* theft of the workers' livelihood was preserved.

Revolutions would not erupt spontaneously, Lenin concluded, nor could revolutions be maintained, for the simple fact that any movement would be violently suppressed. Localized riots, trade unions, and strikes paled in comparison to the power of the capitalist state. Revolutionary struggle—especially struggles against the police or military—required, for Lenin, the organization of professional revolutionaries.

Many members of the Cambodian communist movement, including Pol Pot, viewed themselves as—or at least claimed to be—a "dictatorship of the proletariat." In the years following the revolution, for example, Pol Pot announced in a public speech that victory had been achieved through "the implementation of the Party's dictatorship of the proletariat in all areas of . . . revolutionary activity." However, he cautioned that "we absolutely, without hesitation, apply the dictatorship of the proletariat to our enemies and to the tiny handful of reactionary elements who oppose the revolution, who seek to destroy it, who sell out to the foreign imperialists and reactionaries in order to ruin their own nation, their own people and their own revolution."[42]

From 1960 onward, a secretive vanguard known as Angkar and dominated by Pol Pot began to coalesce.[43] Lenin argues that a vanguard organization "must of necessity be not too extensive and as secret as possible." He elaborates that "a small, compact core, consisting of reliable, experienced and hardened workers, with responsible agents in the principal districts and connected by all the rules of strict secrecy with the organizations of revolutionaries, can, with the wide support of the masses and without an elaborate organization, perform all the functions."[44]

In 1960 Pol Pot took the first necessary step. For the previous three years, Pol Pot had "focused on research, in order to formulate a strategic and tactical line for the Cambodian revolution and draft new, properly Communist statutes to replace those of the proto-Communist [KPRP]."[45] Now, during a secret meeting held at the Phnom Penh railway station between September 30 and October 2, 1960, Pol Pot and a handful of trusted colleagues met to form, in hindsight, what would be called a dictatorship of the proletariat. Indeed, so secretive was this event that neither most veteran Khmer revolutionaries nor their Vietnamese counterparts had any idea as to what was happening.

Since 1951 the Vietnamese communists dictated the conditions of revolution inside Cambodia, and throughout this period veteran Khmer leaders supported, albeit grudgingly, this state of affairs. By 1960, however, the situation was rapidly changing. In the United States–supported Republic of Vietnam (South Vietnam), communist insurgents pressed the DRV for permission to wage armed rebellion. Up to now, the communist leadership in the North had urged patience, for fear of drawing the United States into a protracted ground war. Indeed, since 1954 official policy for the DRV was to limit revolutionary activities in the South to political agitation, and only in 1956 were armed self-defense units formed. However, in 1959 the Vietnamese communists agreed to the use of armed struggle; it was decided that violence was no longer just to be used defensively to protect the party and its bases, but should be used offensively to disrupt and destroy the enemy administration at the most basic levels in the countryside.[46] In the following year, the National Liberation Front (NLF, colloquially known as the "Vietcong") was established. Its purpose was to engage in guerrilla activities, foment a general communist revolution in the South, and contribute to the ultimate reunification of Vietnam. This strategy, however, was predicated on continued access to Cambodia. As Vietnamese forces enlarged their military efforts, numerous transportation routes and bases were established throughout eastern Laos and, especially, eastern Cambodia. Known collectively as the "Ho Chi Minh Trail," these supply chains would prove invaluable both for NLF insurgent activities and for larger military campaigns conducted by the North Vietnamese Army (NVA). Access to Cambodia, though, was conditional upon Sihanouk's assurance or, at the minimum, acceptance of neutrality.

The Khmer communists were once again let down by the Vietnamese, who continued to urge support for the monarch despite his ongoing repression against communists. In 1954, for example, the longtime Khmer veteran Sieu Heng defected. In the aftermath of independence, he saw little reason for revolution. However, rather than simply walking away, Sieu Heng turned informant, routing information on communist activities to Sihanouk's general and police chief, Lon Nol. Over the next four years, Sieu Heng provided the government with the names of Khmer communists living and working in rural areas. Lon Nol, in turn, moved quickly to eliminate the revolutionaries. By 1959 the KRPR lost nearly 90 percent of its rural-based cadre; some were murdered, others quit out of fear, and many more simply disappeared.[47]

It was within this context that the Pol Pot faction assembled in 1960 with the explicit purpose of taking over the communist movement. Symbolically, the KPRP was renamed the Workers' Party of Kampuchea.[48] Tou Samouth was elected party secretary, Nuon Chea as deputy, and Pol Pot as the third-highest-ranking member. The newly established committee offers crucial insight into the rapid and sweeping transformation of the Khmer revolution taking place. The composition of the committee, for example, still favored longtime revolutionaries with ties to the ICP. Pol Pot was the only member of the more radical members to assume a senior position. This would change, however, within the span of three years. In 1962 Tou Samouth disappeared. It remains unclear who arranged for Tou Samouth's apparent murder. One argument, for example, holds that Sihanouk's security policy assassinated the revolutionary, possibly with the assistance of Sieu Heng or even Pol Pot. Regardless of the actual cause, months later, at another secret meeting held in Phnom Penh, Pol Pot was elected secretary-general. Nuon Chea retained the second position, joined by Ieng Sary, So Phim, and Vorn Vet. Significantly, of the twelve Central Committee members, members of the Pol Pot faction held the positions 1, 3, 5, 6, and 11. Son Ngoc Minh, still in the DRV, remained on the committee, while longtime veterans Keo Meas and Non Suon were dropped. Other prominent veterans also failed to be included on the Central Committee.[49]

On March 4, 1963, Sihanouk published a list of thirty-four known and suspected communists. The names had been compiled by Lon Nol and his security police, based on their ongoing surveillance of journalists and eachers. Included on the list were the names of Pol Pot, Ieng Sary, and Son Sen. In the immediate aftermath of the public pronouncement, no arrests were made. However, for those identified, the list sounded a warning note.

Pol Pot and other key leaders had in fact been contemplating a withdrawal to the maquis for some time, as it was becoming all too apparent that political and social change would not be forthcoming through open and democratic processes. On March 31, Pol Pot left Phnom Penh, followed two weeks later by Ieng Sary. They initially stayed at Snuol, a commune on the border of Kratie and Kompong Cham. From there they proceeded to a South Vietnamese communist encampment along the Cambodian-Vietnamese border. For the next seven years, they hid within the jungles of northeastern Cambodia, moving from encampment to encampment, preparing for a peasant revolution.[50]

In 1965 Pol Pot, Keo Meas, and other Cambodian communists were summoned to Hanoi to discuss the role of the Khmer communist movement within the context of the escalating war in Vietnam.[51] For the Vietnamese, the top priority for Indochina remained the defeat of the United States. To this end, the Vietnamese had recently reached an agreement with the DRV that allowed the NLF and other insurgents access to Cambodian territory.[52] In exchange, the DRV pledged to honor Cambodia's independence and borders when the war was over. According to the Vietnamese politburo, the Khmer were to provide military and logistical support.[53] Consequently, the Vietnamese leadership berated the Khmer communists for pursuing a nationalist agenda and for wanting to put the Cambodian revolution ahead of the greater regional conflict. They were informed by Le Duan, secretary-general, that the Khmer's emphasis on "protracted, difficult, and self-reliant struggle" was inappropriate and that the Khmer were to subordinate their interests to those of Vietnam.[54] This meant that the Khmer communists were to work with Sihanouk—even as the Cambodian monarch continued his repression of communists throughout Cambodia.

Pol Pot reportedly said nothing in response to the schooling he received by the Vietnamese. However, the "Vietnamese response to the Khmer party's plan for armed action reconfirmed the suspicion that Hanoi placed its own strategic interests and objectives above its obligations to a fraternal party." Thus, having been rebuffed in Hanoi, Pol Pot traveled to Beijing, where he met high-ranking Chinese Communist Party (CCP) officials, including Deng Xiaoping and Liu Shaoqi.[55] Unlike the Vietnamese, Chinese officials praised the Cambodians for their opposition to US imperialism; nonetheless, they too urged restraint. It was necessary to maintain a wider perspective on events in Indochina, namely, that liberation required collective action and that Sihanouk in particular was allowing vital supplies to pass through Cambodia into southern Vietnam.

The Expanding War

America's overt military involvement in Vietnam was gradual and haphazard, reflecting an ignorance and uncertainty over objective, policy, and strategy. The Democratic Republic of Vietnam (that is, North Vietnam) posed no *military* threat to the United States. However, convinced that the fall of Vietnam to communism would lead to the loss of all of Southeast Asia, a succession of American presidents—from Dwight Eisenhower to Richard Nixon—came to believe that the establishment of a sovereign and noncommunist state in southern Vietnam was imperative.[56] Indeed, Vietnam, itself standing for all of Southeast Asia, became a "surrogate space," as both the country and the war became symbols of American geopolitical policy.[57]

From the signing of the Geneva Accords in 1954 to 1960, only a few hundred military advisers of the US Military Assistance Advisory Group were stationed in South Vietnam. The election of John F. Kennedy, however, paved the way for a greater American presence in Indochina. Patrick Hearden, for example, details how Kennedy "set the tone for the beginning of a bold American policy." Robert Schulzinger expounds that "Kennedy, along with most foreign affairs experts of the late 1950s and early 1960s, believed that the Cold War was a global struggle: events were interconnected, and weakness in the face of communist adversaries' moves encouraged aggression elsewhere."[58]

Throughout December 1960 and January 1961, Edward Lansdale, an air force officer and agent for the Central Intelligence Agency (CIA), traveled throughout South Vietnam in order to gauge the political climate and to inform the Kennedy administration of possible courses of action. His report was channeled to Walter Rostow, a hawkish adviser who had been instrumental in selecting bombing targets in Europe during the Second World War. Rostow was also an ardent anticommunist and believed wholeheartedly in the use of military force to achieve economic ends. In his recent book, *The Stages of Economic Growth: A Non-communist Manifesto*, Rostow concluded, "Nation sovereignty means that nations retain the ultimate right—a right sanctioned by law, custom, and what decent men judge to be legitimacy—the right to kill people of other nations in defense or pursuit of what they judge to be their national interest."[59]

Vietnam specifically, but Indochina in general, was not at the time a top priority for Kennedy. In 1959, for example, Cuban president Fulgencia Batista was removed from power, toppled by a communist revolution led by Fidel Castro who, in turn, began to strengthen ties with the Soviet Union. At the insistence of Rostow, however, Kennedy would give the region a closer look. Lansdale's report had foretold of worsening conditions. Four years earlier, Ngo Dinh Diem had assumed control of South Vietnam. Diem enjoyed the support of many high-ranking American officials, including Kennedy and Senator Mike Mansfield. Now, however, the government of Diem appeared to be faltering as communist activity was intensifying. Compounding the problem was the formation of the NLF and the use of enemy forces along the Ho Chi Minh Trail. Kennedy, confronted with a conflict rapidly intensifying in scale and scope throughout Indochina, was well aware of the political implications. Former US president Harry Truman, for example, was widely condemned by his political adversaries for having "lost" China and for becoming bogged down in Korea.

Kennedy's decision marked the gradual escalation of American military forces in southern Vietnam—a path continued by his successor, Lyndon B. Johnson. To what end remained unclear. It was claimed by the highest echelons of US policy makers that America's ability to halt the spread of communism hinged on the stance taken in Vietnam. The Joint Chiefs of Staff backed an aggressive military response to the deepening NLF insurgency in South Vietnam. Curtis E. LeMay, the air force chief of staff, for example, supported a no-holds-barred use of airborne force. It was his belief that a series of punishing attacks against the North would compel the Ho Chi Minh government to forgo all assistance to their southern comrades and agree to the existence of a sovereign Republic of Vietnam. To Johnson, however, the possibility of an all-out air campaign against the North was worrisome: 1964 was an election year, and while Johnson personally was wary of military involvement in Vietnam, he could ill afford to be seen as soft on communism.

Seeking a middle ground, Johnson agreed to the use of covert military operations, to be held in conjunction with their South Vietnamese allies. Thus it was that on August 2, 1964, an American destroyer, the USS

Maddox, was patrolling the Gulf of Tonkin in support of South Vietnamese commando raids. On that evening three North Vietnamese gunboats appeared, and the *Maddox* opened fire. Two nights later, a second American vessel, the USS *C. Turner Joy*, was reportedly fired upon. It is now generally accepted that there was no battle during the night of August 4–5; at the time, however, the majority of US officials were adamant that the North Vietnamese had launched an unprovoked attack on an American naval vessel. Vowing to protect the "legal principle of innocent passage on the high seas," the United States deployed sixty-four jet fighter-bombers in retaliation, and on August 7, 1964, Congress passed the Gulf of Tonkin Resolution, authorizing the president to use armed force in Indochina.[60]

Sustained aerial bombing campaigns against the North began in mid-February 1965. Repeated sorties, however, failed to deliver the expected results, and, consequently, American tacticians gradually expanded both the list of "acceptable" targets and the frequency of air strikes. Sorties against the North increased from 25,000 in 1965 to 79,000 in 1966 and 108,000 in 1967; bomb tonnage increased from 63,000 to 136,000 to 226,000 over the same period. Casualty rates likewise spiked upward. Vietnamese civilian and military casualties nearly doubled, from 13,000 in 1965 to approximately 24,000 in 1966.[61]

Beyond the immediacy of military operations inside Vietnam, American officials never lost sight of the use of Laotian and Cambodian territories by both the North Vietnamese Army and the National Liberation Front. In 1967 American military advisers initiated Operation Salem House. Whereas American advisers had been in Cambodia, clandestinely, since the early 1960s, Salem House systematized these operations. Teams of six to eight Americans and South Vietnamese would enter Cambodia, seeking tactical intelligence. At first, these teams were limited in their geographic coverage, restricted to the northeastern tip of Cambodia. Over time, however, these operations (renamed Daniel Boone) expanded to encompass the entire Cambodian-Vietnamese border region, and by October 1968 the number of covert missions had increased substantially. The limitations on the number of Americans who could be included were also removed, and the use of antipersonnel mines was permitted. As of 1969 US forces had conducted 454 covert missions in Cambodia, and by the time the missions ceased in 1972, more than 1,885 operations had been conducted.[62]

Cambodian officials, including Sihanouk, publicly condemned these missions. In just one month—October 1969—representatives of Cambodia protested 83 separate incidents of American intervention. Aerial and artillery attacks, ostensibly targeting NLF strongholds, more often destroyed Cambodian villages—houses, schools, bridges—and killed more Cambodian civilians than enemy personnel. Farming was disrupted and livestock killed—both contributing to the ever-present threat of famine.[63]

The Struggle Goes Public

In his seminal essay "What Is to Be Done?" Lenin warns against the "spontaneous element" of revolution, noting that such events, that is, primitive riots or factory strikes, represent "nothing more nor less than consciousness in an embryonic form." For Lenin, these were simply "outbursts of desperation and vengeance" as opposed to indicators of an authentic revolutionary struggle. Nevertheless, spontaneity among the exploited masses could serve as a political salvo in the ongoing struggle. "Political exposures," Lenin concludes, "are as much a declaration of war against the government as economic exposures are a declaration of war against the employers."[64] In 1967 a spontaneous element of desperation and vengeance erupted in Cambodia that would, in hindsight, prove determinant of the Khmer Rouge.

Throughout his long tenure, Sihanouk attempted a delicate balancing act. In 1963, for example, Sihanouk refused US aid, nationalized the import-export sector of the economy, and closed Cambodia's privately owned banks. He hoped, through these steps, to induce stronger relations with China and the Soviet Union and, in the process, curtail the escalating war in Vietnam from expanding further into Cambodia. However, by severing relations with the United States, Sihanouk further crippled Cambodia's faltering economy. Neither China nor the Soviet Union was willing to invest substantial funds into Cambodia; consequently, Sihanouk was forced to make drastic reductions in defense spending, thereby incurring the ire of Lon Nol and the military establishment. Moreover, the nationalization of foreign trade encouraged the commercial elite to trade clandestinely with communist insurgents in Vietnam.

The escalation of the war also translated into increased troop levels throughout the region, causing further economic disruption. In southern Vietnam, for example, recruitment into the NLF quadrupled from 1964 to 1966, climbing from 45,000 to 160,000 new recruits. These troops required food. The end result was that an estimated two-thirds of Cambodian-grown rice was smuggled into Vietnam to (literally) feed the war. Cambodia's economy, dependent principally on the taxes of rice exports, continued to plunge toward bankruptcy.[65]

To forestall economic collapse, military units throughout Cambodia purchased rice from farmers at government-set (and lower) prices. Merchants would then sell the rice on the international market at a higher price, thereby increasing profits for the national treasury. Not surprisingly, most peasants balked at such a scheme, given that Vietnamese communists were paying double the official rate. In response, many farmers began to withhold their harvests, while others refused to grow more than a subsistence level of rice. To counter these practices, the Sihanouk government introduced a new collection system, called *ramassage du paddy*. Under this system, peasants who withheld grain were forced at gunpoint to sell rice at the government price. To ensure compliance, Lon Nol replaced provincial officials with his own men.[66]

By February 1967, protests were breaking out throughout the Northwest. Then, in April, two soldiers were murdered while collecting rice in the village of Samlaut, fifteen miles southwest of Battambang City. This action spurred additional protests. Army posts were attacked, and a local government official was killed. Sporadic fighting continued for four days until Sihanouk responded in force, as both the army and the air force were mobilized to launch a counterattack. In the ensuing melee, tens of thousands of peasants fled, many of whom were pursued and killed by the military. Convinced that the communists were behind the uprisings, Sihanouk offered a bounty for the severed head of any Khmer Rouge (as the monarch derisively called the communists) that was captured. Suspected instigators were publicly shot, and films of the executions were shown throughout the country.[67]

The Samlaut rebellion would later be used, in fact, "rewritten," by Pol Pot to justify the actions undertaken by the Khmer Rouge. Indeed, according to Alexander Hinton, "This incident convinced the Khmer Rouge leadership that it was time to initiate 'armed struggle' throughout the country."[68] On September 27, 1977, for example, Pol Pot explained:

> In 1964, 1965, 1966 and 1967, the struggles developed with great force. Our movement was very powerful. It was in upheaval. In 1964 and 1965, the movement was already strong. In 1966, it became even more powerful. In 1967, it became an extraordinary force. By the thousands, by the tens of thousands, the peasants demonstrated, rose up, marched on the administrative offices of the communes, districts and provinces, in order to regain control of the land. Every form of struggle was used, including petitions and meetings with deputies. But what is especially important, the peasants armed themselves with scythes, knives, axes and hatchets, and other traditional weapons. Weapons in hand, the peasants surrounded police stations and military posts, resorting to revolutionary violence because the ruling classes refused to solve the problem of the lands which they had grabbed from the poor peasants in collusion with the landlords. The ruling classes were the feudalists, the landlords and the capitalists.[69]

Was Pol Pot correct in his assessment? For years scholars have debated at length this question, concluding largely that Pol Pot's assertions are problematic at best.[70] For example, the claim that class divisions throughout Cambodia were a fundamental source of tension and unrest has been demonstrated to be inaccurate. Nor was a landlord-tenant conflict an essential contradiction within Cambodian society. As Hinton concludes, "The revolutionary potential of the Cambodian peasantry does not seem to have been as great as it had been in China and Vietnam, where there were more poor and landless peasants, land was more concentrated in the hands of rich peasants and landlords, and consequently, there was more economic exploitation." Rightly or wrongly, however, for the Khmer Rouge leadership, Samlaut seemingly marked the culmination of years of political struggle, noting the importance of "propaganda and educational work" conducted by the party. The year 1968 therefore was a time of transition, for it signaled the time for revolutionary violence. Had not Lenin declared that to "smash" the "bureaucratic-military state machine" is "what is truly in the interests of the people"?[71] On January 17, 1968, the CPK's "revolutionary army" was officially formed, marking the onset of armed struggle.

Recruitment

The establishment of the Khmer Rouge as a military force coincided with the escalation of the greater Indochina conflict. In 1969 Richard M. Nixon ascended to the presidency of the United States. As part of his over-all approach to "end the war and win the peace," Nixon was prepared to expand American military operations while simultaneously, paradoxically, withdrawing American troops. Reflecting an admixture of Orwellian and Machiavellian logic, Nixon—in partnership with his national security adviser Henry Kissinger—initiated a policy of "Vietnamization." The idea was to turn the war over to South Vietnamese forces. This would entail also a staged de-escalation of American ground forces. However, such a transition would require an expansion of American military operations. Key to this policy shift was the decision to eliminate suspected NLF sanc-tuaries within Cambodia. Consequently, on March 15, 1969, Nixon autho-rized the use of B-52s to carpet bomb "Base Area 353" inside Cambodia, an area long suspected as harboring the DRV's and NLF's command-and-control post known as the Central Office for South Vietnam.[72] This was the beginning of a fifteen-month bombing campaign in Cambodia that would become known as Operation Menu.[73]

In that period, more than thirty-eight hundred B-52 sorties were flown over Cambodia, dropping more than one hundred thousand tons of bombs.[74] Strategically, the bombing was ineffective, as these raids did not seriously affect the ability of the NLF or the DRV to continue their mili-tary operations in South Vietnam. When news of the bombings became public in the United States, however, American officials claimed that the operation was a success and that the targeted areas were not inhabited by Cambodian civilians. Indeed, Nixon and Kissinger repeatedly stated that the areas bombed were "unpopulated."[75] Moreover, both Nixon and

Kissinger would later claim that Sihanouk approved of, or perhaps even encouraged, the carpet bombing of his country—a claim widely disputed by most historians.[76]

Nixon's escalation of the war was given impetus in 1970 by the coup of Sihanouk. Throughout the late 1960s, the political facade of the prince was slowly crumbling. Opposition from both the Left and the Right formed a political vice from which Sihanouk was unable to extract himself. As David Chandler details, during this time Sihanouk busied himself making feature films over which he exercised total control as writer, director, producer, and leading actor.[77] Perhaps this gave Sihanouk the semblance of control he lacked in real life; perhaps it served as a subconscious metaphor in which Sihanouk was forever the leading actor on Cambodia's stage. Regardless, the plot had become too complex, too convoluted. Sihanouk's own contradictions became more pronounced; rather than providing resolution, they only twisted the story line further. As the end drew near, for example, Sihanouk attempted to repair the ties he had severed with the United States years earlier. Yet he also continued to affirm his support of the DRV.

The end came quickly. While traveling to France, Sihanouk had entrusted his government to Lon Nol and his pro-Western deputy prime minister, Prince Sisowath Sirik Matak. In Sihanouk's absence, Lon Nol and Sirik Matak launched attacks on the Vietnamese communist positions, organized anti-Vietnamese demonstrations, and reestablished ties with various noncommunist groups. Sihanouk, upon learning of these actions, condemned both Lon Nol and Sirik Matak. In response, Sirik Matak pressured Lon Nol to depose Sihanouk, and, on March 18, 1970, the National Assembly voted eighty-nine to three to remove Sihanouk from power.[78]

The coup d'état was a turning point in the geopolitical chess match. Initially, Chinese leaders sought to align themselves with the government of Lon Nol and Sirik Matak. Crucial to this strategy was the necessity of retaining DRV access to bases in Cambodia. In essence, the Chinese were willing to postpone the Khmer communist revolution in order to help the Vietnamese defeat the United States. This too was the immediate intention of the DRV. Refusing, however, to work with the Chinese, Lon Nol adopted a hard-line anti-Vietnamese and anticommunist position. In part, this reflected Lon Nol's own political leanings, but it also reflected his misreading of the international stage. Lon Nol believed, naively perhaps, the rhetoric of Nixon. He supported the expanded US military presence on Cambodian soil, the ongoing bombing campaigns, and the presence of thousands of troops of the Army of the Republic of Vietnam (ARVN). Lon Nol also believed in Nixon's promise that military and economic aid would be forthcoming.

Sihanouk similarly made a fateful decision. The leadership in China—having been rebuffed in their overture to Lon Nol—encouraged Sihanouk to form a military alliance with the Vietnamese and Cambodian communists and to lead a government in exile.[79] Sihanouk, as Arnold Isaacs explains, was far too clear-eyed not to have realized, even in these early weeks, that he was tying himself to interests that were mortally dangerous to Cambodia's survival.[80] Cold War calculus, however, forced the prince into a Faustian bargain. Having received no support from the United States, Sihanouk had few options. In response to the coup, Sihanouk issued an appeal to the Cambodian people, whereupon royalist supporters would join the Khmer Rouge in a unified effort to defeat the Lon Nol government. More formally, on March 23, 1970, Sihanouk announced the formation of the National United Front of Kampuchea (Front Uni National du Kampuchea), a political and military coalition of royalists and the Khmer Rouge, committed to destroying Lon Nol's republican forces. Two months later, the Royal Government of the National Union of Kampuchea (Gouvernement Royal d'Union Nationale du Kampuchéa) was announced. Sihanouk assumed the post of GRUNK head of state, while Penn Nouth was designated as prime minister. Other high-ranking positions were occupied by Khmer Rouge cadre: Khieu Samphan was designated deputy prime minister, minister of defense, and commander in chief of the GRUNK armed forces; Hu Nim served as minister of information; and Hou Yuon assumed the positions of minister of the interior, communal reforms, and cooperatives.[81]

Both Sihanouk and the Khmer Rouge leadership recognized the tenuous basis of their alliance. The Khmer Rouge continued to hold Sihanouk responsible for the war in Cambodia, but well understood his popularity. Pol Pot, consequently, used the popularity of Sihanouk for propaganda and recruitment purposes. Sihanouk likewise understood that his role in the alliance was little more than titular figurehead. He gambled, however, that he might use the arrangement as a means of deposing Lon Nol and eventually returning to power.

The geopolitical machinations of China and the United States would reverberate across the fields and forests of Cambodia. With Sihanouk removed, and the more pliable and pro-American Lon Nol in power, Nixon expanded even more the American military presence in Cambodia. On April 30, 1970, Nixon announced to the American public that US ground forces, accompanied by the ARVN, had made a strategic "incursion" into Cambodia. Nixon explained that "North Vietnam [had] increased its military aggression," especially in Cambodia, and that "to protect [Americans] who are in Vietnam and to guarantee the continued success" of US operations, the time had come for action. Nixon was disingenuous when he explained that "American policy [had] been to scrupulously respect the neutrality of the Cambodian people." No mention was made, for example, of the ongoing covert operations dating back to the mid-1960s or of the bombings associated with Operation Menu. Rather, Nixon avowed that the United States had "maintained a skeleton diplomatic mission of fewer than 14 in Cambodia's capital" and that "for the past five years [the United States had] provided no military assistance whatsoever and no economic assistance to Cambodia." North Vietnam, Nixon asserted, was guilty of interference in the sovereignty of Cambodia, North Vietnam had established military sanctuaries along the Cambodian border with South Vietnam, and these sanctuaries contained "major base camps, training sites logistics facilities, weapons and ammunition factories, airstrips, and prisoner-of-war compounds." Nixon further explained that Cambodia "sent out a call to the United States" for assistance and that without American support, Cambodia would become a vast enemy staging ground and springboard for attacks on South Vietnam.[82]

Employing the euphemistic term *incursion*, Nixon stressed that ongoing military operations did not constitute an *invasion*. The purpose, Nixon stated, was not to occupy Cambodian territory but to drive the Vietnamese communists out of the country. And wary of Soviet or Chinese responses, Nixon avowed that the actions were "in no way directed to the security

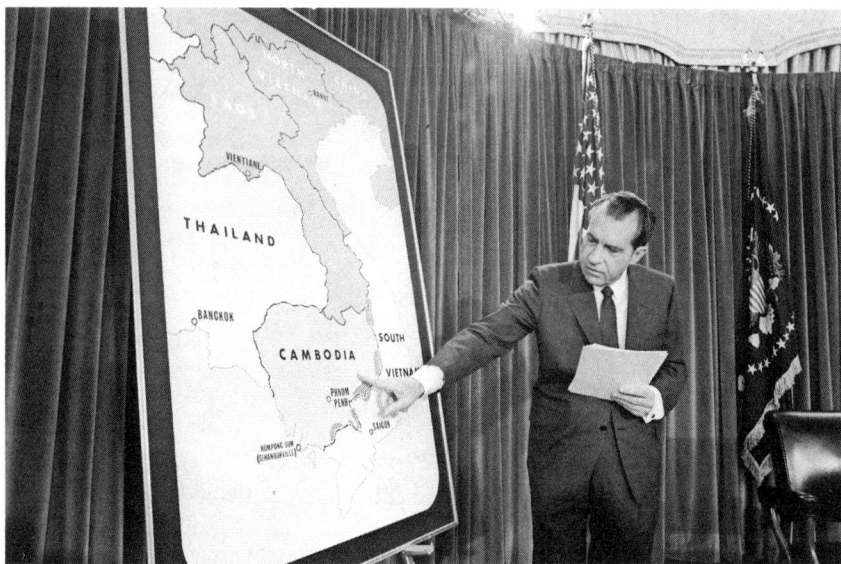

1. President Richard M. Nixon explaining the American invasion of Cambodia in April 1970 during a nationwide television address. Courtesy of the Richard Nixon Presidential Library and Museum.

interests of any nation" and that any government that chose to use the incursion as "a pretext for harming relations with the United States" would be doing so on its own responsibility and on its own initiative. Nixon then repeated that the United States undertook the incursion "not for the purpose of expanding the war into Cambodia, but for the purpose of ending the war in Vietnam and winning the peace."[83]

On July 27, 1970, Nixon announced the resumption of B-52 carpet-bombing raids over Cambodia; they would continue until the US Congress called a halt to all American military operations in Cambodia in 1973. By this point, Nixon was committed to a strategy of indiscriminate bombing, solely as a means of extricating himself from an untenable political position, namely, the fear of becoming the first US president to "lose a war." According to Secretary of the Air Force Robert Seamons:

> The President wanted to send a hundred more B-52s. This was appalling. You couldn't even figure out where you were going to put them all,

you know. . . . I think it was at the same time the President was going over to Moscow . . . so, anyway, a message was sent to the airplane—this was that timely—as to why we couldn't send those B-52s over there. As I understand it, the response when [Nixon] touched down really burned the wires, and he said he wanted them over there. . . . The total never did quite reach one hundred, but it was a pretty large number.[84]

America's bombing campaign of the spring and summer of 1973 was the most brutal and concentrated display of firepower yet. In March 1973 American B-52s dropped more than 24,000 tons of bombs on Cambodia; by April the tonnage increased to 35,000 tons, and in May the figure topped 36,000 tons. According to Shawcross, the bombing of Cambodia had become so intense that the Seventh Air Force faced serious logistical problems. At one stage, B-52 sortie rates were as high as eighty-one per day. In Vietnam, the maximum had been sixty per day. By the time the air campaign was halted in late 1973, American B-52s had dropped more than 260,000 tons of bombs on Cambodia—a figure that does not include the tonnage dropped by other American fighter planes.[85]

Both Nixon and Kissinger maintained their charade that the bombing campaign was targeting only "legitimate" targets (for example, NVA and NLF sanctuaries) in remote regions of Cambodia that were "largely unpopulated." Journalists and officials working within the US Embassy in Phnom Penh knew otherwise. In 1973, for example, Arnold Isaacs, a correspondent for the *Baltimore Sun*, described the devastation along a highway outside of Phnom Penh: "Once, pleasant villages had stood almost shoulder-to-shoulder on that highway. Now they were not just ruined, but obliterated. For five miles, not a house still stood on either side of the road, or as far away as one could see across the fields. No trees were left, just broken stumps. In a few places grass had begun to grow again, but most of the land was blackened and dead. It was as if the bombers had sought to destroy the earth itself."[86]

The air campaign was a brutal, senseless operation that inflicted a massive loss of life on Cambodia. Estimates of Cambodian casualties range from 150,000 to nearly 750,000.[87] Moreover, the bombing campaign further devastated an already deteriorating infrastructure. William

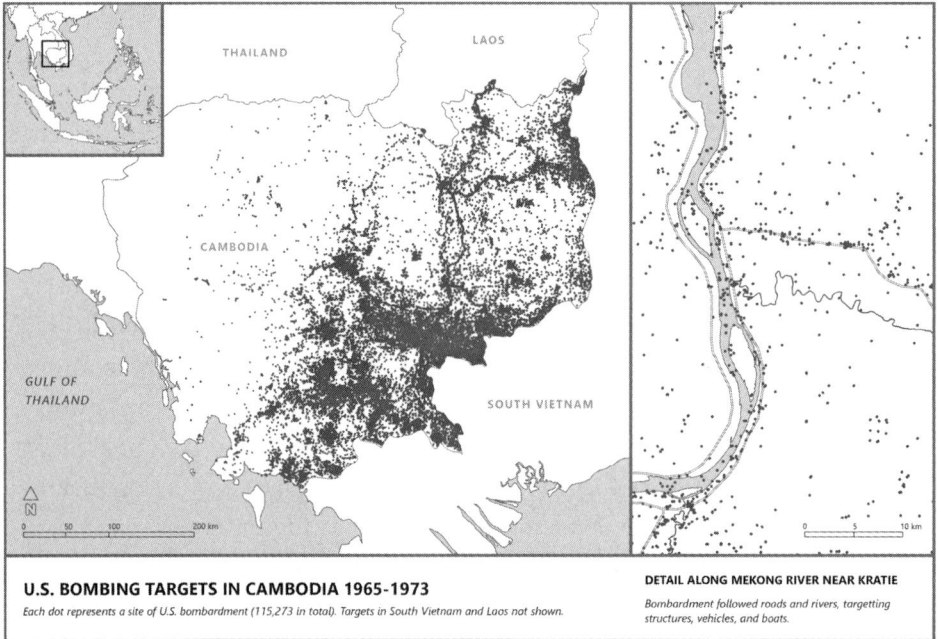

U.S. BOMBING TARGETS IN CAMBODIA 1965-1973
Each dot represents a site of U.S. bombardment (115,273 in total). Targets in South Vietnam and Laos not shown.

DETAIL ALONG MEKONG RIVER NEAR KRATIE
Bombardment followed roads and rivers, targetting structures, vehicles, and boats.

2. American bombing of Cambodia, 1965–73.

Shawcross details the lingering effects of the bombing campaign: "Eighty percent of the country's prewar paddy fields had been abandoned, and the government's own figures showed that in 1974 rice production was only 65,000 metric tons—as opposed to 3.8 million tons in the last year before the war." Henry Kamm concludes that "with the callous disregard of the interests of the Cambodian people that marked all of America's wartime involvement in that country, and in full knowledge that Cambodia's demented and corrupt regime could only prolong their people's suffering, America did all that it could to drag out senselessly the life of a hated government and a war that Washington knew was lost."[88]

The air war did not bring victory to either Lon Nol's republic or the United States. It did create a groundswell of support for the Khmer Rouge—a factor that was widely known but covered up by high-ranking US officials. On May 2, 1973, for example, the Central Intelligence Agency's director of operations provided details on a new recruiting drive launched by the CPK:

Khmer Insurgent (KI) cadre have begun an intensified proselyting [*sic*] campaign among ethnic Cambodian residents in the area of Chrouy Snao, Kaoh Thom district, Kandal province, Cambodia, in an effort to recruit young men and women for KI military organizations. They are using damage caused by B-52 strikes as the main theme of their propaganda. The cadres tell the people that the Government of Lon Nol has requested the airstrikes and is responsible for the damage and the "suffering of innocent villagers" in order to keep himself in power. The only way to stop "the massive destruction of the country" is to remove Lon Nol and return Prince Sihanouk to power. The proselyting cadres tell the people that the quickest way to accomplish this is to strengthen KI forces so they will be able to defeat Lon Nol and stop the bombing. . . . This approach has resulted in the successful recruitment of a number of young men for KI forces. Residents around Chrouy Snao say that the propaganda campaign has been effective with refugees and in areas of Kaoh Thom and Leuk Dek districts which have been subject to B-52 strikes.[89]

The carpet bombing "gave the Khmer Rouges a propaganda windfall which they exploited to the hilt—taking peasants for political education lessons among the bomb craters and shrapnel, explaining to them that Lon Nol had sold Cambodia to the Americans in order to stay in power and that the US, like Vietnam and Thailand, was bent on the country's annihilation so that, when the war was over, Cambodia would cease to exist."[90] As explained by one survivor who experienced the bombings in Svay Rieng Province: "Then in 1972 B-52s bombed three times per day, fifteen minutes apart, three planes at a time. They hit houses in Samrong and thirty people were killed. There were no troops in these villages. At that time there were some Vietnamese [communist] troops on the border [nearby], but they didn't bomb the border: they bombed inside it, people's houses." Another villager who joined the communist forces in 1970 recalls: "I saw them [the bombs] being dropped at Andaung Pring [village]. . . . The bombs came tumbling down in a big clump . . . right onto Andaung Pring, and that time villagers were killed in amazing numbers. . . . The bombs fell in the village, setting fire to people's houses and killing them. . . . [S]ometimes they didn't even have the time to get down out of their houses. . . . The bombing was massive and devastating, and they just kept bombing more and more massively, so massively you couldn't believe it, so that it engulfed the forests, engulfed the forests with bombs, with devastation."[91] Chhit Do, a former Khmer Rouge subdistrict chief, likewise remembers the bombing campaign and the "lessons" taught by the Khmer Rouge:

> They did use it [the bombing] to stigmatize the US. They said that all this bombing was an attempt to make us an American satellite, a manifestation of simply American barbarism, because, after all, as they pointed out, we had never done anything to these Americans, the people had never done anything at all to America. The Khmers didn't even have any airplanes and here the Americans had brought theirs to bomb us, causing great pain to us, with their war. Their country was way over there somewhere and here they had come to interfere with us. . . . [The] propaganda was that this guy Lon Nol had already sold the county to the Americans, because Lon Nol wanted power, wanted to be President.[92]

Chhit Do concludes:

> The ordinary people were terrified by the bombing and the shelling, never having experienced war, and sometimes they literally shit in their pants when the big bombs and shells came. Artillery bombardments usually involved 200–400 shells per attack, and some people became shell-shocked, just like their brains were completely disoriented. Even though the shelling had stopped, they couldn't hold down a meal. Their minds just froze up and [they] would wander around mute and not talk for three or four days. Terrified and half-crazy, the people were ready to believe what they were told. What [the Khmer Rouge] said was credible because there were just so many huge bombs dropped. That was what made it so easy for the Khmer Rouge to win the people over. . . . It was because of their dissatisfaction with the bombing that they kept on cooperating with the Khmer Rouge, joining up with the Khmer Rouge, sending their children off to go with them, to join the Khmer Rouge.[93]

Terrorized, traumatized, angered by the intense bombing campaign, thousands of young men and women rallied to Sihanouk to join forces with the Khmer Rouge in an attempt to restore the prince to power. One survivor recalls: "On the river many monasteries were destroyed by bombs. People in our village were furious with the Americans; they did not know why the Americans had bombed them. Seventy people from Chalong joined the fight against Lon Nol after the bombing." Another remembers that "the town of Chantrea was destroyed by US bombs. . . . The people were angry with the US and that is why so many of them joined the Khmer communists."[94]

The aerial bombardment of Cambodia by the American military thus provides a necessary—and transnational—corrective to the Standard Total View, one that calls attention away from the material conditions on the ground to the imposed violence from above. As Hinton writes, "While scholars continue to debate the [number of disaffected peasants], the extent of landlessness, and the overall degree of peasant support for the Khmer Rouge," there is little doubt that conditions were such "for Pol Pot to build a viable recruitment strategy targeting poor children . . . especially after the overthrow of Sihanouk and the ensuing civil war." Without these events, Hinton concludes, "it is doubtful the Khmer Rouge would have come to power; economic conditions alone were not severe enough to generate widespread support for the movement."[95]

Conclusion

America's escalation of the war into Cambodia proved decisive for the eventual victory and subsequent maturation of the CPK. Indeed, as Anthony Barnett concludes, "The Pol Pot regime would not have emerged in the form it took without the war from 1970–1975, when US intervention in Vietnam spread across the whole of Indochina."[96] Whereas in 1970 Khmer Rouge forces were described as "marginal," by 1972 these forces were estimated to have grown to more than 20,000. Indeed, some US officials presented figures between 35,000 and 50,000, while some CIA estimates placed Khmer Rouge forces at more than 150,000.[97] Such an account, however, is far from straightforward, for embedded in the conflict were several other smaller wars that ebbed and flowed across city and village, rice field and rubber plantation. From 1970 to approximately 1972, the bulk of the fighting against Lon Nol's Forces Armées Nationales

Khmères (Khmer National Armed Forces) was conducted by Vietnamese communist forces, either the NLF or the NVA. Military campaigns often targeted prime rice-growing regions, thereby denying enemy forces much-needed provisions. When Republican forces were defeated, the Khmer Rouge moved in to establish "liberated zones." This enabled the CPK and its military, the Revolutionary Army of Kampuchea, to consolidate its control and to carry out the political and military training necessary for the thousands of recruits who were joining. Communist party schools were established, staffed by young male and female cadre; cooperative farms were likewise formed, as the CPK began to implement resettlement schemes. Even at this date, the strategic importance of agriculture and especially rice was understood.

The CPK's rise to power was bolstered also by returning Khmer communists—the Khmer Vietminh. Many of these veterans had lived for years in exile in the DRV. They had engaged in political studies of Marxist-Leninist ideology; many had received military training. Now they saw an opportunity to actively rejoin the revolution within their own homeland. Most, however, were unaware of the cosmic changes that had taken place within the Khmer communist party or that they were to serve as pawns for the Pol Pot faction. To the ranking leadership of the CPK, the Hanoi-trained Khmer were viewed with suspicion. However, they also offered an opportunity to provide further training to new recruits. Accordingly, upon their return, the veteran communists were disarmed and assigned low-ranking positions. Within months, however, they were also gradually purged from the party. Ultimately, approximately nine hundred of these "Khmer Vietminh" had been killed by Pol Pot loyalists.

From 1973 onward, the CPK steadily, relentlessly "liberated" Cambodia and established base areas from which to operate. By 1974 only the national capital, Phnom Penh, and a handful of provincial capitals remained outside the orbit of Khmer Rouge control. The people in these towns, Slocomb writes, were fed by insufficient airdrops of United States Agency for International Development (USAID) rice, while just a few miles away their relatives were growing rice for the Khmer Rouge.[98] Slocomb's observation is a fitting end to the inglorious beginning of Democratic Kampuchea.

3

Reconstruction

With Sihanouk's fall, the Vietnam War, in the words of Arnold Isaacs, "fell on his helpless country like a collapsing brick wall."[1] Sustained and indiscriminate bombing, combined with brutal fighting between Lon Nol's troops, the Vietnamese communists, and the Khmer Rouge, exacted a horrifying toll on Cambodia's population, engendering a new expression: "The land is broken."[2]

By war's end, approximately one-third of the country's bridges were destroyed, two-fifths of the road network was unusable, and the railroad was inoperable. Much of the country's productive infrastructure, including its lone oil refinery near Kompong Som, had stopped working. Only 300 of 1,400 rice mills and 60 of 240 sawmills were functioning, and both timber and rubber production—Cambodia's major prewar commercial products other than rice—had declined to only one-fifth of prewar production levels. Moreover, upwards of half of Cambodia's livestock had been killed, either through fighting or bombing or as a food source for the starving people.[3]

Beyond the physical destruction, Cambodia's economy was in ruin, shattered by misplaced foreign loans and governmental corruption that flourished in the waning months and years of the war. According to William Shawcross, the United States had begun selling to Cambodia surplus American agricultural products—wheat, flour, vegetable oil, tobacco, cotton—under the "Food for Peace" program. These commodities were purchased with Cambodian riel, which were then placed in a blocked account in Phnom Penh and used to pay the salaries of Lon Nol's military. The "sale" of American agricultural commodities, therefore, not only undermined Cambodian farmers, but also financed a military that was riven with corruption. Officers within the military padded their manpower lists with "ghost" soldiers, people who existed in name only. Estimates placed the number of phantom soldiers somewhere between forty and eighty thousand, representing up to two million dollars a month that ended up in the pockets of corrupt officers. And the landscape of Phnom Penh was a visual reminder of uncontrolled corruption. Haggard and orphaned children shared the streets of the capital with newly purchased Mercedes, Peugeots, Audis, and other luxury cars; starving and traumatized refugees begged in front of newly constructed villas that housed the corrupt generals and politicians.[4]

The specter of famine was ever present but unequally experienced throughout Cambodia. For many Cambodians, food was nonexistent, because of corruption, economic inefficiency, infrastructure collapse, and the destruction of farms and fields. For others, food was available—but unaffordable, because of rampant hyperinflation, exorbitant prices, and declining wages. American policies, likewise, directly led to malnutrition, starvation, and death. The United States, for example, consistently kept rice imports to a bare minimum, supposedly to prevent "food riots" among the starving people and to "encourage" greater domestic rice production. How the Cambodian peasantry, under constant aerial bombardment, was to plant and harvest rice was not specified.[5]

The proximate reason for the lack of food imported to Cambodia, however, was the result of deliberate political spin maneuvering of the Nixon administration. As the months dragged into years and the plight of Cambodia's people steadily deteriorated, American officials refused to concede that they were losing yet another country to communism. Consequently, all talk of a "refugee problem" was drowned out by the rhetoric of an American and Lon Nol victory and the salvation of Cambodia from communism. Indeed, by keeping rice imports low, Washington was able to disguise the grave conditions endured by the masses of Cambodians. Isaacs is blunt in his conclusions: "Long after it was apparent to everyone else that civilian suffering was acute and growing worse, and that the Khmer government was neither competent enough nor concerned enough to do anything about it, American officials continued to deny any need for a major relief effort. From the start of the war almost to its end, instead of food and medicine the US government supplied only a long list of statements declaring, in absolute contradiction to all the evidence, that Cambodia's refugees were being adequately cared for."[6]

Conditions for the sick and wounded—increasing daily as the war intensified—also worsened. Of the twenty-nine civilian hospitals that existed in 1970, only thirteen were operating a year later; the rest had been destroyed by ground fighting or by carpet-bombing campaigns. And of those hospitals still functioning, space and supplies were desperately short: patients slept on cots, rush mats, wooden benches, or the floor. Faced with a severe lack of antibiotics, antimalarial drugs, dressing materials, and surgery equipment, doctors and nurses pleaded for assistance from American advisers to no avail. By 1971 hundreds of Cambodians were dying every day for lack of proper treatment; public health specialists and relief agencies were reporting rising malnutrition and vitamin deficiency. Shawcross describes one Phnom Penh hospital, where 15 percent of all infants were dying of an easily controlled gastric disorder because of a lack of appropriate medicine.[7] He elaborates:

> In the camps and in the streets, in the cardboard shelters, in the Cambodiana Hotel refugee center, one could see sick children everywhere. Those who suffered from kwashiorkor, extreme protein deficiency, had distended bellies and swollen hands, feet and ankles. Their hair was falling out or turning light brown, and so was their skin; they behaved listlessly as one might expect. Other children had simply far too little to eat to be able to grow properly and were suffering from marasmus. Their matchlike limbs hung over the empty skin folds of their bodies, they had almost no muscular control, and eight year-olds looked like shriveled babies.[8]

American policies, again, contributed to the malaise of the Cambodian people. In 1969 Cambodia had imported US$7.8 million worth of drugs, paid for by exports of rice and rubber. By 1971, with demand for medicine and other supplies increasing at an astronomical rate, Cambodia was able to import only US$4.1 million worth of materials. On the one hand, the Cambodian government's inability to import vital medical supplies was connected to the war-related decline in agricultural productivity and the coincident agrarian policies put in place by the Nixon admin-istration. On the other hand, this inability was resultant from the fact that pharmaceutical supplies, specifically, were not included under the USAID Commodity Import Program. Cambodian officials repeatedly asked US officials to include these drugs on the list of permissible imports. And repeatedly, American officials declined, espousing the same political rhetoric that disavowed a growing crisis of starving refugees.[9]

In this chapter I put forward the unconventional argument that the policies and practices of the Communist Party of Kampuchea are best understood as constituting a program of postconflict reconstruction. The Standard Total View holds that Cambodia was shattered by "bizarre" or "irrational" policies, that three years, eight months, and twenty days of genocidal rule left the country in a state of economic ruin and political collapse and a population traumatized by unimaginable violence. While not downplaying the violence unleashed by the Khmer Rouge, it must be acknowledged that Cambodia was devastated *prior* to the CPK assum-ing power. To be sure, key policies put forward by the CPK compounded the living horror that typified Democratic Kampuchea. But these were imposed on top of a land that had been subject to the most atrocious aerial campaign waged against a country in the history of modern warfare. It is only from the perspective of CPK policies as a program of postconflict reconstruction that the day-to-day functions of Democratic Kampuchea's political economy can be properly examined. To this end, the policies of the CPK "can be seen as some sort of extreme, but comprehensible response to the situation in Cambodia after 1975," for as Anthony Barnett concludes, "Had there not been a degree of plausibility and rationality for the [Democratic Kampuchean] state, the majority of cadre would not have gone along with them at the beginning."[10]

Postconflict reconstruction conventionally refers to the rebuilding of a state—and its attendant apparatuses—in the aftermath of war. John Hamre and Gordon Sullivan, for example, define postconflict reconstruction as "that which is needed to help reconstruct weak or failing states primarily after civil wars."[11] William Flavin likewise distinguishes between "conflict termination" and "conflict resolution." Conflict termination refers to the formal end of fighting, although Flavin is quick to note that this does not necessarily mean the end of violence.[12] Indeed, belligerents may continue the conflict, albeit through guerrilla fighting or other subversive practices. Conflict resolution, conversely, is a long-term process that involves primarily civil activities such as social reconciliation, civil administration, governance, public security, and infrastructure development. For the Khmer Rouge, April 17, 1975, marked the termination of conflict and, by extension, the beginnings of conflict resolution. Understanding how this transition was to be accomplished will therefore provide insight into the subsequent social and spatial organization of Democratic Kampuchea's political economy.

An Ominous Beginning

On May 20, 1973, as the US bombardment approached its peak, the CPK launched a "cooperativization" program. Under this system, land was collectivized, and the products of the labor of peasants—organized into groups of ten to thirty families—were to be confiscated by the authorities. This marked a new phase of the Cambodian communist revolution, a transition that aligns with war communism.

War communism, as a revolutionary practice, emerged in the Soviet Union in response to civil war. In the aftermath of the Bolshevik Revolution, decisions were put forward by Soviet planners, framed within the contours of Marx's account of dialectics and the transition to communism. It was understood, for example, that communism entailed the abolition of the labor market, that there would be a period in which the revolutionary party would assume control over labor power, and that labor was conceived as a service to be performed rather than a commodity to be bought and sold. However, the Soviet revolutionaries also recognized that it was impossible to simply conscript civilian labor. Instead, other means had to be found to organize and control labor in a useful, effective manner. On Lenin's instructions, Leon Trotsky developed a doctrine of labor militarization, which was subsequently published in *Pravda* on December 17, 1919. Under the concept of labor militarization, Trotsky proposed that the methods used to build the Soviet army be applied to economic programs. Wherever possible, for example, "military labor armies" would be put to

work in industrial areas, taking control of the organization and administration of both civilian and conscripted labor. Under war communism and
a militarized labor system, not only were workers and peasants expected to
become soldiers, but soldiers were expected to become workers.[13]

At war's end, the CPK encountered similar conditions to those experienced by the Soviets in 1917. Years of conflict, corruption, and foreign
interference had wreaked havoc on Cambodia's physical infrastructure.
Moreover, from the CPK's perspective, society itself had been compro-
mised. Consequently, the Khmer Rouge leadership embarked on their
own program of war communism, one that entailed the militarization of
all facets of society.[14]

Following their victory of April 17, 1975, the Communist Party of
Kampuchea began forcibly evacuating Phnom Penh, the capital of Cambodia. Upwards of three million people—more than half of whom were
peasants who had fled the fighting during five years of civil war—were
relocated onto cooperatives and work camps in neighboring provinces.
Many were forced to walk; others were transported by truck or train. It
was apparent that little planning went into the specific details of evacuation—there was scant coordination, and the resultant death toll, while not
accurately known, was substantial. Survivors recall the brutality and violence that occurred. Vatey Seng, for example, was a thirteen-year-old girl
living in Phnom Penh when the Khmer Rouge arrived. Seng recalls that
"the Khmer Rouge proclaimed through loudspeakers that all people had
to evacuate from the city immediately because American planes would
drop bombs onto the city soon." Families were given just minutes to collect whatever possessions they could carry; they were told that they would
return in three days and that the evacuation was a precaution—a safety
measure. Seng continues: "Thousands of people were walking toward
the outside the city. They carried bags of belongings by shoulders or held
on their heads. . . . Some pushed hospital beds with patients who were
mourning of pain. All patients were also forced against their will to leave
hospitals although their health conditions were very critical. . . . Along the
road there were corpses of former government soldiers and their families
that perished during the confrontation days ago. It looked very tragic and
horrifying, and the smell was so rotten."[15]

François Ponchaud, a French missionary in Cambodia between 1965 and 1975, lived through the evacuation of Phnom Penh. His question, formulated on April 17, 1975, continues to challenge scholars today: "Why had the Khmer Rouge done this? Why had the victors evacuated 2.5 million of their fellow countrymen?"[16] In response, various explanations have been forwarded—some derived from statements of Khmer Rouge cadre, others formulated from textual analysis of CPK documents. During the evacuation, for example, both Khmer Rouge soldiers and officials—as Seng's narrative relates—forwarded the very plausible explanation that American planes were about to bomb the city. Indeed, given the legacy of indiscriminate American bombing, such as scenario was at the time all too likely.

Other scholars maintain that the Khmer Rouge leadership was "antiurban," and cities were targeted as exemplars of all they held evil. Kevin McIntyre, for example, concludes that "in the swidden politics of the Khmer Rouge, Phnom Penh . . . and other cities and towns were slashed and sometimes burned to clear the brush for the new growth of Cambodian society." This "antiurban" explanation in fact has become commonplace and is a defining component of the Standard Total View. Under the Khmer Rouge, it is presumed, cities were anathema to their supposed attempt to create an agrarian utopia. Consequently, cities were emptied out, devoid of life and economic function. Hence, Karen Coates is able to write, "Phnom Penh was an extinguished city after the Khmer Rouge swept through in 1975. A city abandoned. The Paris of the Orient, silenced and shamed."[17]

The "empty Khmer Rouge city" thesis is attractive in its simplicity, but factually incorrect. The leadership of the CPK, far from promoting an antiurban bias, evacuated cities as part of their broader program of postconflict reconstruction. As detailed in chapter 4, a central task in the aftermath of war was to jump-start the economy. This would entail the repair of badly damaged infrastructure (for example, roads and bridges) but also the restoration of the country's agricultural sector. Under intense bombing, many farmers had fled to the cities, their farms neglected. Consequently, as the Khmer Rouge liberated areas from 1971 onward, peasants were relocated from the cities and into agricultural cooperatives. In

1973, for example, Khmer Rouge soldiers seized half of Kompong Cham City, taking fifteen thousand townspeople into the countryside with them. Later, in March 1974, just weeks before the fall of Phnom Penh, Khmer Rouge forces emptied the former capital of Oudong, dispersing more than twenty thousand former residents throughout the countryside.[18] Certainly, many of these movements were violent, and urban residents, refugee or otherwise, were forced at gunpoint to evacuate the cities.

As the CPK assumed its vanguard role in an attempt to build socialism—but also to establish the conditions necessary for their planned communal society—it was essential to fundamentally alter the existing socioeconomic organization of Cambodia. Initially, peasants were organized into "mutual aid teams" (*krom provas dai*). Under this system, effective control—but not ownership—of land, stock, and equipment remained in peasant hands; usury and rental payments were abolished; and taxation was relatively light. Later, but especially after April 1975, these were merged into larger "low-level cooperatives" (*sahakor kumrit teap*) and, finally, into "high-level cooperatives" (*sahakor kumrit khpuos*).[19] Similar to the practice of collectivization in the Soviet Union and the People's Republic of China, the CPK viewed cooperatives as a spatial practice that could, in theory, increase agricultural productivity and thereby garner greater surplus with which to spur industrialization.[20]

A speech delivered in 1976 captures the belief among leaders of the CPK that the revolution was transitioning from a period of conflict termination to conflict resolution. Addressing an assembly of cadre, the speaker, most likely Pol Pot, explained: "In 1970 the Party had over 4,000 people throughout the country. Our armed forces were small too. . . . The world said we were weak, small, few; how could we win?" The speaker then explained that "we organized forces, attacked, and won in a period of five years. This was because of the Party. If the Party had not been absolute, with no correct line on strategy or tactics, we would not have won like that." The message was clear. The CPK had developed a "correct" strategy for the revolution, one that led to a quick and decisive victory over militarily superior forces. Indeed, so resounding was the victory that it was accomplished more rapidly than any other struggle—a blatant and obvious reference to their onetime Vietnamese mentors. Such revolutionary will, coupled with a proper attitude and approach, would ensure a positive change in the lives of ordinary Cambodians. According to the speaker, "We want our country to advance very quickly so that our people advance." However, there was a reason for such a hastened timetable: "If we are not strong and do not leap forward quickly, outside enemies are just waiting to crush us. . . . For that reason we must strive to move fast."[21]

A Revolution Transformed

For Marx and Engels, the modern state was inseparable from capitalism; indeed, as a system of social organization, the state was but a concrete manifestation of the ruling class. The modern state, in other words, was nothing less than a *dictatorship of the bourgeoisie*. Engels elaborates, "The state is therefore by no means a power imposed on society from the outside; just as little is it 'the reality of the moral idea,' 'the image and reality of reason,' as Hegel asserts. Rather, it is a product of society at a certain stage of development; it is the admission that this society has become entangled in an insoluble contradiction with itself, that it is cleft into irreconcilable antagonisms, which it is powerless to dispel."[22]

The problem of the "bourgeoisie" state was most directly addressed by Lenin, notably in his 1917 essay "State and Revolution," written on the eve of the Bolshevik Revolution. Here, Lenin puts the problem of the state concretely, arguing that both the bureaucracy and the standing armies are bourgeois parasites on society. As such, it is necessary for the proletariat to concentrate their forces on the destruction of state power "and to regard the problem, not as one of perfecting the state machine, but one of *smashing and destroying it*." By way of support, Lenin calls attention to *The Communist Manifesto*, where Marx and Engels declare: "The proletariat will use its political supremacy to wrest, by degrees, all capital from the bourgeoisie, to centralize all instruments of production in the hands of the state, i.e., of the proletariat organized as the ruling class, and to increase the total of productive forces as rapidly as possible."[23]

The implications for our subsequent interpretation of CPK policy and of the space economy of Democratic Kampuchea are many. Lenin explains that "if the state is the product of irreconcilable class antagonisms, if it is a power standing above society and 'increasingly alienating itself from it,' it is clear that the liberation of the oppressed class is impossible, not only without violent revolution, but also without the destruction of the apparatus of state power which was created by the ruling class and which is the embodiment of this alienation."[24] It is on this basis that the CPK's penchant for "smashing" must be interpreted.

Marxist political philosophy, but especially as retheorized by Lenin, holds that it is neither possible nor desirable to reform or to remold the capitalist state following revolution. According to Marx and Engels, previous revolutions failed precisely because the revolutionaries attempted to co-opt or reform the state. In the *18th Brumaire*, for example, Marx concludes that previously, "all revolutions perfected this machine instead of smashing it." Heretofore, Marx opined, revolutions failed largely because the existing state—a concrete manifestation of class rule—was appropriated by revolutionaries as opposed to being dismantled. This is a theme picked up and expanded by Lenin, who would write, "All the revolutions which have occurred up to now have helped to perfect the state machine, whereas it must be smashed, broken." For Lenin, revolutionary violence was administered violence; it was not a condition of anarchy. He explains that "the proletariat needs . . . the centralized organization of force, the organization of violence, for the purpose of crushing the resistance of the exploiters and for the purpose of leading the great mass of the population . . . in the work of organizing socialist economy."[25]

It is telling, therefore, that the notion of failed revolutions should assume such a prominent place in Pol Pot's momentous speech of September 1977. Throughout the course of two thousand years of history, according to Pol Pot, Cambodia was witness to a series of class-based revolutions. In previous slave societies, for example, Pol Pot explained that the "exploited class struggled against the exploiting class," but, he cautioned, "this struggle was not guided by a correct line." Likewise, he identified a revolutionary struggle against feudalism. Victory, again, "was temporary, because those who were the victors did not possess a correct line to really liberate the country and really liberate the people, the exploited masses who comprise the peasant class." Failings, according to Pol Pot, stemmed from the fact that those who overthrew the previous class "made themselves warlords and ruled like kings and viceroys, and they became the new exploiters of the peasant class."[26] Pol Pot's interpretation thus falls squarely in line with that of Lenin vis-à-vis the state following a socialist revolution. The dialectic transformation from a feudalist-capitalist society to a communist society entails, on the one hand, the complete annihilation of the previous state and, on the other hand, the establishment of a transitory form of government that, at a certain point in the future, would simply wither away, thereby leaving in place a classless, communist society free of exploitation, oppression, and alienation. The immediate concrete objective of the socialist revolution, therefore, is the material obliteration of the capitalist state and, by extension, the social relations that constitute the state. To posit a rigid separation between a "revolutionary" phase and a "postrevolutionary" phase is therefore a serious misreading of Marxist-Leninist doctrine and leads to a gross distortion of Democratic Kampuchea.

Only with the complete annihilation of the former regime is a transition to communism possible, for the elimination of capitalist relations of productions—including those of governance—marks the beginnings of a new phase of the revolution. Thus, it is not unexpected that a captured Khmer Rouge document dated 1975 reads, "The immediate goal of the party is to lead the people to succeed in the national democratic revolution, to exterminate the imperialists, feudalists, and capitalists, and to form a national revolutionary state in Cambodia." The document continues, "The long range goal of the party is to lead the people in creating a socialist revolution and a communist society in Cambodia."[27] In short, leading members of the CPK viewed themselves as forming a dictatorship of the proletariat. They also acknowledged that conditions for revolution had not been optimal—that the people had not yet adopted a proper political consciousness. An immediate postrevolutionary task, therefore, was to "build socialism" among the masses.

The concept of "building socialism" is derived also from the writings of early Russian Marxist economists who realized that revolutions do not always take place after the final phase of capitalist transformation, and, therefore, the concentration of productive forces must be achieved under revolutionary control.[28] Consequently, in order to achieve socialism and proceed toward a communist society, transitional phases must be identified and overcome. Thion argues, however, that the CPK grossly misunderstood the idea of transitional phases as "reformist" or "revisionist." Such a strategy, for the top echelon of the CPK, was to be avoided. Rather, the CPK leadership believed that they would be able to jump over the transition phases—to bring about a *super* "great leap forward"—and thus build socialism through the hard work and sacrifice of its citizens.

With this argument I am in general agreement. The CPK did believe vociferously that anything was possible on the condition that a proper revolutionary consciousness could be cultivated among its populace. As such, it was theoretically possible, from the CPK's vantage point, to proceed rapidly in their quest to bring about a communist society. For the Khmer Rouge, therefore, 1975 would mark the transition from one form of sociospatial organization to another. The objectives of the CPK, consequently, also underwent a transformation. Previously, the goal was to wrest power from the previous regime; now it would become the obliteration—the smashing—of the former state and the construction of a new form of democratic governance. How this was to take place, though, depended greatly on how the CPK positioned Democratic Kampuchea within the global political economy. As a newly independent state, Democratic Kampuchea was economically, politically, and even militarily vulnerable. Having achieved, in their minds, a momentous victory against imperialism and capitalism, many CPK leaders were loath to rush into any multilateral relations or regional alliances that would jeopardize their hard-won independence. During a meeting of high-level officials on January 9, 1976, for example, it was noted that "our goal of development in the future is to go even faster. But at the same time, there remain many serious problems to solve, both inside and outside the country. If we take attitudes immediately, there may be many mistakes. If we do not yet do so, we are not wrong, we are just a little slow." The document continues: "That we are not immediately announcing our stances has two aspects. First, we remain quiet, and they may ask, how are we serving the world movement? Second, when we do have our attitudes, they will support us. This shows that we have a mature policy. . . . The important thing is the factor of our acting on our own. If we can defend our borders, build a strong army, build a prospering economy, the Party leads firmly and the people are comfortable and happy, then there are no problems."[29] In this document, the CPK is referring most likely to other member states of the Non-Aligned Movement. As detailed in the next section, Democratic Kampuchea positioned itself in line with the Non-Aligned Movement, and the aforementioned document affirms that the CPK leadership stressed "self-reliance" and "self-mastery" not out of some irrational or unfounded decision, but rather because the principles of nonalignment appeared to offer a viable economic path to prosperity.

The International Stage

On December 14, 1975, a constitution was drafted for Democratic Kampuchea; to the world, this event signaled the arrival of the Communist Party of Kampuchea on the world stage. Administratively, the constitution declares that Democratic Kampuchea "is an independent, united, peaceful, neutral, non-aligned, sovereign and democratic state with territorial integrity."[30] From the outset, therefore, it was clear that, at least rhetorically, the CPK adhered to the position advocated by other international members of the Non-Alignment Movement.

In the early years of the Cold War, representatives of former colonial powers sought to forge an independent path, free from the dictates of either American capitalism or Soviet socialism.[31] Known as the Non-Aligned Movement, this movement became a powerful political force that proclaimed a commitment to nationalism, the preservation of national dignity, and the realization of national power. Moreover, the Non-Aligned Movement connoted an alliance with the forces of regionalism, national independence, the struggle for a new economic order, social and economic progress, and self-reliance.[32]

A defining moment of the Non-Aligned Movement occurred in 1955 at the Asian African Conference, held in Bandung, Indonesia. In attendance were twenty-nine independent countries, including Sihanouk's newly liberated Cambodia. Significantly, the Bandung Conference marked the first time that former colonies of Asia and Africa "assembled to discuss common problems and attempted to formulate a united approach to international relations."[33] Nation building was foremost among the topics discussed, as participants vowed to oppose colonialism and neocolonialism through peaceful means.

Throughout the 1960s and 1970s, the aims of the Non-Aligned Movement broadened considerably. On the one hand, members addressed specific conflicts, including the British and French invasion of Suez and the Russian invasion of Hungary, while, on the other hand, members focused attention more generally on the problems of economic development, especially those arising from heightened uncertainty in the international economy.[34] Indeed, by the 1970s, the problems of economic development were in many respects paramount. As Robert Potter et al. explain, many if not most of the newly independent states lacked the capital to sustain their economies, let alone expand or diversify; many states also remained trapped in the production of one or two primary commodities, the prices of which were steadily falling in real terms, unable to expand or improve infrastructure. In light of these structural conditions, participants at the 1974 conference, held in Algeria, called for efforts to create a new economic world order. This attempt was predicated on a crucial distinction that was made between "anticolonialism" and "anti-imperialism." As Singham explains, "Until the end of World War II, the political form of imperialist exploitation was colonialism in that it sought outright control over the subject peoples of Asia, Africa, and the Americas. . . . World War II, however, resulted in the great awakening of colonial powers who proceeded to demand and obtain political independence for their countries. . . . The end of colonial rule did not negate imperialism. While one saw the decline of the colonial powers in Europe one also saw the emergence of a newly reconstructed capitalism led by the United States."[35] Accordingly, for many members of the Non-Aligned Movement, it was imperative to identify a path toward development that did not result in a form of neocolonialism. This meant that states by necessity were to avoid becoming entangled in asymmetric foreign and trade relations.

In August 1976, the Fifth Summit Conference of Non-Aligned Countries was held in Colombo, Sri Lanka. In attendance were representatives of Democratic Kampuchea, including Khieu Samphan, president

of the Presidium of Democratic Kampuchea, who declared that "Democratic Kampuchea resolutely remains in the great family of non-aligned
countries."[36] The context of the summit is important in understanding
subsequent CPK policy. Throughout the early to mid-1970s, many lib-
eral economic strategists and financial institutions advocated the view
that developing countries could and should pay for essential imports by
borrowing extensively from private banks; in turn, numerous developing countries borrowed sizable amounts to engage in the importation of
industrial goods. High levels of indiscriminate borrowing contributed to a
worldwide debt crisis—a problem that was compounded by the decision of
the Organization of Petroleum Exporting Countries to raise the price of
oil.[37] It is no surprise, therefore, that participants at the Colombo conference, including representatives of the CPK, debated at length alternative
paths to economic growth.

The attitudes and positions of the CPK in response to the Fifth Summit
are revealed in a text later published by the embassy of Democratic Kampuchea in Berlin, East Germany. According to this document, the summit
had "achieved brilliant victories," including the adoption of a number of
policies that "reinforce the principles of non-alignment, enhance the role
of this Movement and confirm the resolute solidarity of the non-aligned
countries in the common struggle against imperialism, colonialism, neo-
colonialism and against the interferences, interventions, aggressions and
against the expansionism of the rich great powers, for independence, sovereignty, territorial integrity and the right of each people to determine the
destiny of its nation by itself in full independence and sovereignty." The
text continues: "The people of Kampuchea warmly hails the victories of
the 5th Summit Conference of Non-Aligned Countries which consolidate the non-aligned principles, enhance the non-aligned movement and
strengthen the solidarity within its ranks. . . . In contributing to the revolutionary struggle of the peoples of the world, to the liberation struggle
of the brotherly countries of the Third World and to the strengthening
of the cause of the great non-aligned family, the people of Kampuchea is
determined to carry out the revolution successfully in its own country, to
build up its economy and edify its country according to the principles of
independence, sovereignty and self-reliance."[38]

Two months later, Ieng Sary, deputy prime minister in charge of foreign affairs, spoke before the Thirty-First Session of the United Nations' General Assembly in New York. Following an opening welcome statement, Ieng Sary explained, "The 31st Regular Session of our General Assembly takes place at a time when all the peoples of the world and especially the peoples of the non-aligned countries and of the Third World are waging a victorious struggle everywhere against imperialism, colonialism, neo-colonialism, Zionism and all forms of foreign interference, aggression, expansionism and exploitation, for independence, sovereignty, territorial integrity, for the right to determine their own destiny and for the establishment of a new international economic order on the basis of justice and equality."[39] He continued:

> Dozens of new independent states are arising from the ruins of colonialism, determined to engage in the struggle to defend and consolidate their political and economic independence, their sovereignty and territorial integrity against all acts of domination, exploitation, interference and aggression on the part of the rich great powers. . . . They call forcefully for the establishment of new relations between the peoples and nations, in accordance with the significant changes which have taken place in the world, and based on the principles of mutual respect of independence, sovereignty and territorial integrity, equality, mutual advantage, non-interference in the internal affairs of other states and the right of every people to manage its own affairs.[40]

Democratic Kampuchea, Ieng Sary explained, stood by these principles. Moreover, the people of Kampuchea had participated actively in the struggle against colonialism and foreign aggression. "Together with all the other peoples," he declared, Democratic Kampuchea "has actively taken part in the common struggle against imperialism, colonialism and neo-colonialism in order to liberate itself from all forms of domination, oppression and exploitation." Ieng Sary continued:

> Our people never accepted the yoke of the colonialist and neo-colonialist system which was imposed on us for over a century and against which

our people fought from the beginning, gaining successive victories in a long, difficult and unyielding struggle on the political, military and diplomatic levels, leading to the total victory over the American imperialists' war of aggression on April 17, 1975. This glorious victory is of a great historical significance for the people and nation of Kampuchea, for it marks their total and final liberation from imperialism, colonialism, neo-colonialism and all other forms of domination and exploitation. Our whole nation has regained its soul and its identity.[41]

Democratic Kampuchea's military victory was subsequently interpreted as an international victory for the Non-Aligned Movement as a whole. According to Ieng Sary, "April 17, 1975 is also a victory of the unwavering solidarity with the struggle of the people of Kampuchea shown by the non-aligned and Third World peoples and countries and by all peace- and justice-loving peoples and countries in the world."[42] In so arguing, Ieng Sary presented Democratic Kampuchea not so much as an isolated, autarkic society, but rather as an independent, sovereign state that would interact on the global stage on its own terms. Viewed from this vantage point, the repeated phrases of "self-reliance" and "self-mastery" that appear throughout CPK documents take on a new interpretation. CPK officials were not opposed to cultivating foreign relations. Indeed, as recent documentary evidence clearly shows, throughout 1976 CPK leaders were anxious to expand their international cooperation, especially with those governments associated with the Non-Aligned Movement, but also Western countries such as the United Kingdom, the Netherlands, Denmark, Austria, Greece, Finland, and Italy.[43] As Ieng Sary explained:

> Democratic Kampuchea will always continue to follow a policy of independence, peace, neutrality and non-alignment. . . . As a non-aligned country, Democratic Kampuchea respects and conscientiously practices the principles of non-alignment. . . . Democratic Kampuchea neither participates in any alliance nor in any regional association. She resists the establishment of any foreign military bases on her territory and all forms of intervention and interference with her internal affairs. Our people resolutely defends its independence, national sovereignty,

territorial integrity and its inalienable right to determine its own destiny, for which it has fought so hard and sacrificed so much. At the same time, Democratic Kampuchea continues her efforts to establish and maintain close relations with her neighbors and with all the other countries of the world, based on the strict mutual respect for independence, sovereignty, territorial integrity, of the principle of equality and mutual advantages.[44]

Democratic Kampuchea's allegiance to self-reliance and self-mastery would extend to its participation in the global economy. Ieng Sary clarified that "problems of economic development remain the major preoccupation of our world. . . . [The] present international economic order [is] based on relations of domination, exploitation and dependence [and has] enabled the developed countries to enrich themselves very rapidly and to live in superfluity and wastage, whereas the developing countries get poorer from day to day, and having acquired their political independence, still remain confronted with the dramatic problems of misery, malnutrition, hunger, sickness and illiteracy." Moreover, "The terms of trade continue to deteriorate for these developing countries, because the basic products and raw materials they possess are constantly devaluated. Their indebtment [sic] with all the resulting financial implications is growing in a tragic manner . . . [and] these unequal and unjust relations have led to the importation of the economic and financial crisis of the capitalist world with all its consequences, especially inflation, rising prices, devaluation of currency and a sinking standard of living for the population."[45]

Democratic Kampuchea's participation at the Fifth Summit Conference of Non-Aligned Countries, but especially Ieng Sary's statement before the United Nations, is extremely important in addressing the broad coordinates of governance under the Khmer Rouge. Most significantly, it is necessary to situate the CPK not as an aberration but rather as a mindful participant in a global social movement. And while the reality of CPK practice often failed to live up to its rhetoric, it remains the case that subsequent decisions emanating from the top echelons of Khmer Rouge leadership adhered to the principles established by the Non-Aligned Movement. It is through this framework that we must understand the CPK's attempt to construct its own state apparatus.

Transformations in Governance

As a "dictatorship of the proletariat," the CPK did not attempt to establish a "state," as this political term is commonly understood.[46] Rather, the leadership of the CPK, in principle, envisioned a representative form of governance based on democratic centralism. As with many concepts, there is no singular or essentialist definition of democratic centralism.[47] Further, it is not entirely clear how consistently the term was applied by members of the CPK. Nevertheless, it is possible to identify key components of democratic centralism and to juxtapose them with surviving CPK documents.

Not found in the writings of Marx or Engels, the term *democratic centralism* was first specifically formulated as the organizing principle by both Bolshevik and Menshevik factions of the Russian Social Democratic Labor Party in the early twentieth century.[48] It was Lenin, however, who most effectively formulated the dialectical combination of "democracy" and "centralism" into a principle of political organization.[49] Postrevolutionary society would be governed not by members of the ruling class but democratically, by the workers themselves. Under socialism, according to Lenin, the functions of "state" administration are simplified: a separate managerial class is unnecessary, for the workers themselves will be able to govern. For Lenin, a more representative democratic politics would carry into the economic sphere, whereby the workers, likewise, would assume the decisions regarding production and distribution. Combined, through a worker-led democratic movement, the state would gradually cease to exist. A dialectics of democracy and economic activity in others was *centralized* within the proletariat.

Over time, democratic centralism acquired various meanings, as Marxists in the Soviet Union, the People's Republic of China, and elsewhere adapted or adopted the term for particular uses. Since its inception in 1921, for example, the Chinese Communist Party accepted Marxism-Leninism as its political canon and, consequently, adopted—but also reinterpreted—democratic centralism as a key tenant of its policies and programs.[50] A CCP document from 1938, for example, states, "The minority obeys the majority; party members have complete freedom to discuss and criticize before any issue is decided; after it is decided, everyone must implement the decision of the organization no matter what their view; the subordinate must implement the resolutions and directives of the superior; if they have different views about the resolutions and directives of the superior, they may present their views to the superior, but they must still implement these resolutions and directives before they are changed by the superior."[51]

Democratic centralism was also a key feature of the Democratic Republic of Vietnam. As a revolutionary socialist party infused with Marxist-Leninist ideology, the Communist Party of Vietnam established in the 1950s a bureaucratic-authoritarian state founded on the principles of democratic centralism and the economic policies of Soviet-inspired state socialism. As Jonathan London explains, "The formal institutions the [Communist Party] sought to impose in the 1950s and 1960s were premised on the elimination of political opposition and the subordination of all social activity to the interests of the Party."[52]

In his momentous speech of September 29, 1977, Pol Pot identified the Marxist-Leninist foundation of Democratic Kampuchea. He explained: "We have solidly laid the foundations of our collectivist socialism, and we are continually improving them, while consolidating and developing them." Strikingly, Pol Pot called attention to "the implementation of the Party's dictatorship of the proletariat in all areas of our revolutionary activity. We promote broad democracy among the people by a correct application of democratic centralism, so that this immense force will mobilize enthusiastically and rapidly for socialist revolution and construction, at great leaps and bounds forward."[53] And while this speech marked the first public enunciation of the CPK's underlying political philosophy, key components of Marxist-Leninism, notably democratic centralism, had already informed the establishment of Democratic Kampuchea governing structures. The Democratic Kampuchea Constitution, for example, declared unequivocally in Article 1, "The State of Kampuchea is the State of the workers, peasants and other laborers of Kampuchea." Here, we must not lose sight that the "State" referred to in this article must be understood as a state in the Leninist sense, that is, a communal organization of men and women. This understanding necessarily informs Article 2 of the constitution: "All important means of production are the collective property of the people's State and the collective property of the communally organized people."[54] In other words, and consistent with the broad coordinates of democratic centralism, economic productivity was to be organized by the workers themselves. In practice, this never came to pass, as the policies and programs of the CPK assumed more and more the character of state capitalism. Indeed, it is ironic that the CPK regime would fail in large part because the CPK as ruling class never did allow the masses to control their own destiny. In the beginning, however, there remained the theoretical possibility of greater participation in political and economic decision making by the citizens of Democratic Kampuchea. As detailed in later sections and chapters, apprehension remained among top leaders of the CPK that a sufficient level of political consciousness had not been achieved. Absent a correct consciousness, for the CPK greater participation was all but precluded. Moreover, this sentiment contributed to the purges of those men and women suspected of traitorous and reactionary attitudes.

As stated in the constitution, democratic centralism provided the bedrock upon which legislative, executive, and judicial power was built. Following Article 5, "The legislative power lies with the Assembly of workers, peasants and other laborers' representatives," Article 6 explains that "the Government is designated by the Assembly of the People's Representatives of Kampuchea" and "is fully responsible to this Assembly for all its activities inside and outside the country"; last, Article 7 proclaims that "justice is exercised by the people. The people's courts represent and guarantee the people's justice, defend the people's democratic liberties and punish any act directed against the people's State or violating the laws of the people's State." The importance of democratic centralism was further detailed in Article 6 of the Statutes of Democratic Kampuchea, adopted in January 1976: "The Communist Party of Kampuchea takes the principle of democratic centralism as its organizational foundation." This meant, in theory, "All Party leadership organizations must implement collective leadership and have specific persons holding responsibility"; "All of the various decisions of the Party must be made collectively"; "All echelons of Party leadership organizations must be collectively appointed"; "The minority respects the majority. Lower echelon respects upper echelon. The individual respects the collective. The private respects the organization. The various echelon organizations respect the central organization"; "At the designated times, lower echelon must report to upper echelon on the situation and on work done"; and "Also at each designated time, upper echelon must report to lower echelons regarding the general situation and regarding instructions which they must carry out."[55]

In practice, governance was centralized among a few key individuals who composed the "Standing Committee." Dominated by Pol Pot, Nuon Chea, Son Sen, and Ieng Sary, the Standing Committee was the true locus of sovereign power and literally held the power over life and death. Membership fluctuated, in large part because of internal purges initiated by Pol Pot toward other members suspected of traitorous activities. As of April 1975, the Standing Committee included Pol Pot (secretary-general), Nuon Chea (deputy secretary-general and vice chair of the Military Commission), Ieng Sary (deputy prime minister of foreign affairs), So Phim (secretary, Eastern Zone), Vorn Vet (deputy prime minister for the economy), Ros Nhim (secretary, Northwest Zone), Ta Mok (secretary, Southwest Zone), and Son Sen (deputy prime minister for defense).

The Standing Committee was itself a smaller component of the Central Committee.[56] By statute, the Central Committee was the highest decision-making body in Democratic Kampuchea. Likewise, as a more broadly representative body, the Central Committee was given responsibility to "implement the Party political line and Statute throughout the Party" as well as to "govern and arrange cadres and Party members throughout the entire Party."[57] In practice, though, the Central Committee remained subservient to the dictates of the Standing Committee.

Crucial to any form of governance, but especially that of democratic centralism, are the conditions on which any citizen may (in theory) participate. Within Democratic Kampuchea, both "formal" and "informal" categorizations were used. Most prominent—and not constitutionally binding—was that between "new" (or "April 17") people and "base" people. Here, the latter referred to those people who came under Khmer Rouge control during the civil war, that is, prior to April 17, 1975. In general, these people were considered more loyal and more trustworthy. The category of "new" people, conversely, consisted of people who either did not live in liberated areas prior to the date of victory or did not support

3. CPK leaders riding on a train. First from left, Pol Pot; second from left, Nuon Chea; first from right, Vorn Vet; and second from right, Ta Mok. Courtesy of the Documentation Center of Cambodia Archives.

the Khmer Rouge. Beyond this informal distinction, other, more "legal," qualifications were applied. According to Article 9 of the constitution, "Every citizen of Kampuchea has the full right to enjoy material, moral and cultural life. . . . Every citizen of Kampuchea has all his means of existence fully secured." These rights did not extend, however, to full and equal political participation, despite rhetoric that Democratic Kampuchea was a people's state. Indeed, the 1976 statutes outlined the ideology, membership, structure, and organization of the party.[58] Crucially, Article 1 of the 1976 statutes specifies that "persons who may join the Communist Party of Kampuchea are members of the Party core organizations . . . , male or female, of age 18 and older." However, membership is conditional upon the fulfillment of two criteria. First, prospective members "must have had good and constantly combative activities, tested in successive revolutionary work in the unions, in the cooperatives, and in the Revolutionary Army, following the Party political line, following the ideological stances of the Party, and following the organizational stances of the Party";

"must be of good class pedigree, and in particular hold the worker class stance of the Party, which they have successfully strived to build while inside the revolutionary movement under the leadership of the Party"; "must have [a] good and clean life morals and be good and clean politically, never having been involved with the enemy"; "must examine, question, and take the measure of the opinions of the popular masses inside the framework that those selected into the Party must live or work in the cooperatives, unions, company-level units, or various other units"; and "must have a clear personal history with a verified base of origin, place of residence, and work." This last condition is especially noteworthy, in that it directs attention to the second criteria, the *process* of becoming a member. Thus, the statutes indicate that "many levels of Party organization must collectively examine, deliberate, and decide before permission to join can be granted." In general, this meant that various hierarchies of administrators (as discussed below) were to decide on one's fulfillment of the first set of criteria; these decisions were based in large part on an evaluation of "biographies" that would be gathered from all people throughout Democratic Kampuchea. According to the statutes, a preparatory period was necessary, during which evaluators would (again, in principle) determine whether one was worthy of membership. Moreover, potential party members were required to satisfy ten additional criteria for selection into various party leadership positions. Article 5 clarifies that "to raise the quality of Party leadership and to guarantee its inherent strength and purity of Party politics, ideology, and organization, various criteria must be established as the factors for deliberation in selecting cadre into the various leadership committees of the Party." These included "strong revolutionary stance on the Party political line"; "strong Party revolutionary stance on proletarian ideology"; "strong revolutionary stance on internal Party solidarity and unity"; "strong revolutionary stance on the lines of organization, leadership, and work of the Party"; "strong Party revolutionary stance on revolutionary vigilance, maintaining secrecy, and defending revolutionary forces"; "strong revolutionary Party stance of 'independence, mastery, self-reliance, and self-mastery'"; "strong revolutionary stance in making and examining personal histories and revolutionary life views"; "strong revolutionary stance on class"; "strong revolutionary stance on clean life morals, and politically clean"; and "the capability to build oneself and be receptive to future leadership." Each of these ten criteria contained detailed explanatory remarks as to fulfillment. For example, to demonstrate "strong Party revolutionary stance of proletarian ideology," cadre "must have a correct and strong proletarian class stance in every sector, material, right of power, and life morality"; "have a correct and strong stance of collective ownership in every sector, materials, right of power, and life morality, and live in a regime of collective organization"; "have a high and absolute stance of sacrifice of private ownership in every sector, material, right of power, and life morality"; "have an audacious stance of active combat and endurance of difficulties on all occasions in absolute class struggle in the national defense and national construction of Democratic Kampuchea in the direction of social revolution and building socialism"; and "be vigilant regarding the stance of thick and materialistic personal and private ownership, rights of power, and life morality."[59]

The statute also clarified that individual members could not make decisions by themselves, but only in concert with other members—a key tenant of democratic centralism. Of particular significance is the designation of "rights" (Article 3) afforded to party members. Full-rights status meant that members were permitted to "consider and discuss and join in decision making" on all party affairs, unlike "candidate" members, who were allowed only to participate in meetings, without the right of decision making.[60] Perhaps most significantly, although not enunciated in the 1976 statutes, full-rights status meant "having the decision-making power to eliminate people."[61] Both the Central Committee and the Standing Committee were composed of "full-rights" and "candidate" (or "reserve") members.

Constitutionally, Democratic Kampuchea was to be governed by the Assembly of the People's Representatives (PRA) of Kampuchea. As specified in Article 5, this body was to be composed of 250 members representing workers, peasants, other laborers, and the Revolutionary Army of Kampuchea. Consequently, on March 20, 1976, "elections" were held to appoint men and women to this governing organ, and during the first—and only—congressional meeting of the PRA, held between April 11 and 13, 1976, Khieu Samphan was appointed as chairman of the State Presidium, a position that, under the Constitution, was responsible for representing the State of Democratic Kampuchea both internationally and domestically. Nuon Chea was to serve as chairman of the Standing Committee of the PRA.[62] Apart from the appointments of Khieu Samphan and Nuon Chea, these elections mattered little, as true political power remained vested in the Standing Committee of the CPK.

On March 20, 1976, a suite of ministries to replace the previous government was also introduced.[63] These included the Ministry of Foreign Affairs (headed by Ieng Sary); Ministry of the Economy (Vorn Vet); Ministry of Defense (Son Sen); Ministry of Information and Propaganda (Hu Nim); Ministry of Health (Thioun Thioeun); Ministry of Social Affairs (Ieng Thirith); Ministry of Public Works (Touch Phoeun); Ministry of Culture, Education, and National Studies (Yun Yat); and the Ministry of Interior, Cooperatives, and Communes (Hou Yuon).[64] Pol Pot was appointed as prime minister. In addition, six committees were established under the direction of the Ministry of Economy: agriculture, industry, commerce, rubber plantations, transportation, and energy.[65]

Many of these so-called ministries existed on paper only. Indeed, Boraden Nhem describes the administrative structure of Democratic Kampuchea as an "empty government," noting that many of the ministries were "nominal only and had no notable activities."[66] For a Marxist-Leninist organization, however, this is readily understandable and also explains the indifference exhibited by CPK officials in their smashing of civilian and military officials of the previous regime. On the one hand, the CPK was well aware of potential problems arising from the elimination of former bourgeois workers, administrators, and so forth. During a meeting of the CPK Standing Committee on October 9, 1975, for example, discussion revolved around the dearth of qualified cadre throughout the country.[67] On the other hand, the CPK leadership appears to have taken to heart Lenin's assumption that "capitalist culture has created large-scale production, factories, railways, the postal service, telephones, etc., and on this basis the great majority of functions of the old 'state power' have become so simplified and can be reduced to such simple operations of registration, filing and checking that they can be easily performed by every literate person."[68] In other words, trained and skilled professionals were unnecessary, for life had become so simplified under the previous regime, *anyone could take over.*

In the interim, however, a strong central authority remained necessary, for until the masses had elevated themselves to the appropriate level of political consciousness, a vanguard remained indispensable. Consequently, the tasks of the Standing Committee as well as the various ministries were supported by a host of governmental offices.[69] These were mainly functional units but were essential for the day-to-day operations of Democratic Kampuchea. Notable among the myriad and mysterious offices was "Political Office 870" and "Office S-71" (designated also as Ministry S-71 or simply the "Government Office"). Political Office 870 was tasked with matters of policy, including the coordination of communication between the party center and the various territorial committees (discussed below). S-71, conversely, was responsible for a variety of administrative and logistical functions and included a bewildering array of suboffices, all code-named with the prefix K.[70] K-1, for example, designated a housing compound that contained, for at least part of the time, the residence and workplace of Pol Pot; other key offices included K-3 (Khieu Samphan's residence), K-4 (logistics), K-7 (courier and communications), K-11 (medical affairs), and K-12 (motor pool).

Spatially, the CPK was organized along military lines.[71] Following the coup of 1970, the Khmer Rouge began to build its rank and file through the establishment of a new communist system throughout the countryside. Modeled after their Chinese and Vietnamese counterparts, small guerrilla units known as *korng chhlorb* were organized to both fight and recruit new members. These military units were under the command of a three-person committee consisting of a chief, deputy chief, and member.[72] Throughout the civil war, CPK armed forces were regionally based and largely autonomous.[73] Traditionally, Cambodia was administered following a territorial hierarchy. At the smallest level stood the *phoun* (hamlet) or *phum* (village). Collectively, *phoun* and *phum* would constitute a *khum* (commune), various *khum* would form a *srok* (district), and various *srok* would form a province.

The CPK essentially continued the territorial division of Cambodia for administrative purposes but made a number of modifications. First, the CPK adopted a military administrative unit known as a *phumipeak*, or zone. Previously, a *phumipeak* that encompassed many provinces existed only in the military domain under the form of a "military region." The CPK, however, elevated all civilian administration to the zonal level.[74] These were referred to by cardinal directions, that is, Southwest or East Zone, although each was given a numeric code.[75] Second, each zone was to be composed of *damban*, or regions (also translated as "sectors"). These were largely based on former provinces, but there was no one-to-one correspondence; indeed, many regions crossed old administrative boundaries. Regions were designated by number, often but not always indicating a level of systemization. The Northwest Zone, for example, was composed of seven regions, numbered 1 through 7. The East Zone consisted of five regions numbered 20 through 24. Other regions, however, were less straightforward, reflecting in part the ongoing shuffling of regions between zones.[76] Administrative divisions below the zonal and regional levels conformed to prerevolutionary terminology. Each region was composed of several districts (*srok*), each district was composed of several communes (*khum*), and each commune comprised numerous villages (*phum*). By way of illustration, consider the Northwest Zone. As indicated, this zone was composed of seven regions. Region 5, located north of Battambang City, was divided into four districts, identified as Serey Sophoan, Preah Neth Preah, Phnom Srok, and Thma Puok. Each of these four districts was divided into a number of communes. Phnom Srok, for example, consisted of five communes, while Thma Puok was composed of nine communes. Each commune, in turn, was composed of a number of villages. In the district of Phnom Srok, for example, Sreh Chik commune consisted of fifteen villages.

It is important to stress that communes, districts, regions, and zones were "virtual" in the sense that there was no separate material form to these entities. Working from below, villages had a concrete existence; in turn, an assemblage of villages was *administratively* organized into a commune. Working from the top, zones were administrative territorial divisions that were subdivided into regions and districts, which contained various villages (assembled as communes). Consequently, people materially lived in villages and participated in communal (commune-based)

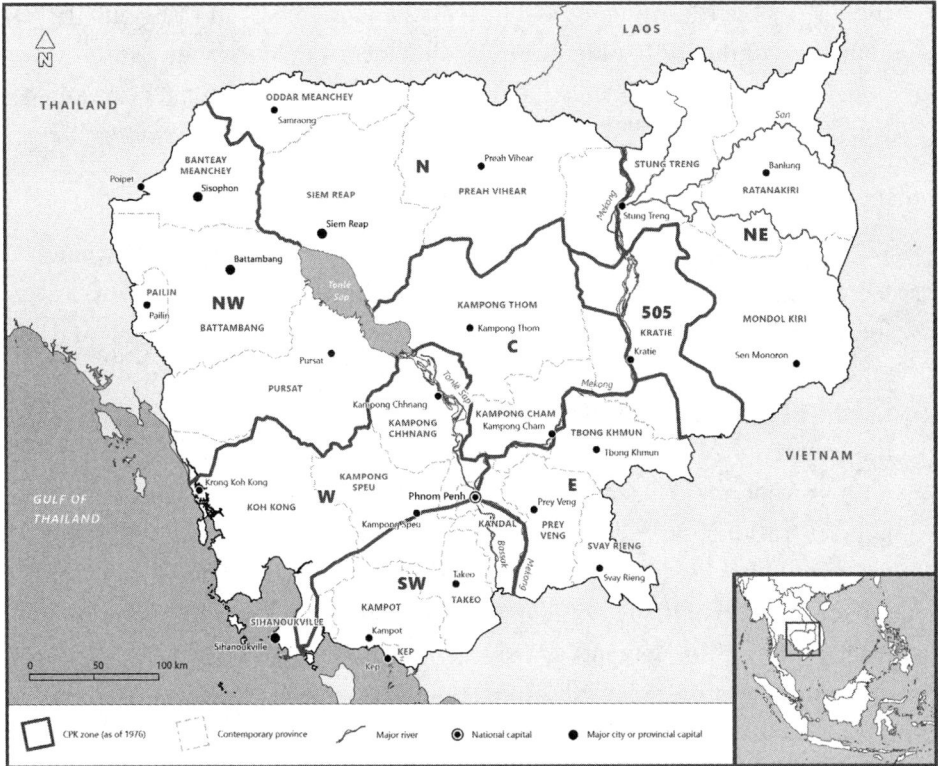

4. Former provincial boundaries and CPK zone-level administrative boundaries, ca. 1976.

activities. Policies would be implemented and administered at the various territorial divisions.

By April 1975 the CPK had divided Cambodia's nineteen provinces into five zones: the Northeast, North, Northwest, Southwest, and East. A "special zone" was also created, to include the area around Phnom Penh. In the ensuing months and years, administrative divisions changed often, usually resultant from internal purges or power plays among CPK leaders. Toward the end of 1975, for example, the Southwest Zone was split into two, forming a new West Zone and a smaller Southwest Zone. The Phnom Penh "special zone" was also dissolved, hereafter categorized as a distinct territory not within the formal administrative structures. Later, two autonomous regions were formed: Region 106, consisting mostly of the former Siem Reap and Oddar Meanchey Provinces, and Region 103, composed of the former Preah Vihear Province. The port facility at Kampong Som was also organized as a separate entity. And still later, toward late 1976 and early 1977, a seventh zone was created when Regions 103 and 106 were merged to form a new North Zone; the old North Zone was renamed the Central Zone.[77]

Each political division was administered by a three-person committee consisting of a secretary, deputy secretary, and member, responsible for politics, security, and economics, respectively. At the commune and village level, the two senior ranking committee members were usually identified as "chief" and "deputy chief." The CPK's spatial organization of the country was pivotal for its administrative practices. The zone committee was responsible for overseeing the implementation of CPK plans and policies throughout its respective zone and for delegating plans and policies to all other levels (for example, regions, districts) in its zone. Likewise, the committees at the region, district, and commune levels fulfilled similar functions of implementing tasks designated by the higher levels. The degree of authority, especially among lower levels of governance, remains unclear. In general, "administrative levels below the zone were more akin to implementing bodies than decision-making ones."[78] However, evidence indicates that for some projects, such as the construction of small-scale canals and dikes, local chiefs had a certain degree of leeway.

Each political division from the commune level up included a variety of three-person committees responsible for specific tasks, including economics, transportation, finance, medical, mobile, military, social affairs, fishing, textile, and security. Here, Khmer Rouge terminology is important. The "economic committee," for example, was responsible for the collection and warehousing of rice; the "finance committee" was tasked with the distribution of all other agricultural products. "Mobile" committees were responsible for the deployment of mobile work brigades to undertake specific projects, such as the construction of a canal, the clearance of forest, or the harvesting of fields. Moreover, not all zones, regions, districts, communes, or villages would include all ten committees. Communes that did not include sizable bodies of water would obviously not have fishing committees. In general, most divisions would have an economic unit, transportation unit, and security unit. Last, the designation of the committees varied widely. In some locales, the standard triumvirate of secretary, deputy secretary, and member was followed; in other areas—and especially at the village or commune level—committee leaders were identified as "chief" or even *me kong* (group mother).[79]

Existing apart from, but still administratively connected to, the hierarchal structure of zone, region, district, commune, and village were cooperatives, ad hoc units of administration that were formed according to a specific need. If, for example, a major construction project was initiated, such as the building of a reservoir, the relevant zone secretary would be responsible for assembling myriad cooperatives to undertake the task. Depending on the expected number of workers required, each region may be called upon to "volunteer" a specified quota of laborers; subsequently, each district would be required to provide a certain amount of laborers. This recruitment system continued to the level of the commune, whereby groups of villagers would be assembled. Conversely, if a project was initiated at the district level, laborers would be recruited only from those communes (and hence villages) of the district involved.

The social organization of Democratic Kampuchea was a direct reflection of democratic centralism. As Herbert Schurmann explains, "The operation of the principle of centralism has seen the creation of a web of organization with vertical chains of command which ultimately merge, like the apex of a pyramid, at the very top." In theory, throughout Democratic Kampuchea, each political division, including cooperatives, was to be self-reliant and autonomous—a structure I identify elsewhere as *integrated autonomy*.[80] In practice, flows of information, supplies, and so on were channeled hierarchically through the three-person committees, with ultimate control overseen by the Standing Committee of the CPK. Lower-level cadre—for example, those governing at the district level—were required to channel all requests via messenger or telegram to their immediate supervisors at the regional level; these cadre would, in turn, forward the request to the zone level, where it would then be routed (often via telegram) to the relevant "ministries" of the CPK. There were to be no "horizontal" relations; hence, a district secretary in the Northwest Zone could not request supplies from a neighboring district secretary, also located in the Northwest Zone. He or she would (in theory) have to route the request through the zone committee (and hence to the Standing Committee) before it would be rerouted to the other district cadre.

This form of sociospatial organization appears exceptionally inefficient and cumbersome but also belies the common misperception that the CPK disdained bureaucratic procedures. The salience—both in practice and in theory—should not be overlooked or discounted. On a practical side, the Standing Committee of the CPK was able to keep tabs on most everything that happened throughout the country. This enabled the top echelon to more effectively centralize its authority and to enact sweeping transformations of the country, for the "centralism" of democratic centralism "arises from the fact that decisions of a higher-level party organization are always binding on lower party bodies and every party member."[81]

As in the Soviet Union and China, leaders of the CPK recognized the inherent problems and contradictions of democratic centralism, notably the disconnect between "democracy" (understood as free and full participation of the masses) and "centralism" (that is, the concentration of decision-making power by those at the apex of the political hierarchy). How, for example, are disagreements between levels resolved? What democratic or participatory roles are provided for the majority of citizens who are not party members?[82]

Awareness of these problems by the CPK is evidenced in various documents, notably a December 20, 1976, report on activities of the party center. In reference to efforts to build political consciousness, the report reads, "We have nourished political consciousness, proletarian patriotism and proletarian internationalism. We have also nourished dialectical materialism as a basis. . . . Proletarian patriotic consciousness and proletarian internationalism can transform people's nature into something new. As for the problem of nurturing a Marxist-Leninist viewpoint, we should allow this to seep in according to our chosen methods." The report indicates, however, that "complete mastery" was not yet attained, as "we have struggled to institute a leadership stance consistent with democratic centralism." What was the cause of these struggles? The report clarifies, "We have purified the surface of the Party and the key organizations to a large extent"—a clear reference to the ongoing purges that had taken place over the previous twenty months; the problem was that the party was unable to "expand key organizations or . . . only expand them slightly." More precisely, party leaders, as evidenced by this report, expressed concern with the expansion of members who exhibited the proper political consciousness. The concern, simply, was that insufficient numbers of citizens had attained the political maturity necessary—from the CPK's vantage point—to fully participate in governance. Solutions proposed included the widespread use of life histories and mandatory study sessions. According to the report, it was thought that membership could expand by 40 percent within the first half of 1977; however, the report cautioned, "If someone's life history isn't good, don't enroll him in the Party, no matter what size [is in his favor]."[83]

Conclusion

When the Khmer Rouge stood victorious on the streets of Phnom Penh in April 1975, they constituted neither a centralized, efficient political party nor a military force.[84] Their victory was the haphazard by-product of the culmination of a series of concurrent revolutions, armed conflicts, and geopolitical machinations. Through their own suppression of dissenters and opposition, the CPK assumed control of a war-torn and exhausted country. They "defeated" the French, the Americans, and the Khmer Republican forces of Lon Nol not because of their own military superiority or political acumen (despite their claims to the contrary) but because of military blunders by Lon Nol, the military prowess of the Vietnamese communist forces, and the failed policies of a long line of American presidents and their advisers. The Khmer Rouge "achieved" victory not because they were united in principle and in ideology with the Cambodian citizenry; in fact, the revolution enacted by the Khmer Rouge was not the end result of a popular uprising.

The leadership of the CPK understood their tenuous hold on power and lack of widespread popular support, let alone loyalty. More to the point: After five years of "popular struggle," not only was the party still a formal secret, but most of the population had not heard of the main leaders of the Khmer Rouge.[85] To this was added a pervasive layer of mistrust and paranoia among the CPK with respect to the Cambodian citizenry.

This is seen most clearly in the fundamental distinction between so-called new people and base people put forward by the Khmer Rouge.

In a series of meetings held from August 20 to 24, 1975, members of the CPK discussed the status and future of their socialist revolution. Minutes of meetings reveal four broad topics of discussion, followed by a series of recommendations. First, it was noted that unequal living conditions between "base" and "new" people were clearly apparent. For the base people, shelters had been prepared, and, for the most part, there was no shortage of food or medicine, except for those living in outlying districts. Here, it was noted, many base people were suffering from diseases. For the new people, conversely, there was a lack of both food and medicine. Overall, the minutes conclude, "Most people feel warmth being with the revolution and are active in [the] country's building movement and crops diversification movement." Regarding the "enemy" situation, it was noted that there had not yet been any military action on behalf of Thailand, although some "Thais illegally came about 3 kilometers into our territory to cultivate rice." To this, an unnamed cadre stated, "We are seeking to smash them." More pressing were possible internal activities, as the report explains: "They have their secret connections contacting each other from one place to another. . . . There are still some persons in our line who have not been completely screened. And they use those individuals to lead people to escape. We have successfully arrested some of them and are carrying out more searches." Third, an update on the Khmer Rouge's military situation is provided. It is noted, for example, that from a political standpoint, "consciousness" and "solidarity" of the soldiers is not a problem, but there is a lack of hammocks and mosquito nets. Last, the economic condition is discussed. Rice was actively being planted, both on "old land" (meaning existing rice fields) and on "new lands." Water management was a concern, as fields around Pursat were badly short of water, while the area around Sisophon was receiving too much water. Beyond rice cultivation, cotton and hemp were being planted, and hemp-weaving factories were being established. Tractor-repair factories were also becoming operational, notably in Mongkul Borei and Thmar Kol.[86]

"Angkar's guiding opinions" are presented in the second half of the minutes. With respect to national defense, the resolution of the political situation of people is deemed crucial. Echoing Lenin's remarks that "our task is not to degrade the revolutionaries to the level of an amateur, but to exalt the amateur to the level of a revolutionary," the CPK determines that "the importance is to settle [the] political situation of people by making them stable-minded and become united with revolutionary authorities." The minute meetings continue that "the revolutionary authorities must . . . control people in all areas—politics, consciousness, and assignment." The means to this end was the continued use of collectives: "People are strong only when collectives are strong." Accordingly, "the issue of people's living standards within collectives must be resolved. Even with new people, we have to help improve their living conditions so that they will be satisfied with the revolution."[87] The building of socialism, in other words, was to be an ongoing process. Recommendations were provided also for economic activities, ranging from the need to relocate workers toward areas suffering from labor shortages to the continued necessity of managing water more effectively.

Overall, the minute meetings of August 20–24, 1975, provide insight into the day-to-day concerns and practice of CPK governance during a period of postconflict reconstruction. Most important, however, they illustrate the pressing need to elevate the political consciousness of the masses to the level of the revolutionaries. Consider, for example, the opinions expressed by Angkar in this document with a report dated September 22, 1975. Here, an unnamed cadre explains:

> As the first step of our Cambodian society, countless changes have been made since the liberation day. In reality, our class has been filled with new and old peasants and workers. New peasants include former civil servants, middle-class, merchants, capitalists, feudalists, and the rich. These new peasants do not have any former political thoughts and any economic base like the previous [regime], and particularly they were like peasants in the countryside. Now they are all based in our liberated areas, and the cities are full of our workers, male and female soldiers, and military. Old workers and new peasants are based in the countryside.[88]

No mention is made of the "smashing" of bureaucrats and former soldiers, although questions were raised as to the viability of recruiting members of the previous regime. The cadre asks: "Is doing so leftist?" The answer would appear to be positive, as it is noted that "all classes have become peasant class, and peasants received assignments in a collective manner." However, deeper in the report, the following statement appears: "We trust our new peasants. Among citizens, we recruit only those we know. They are collective peasants." In fact, in order to recruit workers from the previous regime, it was necessary to ensure that they labor under proper "supervision" and that all workers were to be "re-educated." Trust, in practice, was largely lacking, as revealed by various slogans: "The '17 April' are the vanquished of the war," "The '17 April people' are parasitic plants," and "The new people bring nothing but stomachs full of shit and bladders bursting with urine."[89] Thus, while both "new" and "old" people found their lives radically changed in Democratic Kampuchea, it was the former who were especially singled out for dehumanizing practices and persecution.[90]

A careful evaluation of documents from 1975 and 1976 illustrates the halting steps taken toward a new form of government. On March 30, 1976, for example, top-ranking members of the CPK met to discuss the ongoing administration of Democratic Kampuchea. A list of twelve "decisions" was identified. Some decisions were exceptionally banal. Decision "8," for example, specified various "days commemorating historical events," including the "birth date of the Revolutionary Armed Forces (17 January 1968)," the "day of the great defeat of the air war of the American Imperialists (15 August 1973)," and the "day of the launching of the final offensive (5 February 1961)." More foreboding, however, was the first decision, which specified "the authority to smash [people] inside and outside the ranks." As Chandler explains, this "makes it clear that political murder would henceforth be an accepted means of dealing with perceived opponents of the Party, including its members" and that this decision legitimized, for the CPK, "the 'smashing' (komtech) of such people by the central and regional organs of the government that was about to be installed." As territories were "liberated" by the armed forces of the Khmer Rouge, and especially after April 1975, both civilian and military officials of the former regime were targeted for execution. These "enemies" were to be found predominantly among the "new" people. François Ponchaud, a French missionary living in Cambodia, witnessed firsthand the evacuation of Phnom Penh and the "systematic cleanup," as "civilian and military officials were methodically eliminated."[91]

The decisions made by the CPK on March 30, 1976, markedly illustrate Lenin's assertion that "the substitution of the proletarian state for the bourgeois state is impossible without a violent revolution." As detailed in the twelfth and longest recommendation, "On Preparing and Organizing the State Organizations," the report concludes, "The aim of our revolutionary struggle is to establish state power within the grasp of the worker-peasants, and to abolish all oppressive state power."[92] For the CPK, therefore, it was necessary to remain ever vigilant in the search for internal enemies. Mam Sarun, for example, recounts his experiences following the evacuation of Phnom Penh:

> I found my family near Kieng Svay pagoda on April 27, and we stayed there over a month. Behind the pagoda the Khmer Rouge had written an order on a big blackboard: "All officers from the rank of second lieutenant up must register here, in order to return to Phnom Penh. Professors, students, and schoolteachers must also give their names, but will leave later." Every day I saw many officers come up and sign their names. They were separated from the rest of the people and given plenty of rice; their families stayed inside the pagoda but didn't get much to eat. Then they were taken away and never seen again.[93]

Mam Sarun's experience is far from unique, for throughout the entirety of the regime, Khmer Rouge cadre sought out members of the former regime. In the evenings, announcements were broadcast over the radio or made at propaganda meetings that "we have beaten the enemies outside, the Americans and their lackeys. Now we must defeat the enemies within, for there are still some left." To be associated with the former region was to be considered an enemy. As a former Lon Nol soldier explains, "The Khmer Rouge were very well informed about us all. Nobody could hide his true identify for long."[94]

Deception was often used to ferret out suspected enemies. At nightly "education" and "self-criticism" sessions, Angkar would request the assistance of any person who had particular skills, such as former teachers or doctors. Their talents, Angkar explained, were needed in support of the revolution. Often, extra rations were promised. Those who identified themselves were taken away. Militias (*kang chhlop*) were also formed, often composed of young boys and girls. Their task was to eavesdrop among the villagers and to listen for any words or phrases that might signal a "traitorous" past. As one survivor recalls:

> The children mingled with us; we thought they were the villagers' boys, but when one or another member of our group was summoned and then disappeared, we realized that they were reporting what we said to the Angkar. We gradually learned who had been told to spy on us, and we took refuge in silence. The Angkar told us, "If you want to live, surround your house with a wall of [kapok] trees." Everybody understand that that meant a wall of silence. . . . Even at night children hid under the houses on stilts, with orders to report any words spoken by the people inside.[95]

Most scholars and commentators of the Khmer Rouge have interpreted these actions as evidence of a pervasive anti-intellectual and antiprofessional bias among the CPK. However, this is not entirely accurate, for the underlying motive—at least from the vantage point of members of the upper echelons of the CPK—was to smash the former state, to eliminate those "parasites," the bureaucrats and soldiers of the exploiting class, who remained burrowed in the political body of the proletariat. As Lenin explained, "But to smash the old bureaucratic machine at once and to begin immediately to construct a new one that will enable all officialdom to be gradually abolished is not utopia. . . . [I]t is the direct and immediate task of the revolutionary proletariat."[96] To this end, between 1975 and 1979, the CPK embarked on a series of postconflict reconstruction policies in an attempt to "build" a socialist state. Internationally, the CPK claimed to support the Non-Aligned Movement; accordingly, CPK officials championed a commitment to peace, neutrality, and territorial integrity. Far from seeing Democratic Kampuchea as an isolated, autarkic state, members of the CPK professed a deep and profound commitment to the Non-Aligned Movement. Domestically, a new constitution was drafted, proclaiming social justice, liberty, and equality for all citizens of Democratic Kampuchea. Professing a commitment to democratic centralism, elections were held, a representative assembly was formed, and government officials were appointed. On paper Democratic Kampuchea was a model of progressive politics. In practice, the CPK leadership laid the foundation for a thoroughly repressive state apparatus committed to the generation of surplus capital. It is to this component we now focus attention.

4

Production

In this chapter I provide a detailed discussion of the generation of surplus value under the Communist Party of Kampuchea. I argue that, rhetoric aside, the political economy of Democratic Kampuchea was neither Marxist, socialist, nor communist and that the economic system planned and implemented by the CPK was an exploitative system of production for exchange. Despite the brutal elimination of landlords and private property, class distinctions in Democratic Kampuchea were not eliminated; indeed, exploitation remained, in that the surplus labor produced by the workers was appropriated and distributed not by the workers themselves, but rather by the state apparatus. This argument provides the material foundation for an understanding of the CPK's conceptualization of nature and in so doing addresses specifically how the Khmer Rouge's attempt to transform nature was necessary—and necessarily wrong—in their greater objective of building a socialist consciousness. To fully articulate the CPK's attempt to accumulate capital through the production and exchange of rice specifically, it is necessary to first situate rice production more broadly within the Cambodian context.

Rice Systems in Cambodia

Rice is an extremely adaptable plant. It thrives in swampy, low-lying areas but also grows well in arid, hilly environments. Compared with other crops, rice also has many advantages. Rice is a relatively high-yield crop, even under adverse conditions. In fact, provided an adequate water supply, nitrogen-fixing organisms (which occur naturally in paddy fields) enable farmers to harvest upwards of two tons per hectare per year without applying any mineral fertilizers. In areas where highly developed farming techniques are used, annual yields may approach seven tons per hectare. Also, rice has a high-yield-to-seed ratio. Under proper conditions, each plant can produce two thousand grains; by comparison, wheat, barley, and rye may give rise to only four hundred or so grains per plant.[1] The cultivation of rice, moreover, does not significantly deplete the fertility of soils. Indeed, if fields are continuously planted, soil fertility does not diminish over time but in fact increases. Relatedly, double-cropping techniques may significantly increase yields without significant depletion of soil fertility.

Rice has long been a staple in Khmer society. Khmer farmers have been growing low-land, rain-fed rice for at least two thousand years, and irrigated rice has been cultivated for at least fifteen hundred years.[2] And over the millennia, farmers have developed and refined countless farming strategies based on a combination of seed selection, planning techniques (for example, broadcast or transplanting), and water management. Quick (or early) maturing varieties, for example, are best suited for conditions where the availability of water is uncertain or insufficient. These varieties, because of a short-growing cycle, also permit double-cropping. However, the yield for quick-ripening varieties is often significantly less than it is for late-maturing varieties.

Given the complexities of rice production, indigenous knowledge is of great importance. Cultivation techniques, for optimal harvests, need to be adapted to local conditions, including topography, precipitation, and soil. Cambodia's climate is monsoonal, with distinct wet and dry seasons. Sometime around May the "mango washing rains" (*plieng daem vorsa*) arrive. These showers bring welcome relief to the end of the dry period and generally mark the onset of rice production.[3] The timing, however, is irregular, and farmers must make adjustments to their planting schedule accordingly. Precipitation amounts also vary widely. Whereas most of the prime rice-growing regions of Cambodia receive between 1,250 and 1,750 mm annually, other areas experience more or less. The coastal areas surrounding the Cardamom Mountains, for example, receive upwards of 4,000 mm per year. To these differences, one must add variation in soil, slope, and hydrology. Given the multiple combinations of these variables, it is perhaps not surprising that more than two thousand traditional varieties of rice have been identified as being unique to Cambodia.[4] This makes for an exceptionally diverse agricultural landscape. Throughout Cambodia, it is not uncommon to see a range of activities occurring in close proximity. In one field, for example, farmers may be planting rice, while in a nearby field farmers are harvesting rice, and still other fields may be fallow.

Despite this diversity, Cambodia's rice ecosystems may be classified into four broad categories: rain-fed lowland rice, dry-season rice, deepwater rice, and rain-fed upland rice. The most prevalent type, constituting approximately 86 percent of all land cultivated to rice, is rain-fed lowland rice (*srov tumneap*). Geographically, rain-fed lowland rice is widely distributed, although it is predominant around the Tonle Sap Lake and Tonle-Bassac River system and along the Mekong River. By definition, rain-fed lowland rice is almost completely dependent on local rainfall for its growth. Small-scale irrigation methods may be used, however, either to increase water available in times of drought or as drainage in times of excess rainfall.

The typical landscape associated with rain-fed lowland rice appears as a patchwork of irregular fields separated by small earthen bunds (*phleu sre*). These mounds—which require constant maintenance—are used primarily on flatlands and serve two functions: to retain water for weed control and for crop growth. The field size is often related to physical conditions, such as soil fertility and land gradient; however, a legacy of social relations, inheritance practices, and so forth also affects field size.[5]

Local topography is a significant variable in the cultivation of rain-fed lowland rice. Morphological variation, even on the order of a few meters, has a strong influence on growing cycles. In part, this is related to the amount and duration of water availability, in that the yields of rain-fed lowland rice production are a function of a plant maturation–water depth relationship.[6] For example, since lower fields remain flooded longer, a correspondingly longer growth period is permitted. This inverse relationship between slope height and standing water enables farmers to determine which variety to plant in order to "match" the maximum experienced water.

In Cambodia rain-fed lowland rice is classified according to the elevation of the fields. High fields (*srai leu*) are those fields located relatively higher in elevation; lower down the slope are middle fields (*srai kandal*) and low fields (*srai kraom*). In upper fields, where the deepest standing water is usually in the range of twenty to thirty centimeters, early-maturing varieties (*srau sral*) are planted. Harvested late in November or early December, these are typically drought tolerant. In terms of quality, these varieties are considered good "subsistence" rice. For medium fields, the average water depth ranges between twenty and forty centimeters, and medium to medium-late maturation varieties (*srau kandal*) are planted. These are harvested later in the year, usually around mid- to late December, and are generally thought to be the best cooking rice. These varieties also normally enjoy the highest market price. Last, in those fields where the deepest standing water ranges from forty to upwards of fifty centimeters, late-maturing rice (*srau thungu*) is planted. These varieties are considerably more flood tolerant and are known for having a good cooking quality. Harvesting of these fields usually occurs in January or February.[7]

The cultivation of rain-fed lowland rice is conditioned by the onset of the monsoonal rains, normally arriving sometime between March and May. Once the hard, sunbaked fields have been thoroughly soaked by rain, field preparation begins. Typically, farmers plow the field twice, followed by harrowing. The timing of seedbed establishment depends mostly on the onset and amount of precipitation. If early rains are adequate, late-maturing varieties are seeded first (from mid-May to early June), followed by medium- and quick-maturation varieties.[8]

The actual planting of rice seedlings takes one of two forms. Transplanting rice is a process whereby pregerminated rice seedlings are sown first in small, carefully tended nurseries (*santoung*). After twenty to thirty days, the "baby rice" (*samnap*) is bundled and transplanted into the primary rice fields in a series of carefully aligned rows. The second form of planting consists of broadcast sowing. Here, the pregerminated rice seedlings are sown directly onto the primary rice fields. This technique is common where labor shortages exist.[9] Upon maturation, harvesting is done by hand. Rice plants are bundled and sun-dried for two to three days, after which the rice is threshed, winnowed, and dried. Traditionally, rice yields are divided by farmers into three uses. A certain portion will be set aside and stored for the next year's planting. The remaining yield will be divided into household use and rice to be sold.

Dry-season rice accounts for approximately 8 percent of Cambodia's rice ecosystem. Fields are generally located along rivers and exhibit considerable variability with respect to cultivation techniques. However, because of more active water-management practices, dry-season rice often registers some of the highest yields. Broadly speaking, dry-season rice cultivation falls into two categories: recessional rice and irrigated second-crop rice. The first type illustrates well the adaptations of farmers to local topography and flooding. During the rainy season, many areas are seasonally flooded for three to five months. As these floodwaters recede, lands higher in elevation gradually appear. Through small-scale terracing and staggered sowing, these upper regions are planted, followed by lower areas, as waters continue to recede. This form of sequential cultivation may begin as early as late October and as late as February, depending on the timing of precipitation and the rate of water recession. A second form of dry-season rice cultivation refers to the use of irrigation practices to permit the double-cropping of fields. For example, if a rain-fed rice crop was harvested in early October and adequate water is still available, rice seedlings may be broadcast or transplanted onto the field.[10] As detailed later, it was the objective of CPK planners to greatly expand through irrigation the amount of dry-season rice.

Two other forms of rice cultivation are prevalent throughout Cambodia. Deepwater rice refers to the cultivation of rice in low-lying areas and depressions and in some respects mirrors recessional forms of dry-season rice. The relationship between topography and precipitation is also paramount. Following the onset of the summer monsoon, water levels in low-lying areas generally begin to rise between July and August; maximum depths are usually registered between September and November. Rice is planted as the water recedes, usually between November and early January, and is adjusted to the rate of recession, which may be either gradual or rapid, depending primarily on soil type.

The ecology of deepwater rice is exceptionally diverse, owing to microvariations in topography and soil. A bowl-shaped depression, by way of illustration, may exhibit considerable subsurface variation; consequently, the depth of the water will vary tremendously, based on the slope. This in turn impacts not only overall water depth but also the deposition of silt and nutrients. The lower reaches of the depression, for example, tend to receive the most deposition and hence exhibit higher yields than upper slopes. On the other hand, differences in elevation (based on slope) influence both the rate of water-level rice and recession as well as the duration of flooding. This will impact the type of rice planting (based on timing of maturation) and thus overall yield. In general, yields for deepwater rice are comparatively lower than either rain-fed lowland rice or dry-season rice.

A final type of rice consists of rain-fed upland rice. As the name suggests, upland rice, also known as "mountain rice," is grown in hilly or mountainous areas, usually in unbounded, nonterraced fields, with water provided entirely by local rainfall. In Cambodia the cultivation of upland rice is generally conducted as part of a broader practice of shifting cultivation. During the dry season (February to April), trees are cleared and underlying brush is burned. This provides both clearance for planting and natural fertilizers. Seeding generally occurs between April and June; seeds are dibbled using pointed sticks. Harvesting occurs in August. Mixed cropped is also common: maize, sesame, cucumber, sweet potato, pumpkin, cassava, papaya, and banana are typical crops. Compared to other forms of rice cultivation, upland rice registers low yields.[11]

Rice Production under the Khmer Rouge

Prior to the imposition of French colonial rule, rice production in Cambodia was largely subsistence based. Population densities were relatively low, and supplemental nutrition was available through hunting, gathering, and fishing. Many forms of rice farming were practiced, and farmers developed or adapted cultivation techniques suited to local conditions. Beginning in the late nineteenth and early twentieth centuries, French colonial authorities began to implement an agricultural development policy that would dramatically, albeit unevenly, transform Cambodia's agrarian landscape.

Soon after the capture of Saigon in 1859—well before the consolidation of French authority throughout Indochina—the French colonial government authorized and facilitated the export of rice.[12] This was made possible, in part, through the introduction of private ownership and the establishment of large landholdings. Traditionally, all lands were "owned" by the Vietnamese emperor, although decision making was mostly at the village level. Under the French, however, large land grants were made. Land was especially plentiful in the Mekong Delta and was given directly in the form of concessions to French nationals or "deserving" Vietnamese citizens who had loyally served the French. Alternatively, land was auctioned off in large lots to offset the cost of canal building in the Mekong Delta. Over time, Vietnamese landlords—a new aristocracy—became extensions of the French colonial government.[13]

The introduction of an export-oriented agrarian economy dramatically altered existing social and economic relations, but in decidedly unequal ways. In Cochin China, absentee landlords soon gained control of most cultivable land, leading to the emergence of a dispossessed, landless population. Vietnamese peasants were exploited through increased taxes and usury. Rents, for example, usually represented 50 percent or more of the primary rice crop; in some cases, loans extended by the landlord for seeds, equipment, and draft animals could raise the landlord's share to 70 or 80 percent.[14]

The basis of Cambodia's colonial economy, for the French, was to be the export of agricultural products, notably rice and livestock. This was to greatly augment the French agroprocessing facilities and international export trade system centered in Cochin China. More specifically, the French proposed two different strategies with respect to rice cultivation. On the one hand, large-scale rice plantations were established. Located primarily in Battambang Province, these were founded on land concessions given to French settlers. Operationally, the plantations utilized modern farming methods and hired labor. The French colonial government provided extensive agricultural infrastructure to support the plantations, including the widespread use of irrigation schemes. To facilitate exports, a railroad linking Battambang Province with the capital was constructed; from Phnom Penh, rice was then shipped down the Mekong River to Saigon, destined for French markets.[15]

On the other hand, Cambodian farmers continued to cultivate rice using more traditional techniques on small landholdings. Under this system, the French acquired rice for export not through the advancement of rice technology but through taxation. According to David Chandler, Cambodian farmers paid the highest per capita rates of tax in rice, labor, and cash than any other farmers in French Indochina; as such, the rice tax was the largest source of government revenues.[16]

Following independence in 1953, the fledgling Cambodian government assumed control of the large-scale rice plantations in Battambang Province. Moreover, with financial support provided primarily by USAID, numerous irrigation schemes were proposed, and many were implemented throughout the country, but especially in Siem Reap, Kampong Cham, Kandal, and Kampot Provinces. By the early 1960s, the area of rice cultivation expanded to around 2.2 million hectares, while rice production increased to levels approaching 2.3 million tons, with yields approximating 1.1 tons per hectare.[17]

In 1963 Prince Sihanouk refused American aid, and, in the following year, foreign trade—including rice exports—was nationalized and placed under the control of a state monopoly known as the Société Nationale d'Exportation et d'Importation. Rice production, and by extension rice exports, flourished under this nationalized system. Indeed, production levels approached 2.5 to 2.75 million tons; it would peak at 3.8 million tons in 1969.[18]

As the conflict in neighboring Vietnam escalated, so too did greater collusion between the Cambodian government and the Vietnamese communists. This would have a dramatic effect both on rice production in general and on the day-to-day lives of Cambodian farmers. First, a substantial black-market arose, whereby illicit sales of rice, cattle, and other foodstuffs to communist insurgents made large profits for local Chinese and Sino-Cambodian merchants in the towns and smaller ones for Cambodian peasants.[19] It is estimated, for example, that one-third of the 1966 rice export crop was sold or smuggled to Vietnam. Consequently, there was a significant fall in official exports, with a corresponding decline in government rice tax revenues.[20] Thus, to stem the outflow of rice, a decision was made within the Sihanouk government that army units should gather the rice surplus, pay government prices (which were considerably lower than that paid by the Vietnamese) for it, and transport it to government warehouses.[21] This was followed by the imposition of the *ramassage du paddy* collection system (as discussed in chapter 2).

In other respects, the encroaching conflict was more devastating to Cambodia's agricultural sector and its farmers. The sustained aerial campaign of carpet bombing exerted a heavy toll. Rice fields and irrigation systems were destroyed, and livestock were killed. Hundreds of thousands of farmers were also killed or forced to flee. Indeed, by 1974 an estimated 80 percent of the country's prewar paddy fields had been abandoned, and the government's own figures indicated that rice production levels plummeted to 65,000 tons—far short of the peak level of 3.8 million tons registered just five years earlier.[22]

Following their victory in April 1975, the CPK was confronted with a devastated infrastructure. Years of armed conflict left the countryside in ruins; roads and railways were destroyed; farms and fields were left vacant. A traumatized population had been scattered far and wide, with an estimated two million peasants seeking refuge in the capital city. Such conditions would prove daunting to any postconflict government. This observation is in no way meant to excuse or exonerate subsequent CPK decisions; it is to call into question the overly simplistic explanations forwarded.

The Standard Total View holds that the Khmer Rouge, once in power, initiated a series of "bizarre and brutal" policies that led to the death of upwards of two million men, women, and children. Bert Pijpers, for example, begins by noting that the Khmer Rouge *after* being removed from power in 1979 left behind a "legacy of destruction." He notes that hospitals, schools, and factories were destroyed or rendered inoperative; no transport or communication systems remained; and roads, canals, bridges, ports, and railways were extensively damaged by bombing.[23] What he fails to articulate is that these conditions held *before* the CPK assumed victory. And while the Khmer Rouge certainly contributed to the destruction of infrastructure between 1975 and 1979, it is exceptionally disingenuine to excuse the damage wrought by the Americans and Vietnamese.

With respect to the actual policies, Pijpers notes that men and women "were put to work digging canals, constructing dikes and dams, laying out rice fields in rectangular 1 ha plots and trying to grow high-yielding rice varieties under unfavorable conditions. Work had to be done by hand or with simple hand tools." He elaborates that the CPK's overall policy meant "at least two rice crops a year and preferably more; production of other crops was severely curtailed and tobacco and maize fields were turned over to rice; the use of high yielding rice instead of the traditional low yielding varieties; [and] extended production areas by reclaiming tropical forests."[24] Let's consider these in turn.

To begin, the CPK did (as detailed below) attempt to secure at least two rice crops per year. To this end, the CPK sought to *triple* rice production within four years in an effort to achieve three tons of rice per hectare per year. One may question the wisdom of such a rapid increase in productivity in such a short time span; however, the objective of facilitating two crops per year was a policy pursued not only by the French but also by Sihanouk. Likewise, the CPK did replace some tobacco and maize fields with rice. However, two aspects are worth noting. On the one hand, given the severe food shortages in existence in 1975–76, it was entirely rational to forgo the production of tobacco in favor of rice. On the other hand, as explained in greater depth later, rice enjoyed considerable economic advantages and, again, made sound economic sense in 1975–76.[25]

The CPK did promote high-yielding rice varieties. But then again, so too did the French colonial authorities (at least on the plantations) and the Sihanouk administration. Here, though, care must also be taken with respect to national policy and local practice. In the CPK's "Four-Year Plan" (see below), it was decided that "only a very small amount" of hectares of "first-class fields" should produce rice twice a year; the amount under cultivation should, however, "increase on a yearly basis." And while the proposed production schedule of "six and seven tons per hectare for both harvests, according to the soil, and zone and the region" was wildly optimistic, it does indicate that the CPK was aware of the importance of different varieties and the salience of geography for production levels.[26] Indeed, it is noteworthy that a 1976 planning document requests "such charts, lists and figures for certain zones and regions so that those attending this meeting can observe whether these are in accordance with reality or not, and whether they are clear."[27]

With respect to rice production, Boraden Nhem writes that "Democratic Kampuchea did not pay attention to the realities but instead focused

on fulfilling its fantasy." This is misleading and, again, illustrates the crucial nexus between policy and practice. By way of example, documents
indicate that cadre "must grasp the nature of the available soil and the
nature of water resources. Having grasped the geography, we can assign
first-grade land to two harvests and second-grade land to one. In addition, we must estimate the water-power available. We must know where
to construct dams and where to dig canals." The document illustrates this
with reference to various locations: "In Region 1, we must decide what to
do about Stung Sangker; if we dug a canal, how many hectares would it
serve? If we dug two canals, how many hectares would they serve . . . ?"[28]
Consequently, it is somewhat premature to conclude that CPK policies
were so detached from reality as to be viewed as irrational.

Pijpers concludes that the Khmer Rouge did not take into consideration Cambodia's "difficult soil conditions and the great variations
between the wet and dry seasons," and, as such, rice cultivation under the
Khmer Rouge "was a total failure."[29] At a national level, the CPK did in
fact take into consideration these geographic variations; indeed, the preparation of soil surveys, maps, and other schemata was called for. Here, the
crucial question becomes: What happened in the transmission of policy
from the national to the local level? Thus far, no satisfactory analysis has
been performed.

Finally, Pijpers critiques CPK policy for converting tropical forests
to rice cultivation. Given the legacy of deforestation, both under French
colonial policy and in contemporary practice, one would be hard-pressed
to forward this as a uniquely poor policy advocated by the CPK. Rather,
it is more appropriate to recognize that at a national level, CPK policy
actually followed most development practices put forth from the 1950s
onward.

What of the implementation of irrigation schemes? Numerous commentators, including Pijpers, have roundly criticized the CPK's promotion
of "a nationwide chessboard of levelled 1 ha plots in productive areas and
in the reclaimed forest" and the "creation of reservoirs by constructing
long dykes along depressions or by damming natural depressions and val-
leys."[30] The so-called chessboard strategy is a well-entrenched myth. It is
accurate that in many locations—most notably in the floodplains of the

5. Forced laborers constructing an irrigation canal. Courtesy of the Documentation Center of Cambodia Archives.

Tonle Sap—extensive rice fields arranged in one-by-one-kilometer grids were established. However, to this one should acknowledge that on a floodplain, a grid-patterned system of dikes and canals is enormously efficient. Indeed, this is why the French utilized similar geometric arrangements throughout their rice plantations in both Cambodia and Vietnam.[31] Further, as Pijpers recognizes, "the standard guidelines were *not followed everywhere and there are small differences as local authorities adapted the standards to local conditions.*"[32]

Rice production under the Khmer Rouge, I have argued, represents not so much a radical break from previous practice as it does a highly augmented continuation of previous efforts. Certainly at the national level, CPK cadre endeavored to increase rice yields through the selection of appropriate varieties, expand the amount of land under cultivation, and achieve double-cropping through the expanded use of irrigation. There is, however, an economic component that heretofore has been overlooked: how increased yields were to facilitate the accumulation of capital. Thus far, most scholars have simply assumed that greater exports would translate into greater profits. And on a superficial level, this is accurate. Such a premature conclusion, though, forecloses a more nuanced analysis that calls into question the philosophic basis of Democratic Kampuchea's political economy.

Surplus Production under the Khmer Rouge

In its "Four-Year Plan," developed between July 21 and August 2, 1976, the CPK identified two economic objectives. The first was "to serve the people's livelihood, and to raise the people's standards of living quickly, both in terms of supplies and in terms of other material goods." This was to be accomplished through the satisfaction of a second and related objective, namely, to "seek, gather, save, and *increase capital* from agriculture, aiming to rapidly expand our agriculture, our industry, and our defense."[33] How, though, under a purportedly socialist system, could surplus capital be generated? Moreover, how could this be possible when money and private property were abolished? The answer is straightforward: Within Democratic Kampuchea, the CPK established an equivalency between rice and money; in so doing, rice was transformed into a representation of value. Once commodified, the production and export of rice were used to generate surplus capital. And while this answer is deceptively simple, it does require considerable elaboration.

Commodities, according to Marx, have a dual character, being composed of both "use values" and "exchange values." On the one hand, commodities, as products of human labor, possess some useful quality for people, and, on the other hand, commodities have exchange values, in that one commodity may be exchanged for another commodity. The use value of a commodity, therefore, stems from the qualitative properties that make it useful, while the exchange value stems entirely from the social homogeneity of commodities, whereby they differ only quantitatively.[34] In a well-known example, Marx considers the relation between the values of two commodities: twenty yards of linen equals one coat. Here, Marx explains that the value of linen is expressed in relation to that of a coat.[35] It is not possible, he notes, to express the value of linen in linen. The value of linen must be expressed, quantitatively, in terms of another commodity.

The first commodity, linen, is expressed as the *relative value*, whereas the second commodity, the coat, constitutes the *equivalent form of value*. The obverse also holds true. It is possible to state that one coat is equivalent to twenty yards of linen. This indicates that "value cannot be grasped within an individual use value."[36]

Marx explains, however, that within capitalism (unlike, say, a barter system), commodities are not simply exchanged (that is, a shirt is exchanged for a bushel of corn).[37] Commodities are produced not because of an immediate need but rather because of a necessity to increase capital. If we return to the CPK's Four-Year Plan, we read of an intention to raise standards of living—but the crucial component is to increase capital in order to facilitate further economic growth. In other words, when we examine more closely the CPK's objective of increased rice production, it was not to provide additional foodstuffs for Cambodia society; instead, it was a means of capital accumulation.

To fully appreciate CPK policy, it is necessary to also situate Democratic Kampuchea's political economy within a broader context of development. Thus far, I have argued that CPK policy represents less a radical break with previous regimes than it does an exaggerated form of preexisting modes of governance. So too should we understand the so-called excessive focus on agriculture.

During the 1950s and 1960s, many former colonies, but especially those adhering to the Non-Aligned Movement, embarked on a particular economic strategy known as import-substitution industrialization.[38] Proponents of ISI argued that lesser-developed countries should initially substitute domestic production of previously imported simple consumer goods and then substitute through domestic production for a wider range of more sophisticated manufactured items.[39] In other words, advocates of ISI promoted an economic strategy predicated on self-sufficiency. Variously understood within broader theories of dependency or underdevelopment, the argument was this: For decades, if not centuries, the economies of colonies were held in check by unfair trade arrangements and production processes that consigned the colonies to positions of subservience within the global economy. Colonies and former colonies were historically forced to import most of their manufactured goods in return for the export of primary products, such as sugar, bananas, coffee, tea, and cotton. Under ISI, these unequal relations were to be inverted. Governments of former colonies would protect their domestic industries and by extension encourage the production of domestic consumer goods. Revenue saved from not having to import these goods could then be used to purchase other manufactured commodities that could not be produced given the country's overall level of industrialization.

From the 1950s onward, several governments, notably South Korea and Taiwan, used these strategies to obvious success. Typically, governments would erect tariff barriers or quotas on the importation of certain commodities; this would constitute the first step on the path toward industrialization. Indeed, for proponents of ISI, to industrialize, given the existence of already industrialized and highly productive economies, many former colonies sought to protect their economies from imports (largely from the West) and concentrate on putting in place new economic activities.[40]

In practice, ISI constitutes a form of self-imposed isolation, and it is this economic strategy I maintain the CPK initiated from 1975 onward. An internal document dated May 8, 1976, states clearly, "We will decrease importing items next year, including cotton and jute, because we are working hard to produce ours. We will import only some important items such as chemical fertilizer, plastic, acid, iron factory, and other raw materials." According to this document, such a strategy was deemed most appropriate; indeed, to solve the currency problem, it was determined that solutions were not to be found "by taking loans from the West or Eastern Europe," for in so doing the CPK would lose their "self-reliant stance."[41]

Having adopted a policy of import substitution, the CPK next directed its attention to those items that could be effectively produced, both for domestic consumption and for foreign trade. On the home front, plans called for the promotion of items necessary to facilitate the people's livelihood: plates, pots, spoons, mosquito nets, shovels, hoes, and so on. In practice, most of these industries never materialized, although textile factories and some machine shops were in operation. Internationally, documents indicate that the CPK was receptive to any number of goods but that economic efficiencies would be the determining factor.

Within a system of production for exchange, it matters little if linen or coats are produced; whichever offers the best opportunity for capital accumulation will, in principle, be produced. Marx refers to this tendency as "indifference to use value," and the CPK was in many respects indifferent to use value. A documented titled "Report of Activities of the Party Center according to the General Political Tasks of 1976" notes, "We can export and sell many products such as kapok, shrimp, squid, elephant fish, and turtles. All of these products can earn foreign exchange. There are great possibilities for exporting peanuts, wheat, corn, sesame, and beans. The objective would be to save up these products for export. Almost anything can be exported, so long as we don't consume it ourselves, but set it aside."[42] The report further details that "we have the potential to achieve full quotas in rubber, cement, railroads and salt. We have progressed nicely, almost with empty hands. We have achieved good results. But the possibilities are even greater. We must expand the Plan. Our line is to stress industry and the working class as the basis."[43]

Faced with a seemingly indifferent choice, how then are decisions made, especially at the national level? Adam Smith (1723–90) and David Ricardo (1782–1823) both envisaged a global division of labor in which each country would freely choose the commodities it was most suited to produce and freely exchange its optimal commodity for the optimal commodities of others.[44] Indeed, following Ricardo, when a country specializes in producing commodities for which it possesses a comparative advantage, trading its surplus for other commodities produced more efficiently elsewhere, then the international economy operates more efficiently.[45]

For the CPK, agriculture—but especially rice—was determined to be the country's comparative advantage. During a speech delivered in June 1976 at an assembly of cadre of the Western Zone, the speaker (most likely Pol Pot) discussed the importance of rapid agricultural development. The speaker explains, "National construction proceeds along the lines laid down by the Party. The important point of this is building up our agriculture, which is backward, into modern agriculture within ten to fifteen years." This point is developed in greater length in the Four-Year Plan, whereby it is noted that Democratic Kampuchea is replete with "such things as land, livestock, natural resources, water sources such as lakes, rivers and ponds" and that these "natural characteristics have given us great advantages compared with China, Vietnam, or Africa. Compared to Korea, we also have positive qualities." Paramount among these, of course, was agriculture. According to the Four-Year Plan, "We stand on agriculture as the basis, so as to collect agricultural capital with which to strengthen and expand industry." This was no desire to construct an agrarian utopia but instead a pragmatic course of action based on capitalist principles. Indeed, it was simply a continuation of policies advocated by the former French colonial government and that of Sihanouk. From a competitive standpoint, rice was the clear choice. And while other agricultural products were identified, including rubber, corn, beans, fish, and forest products, these were largely gratis. The CPK argument was profit based: "For 100,000 tons of milled rice, we would get [US] $20 million; if we had 500,000 tons we'd get $100 million. . . . We must increase rice production in order to obtain capital. Other products, which are only complimentary[,] will be increased in the future."[46]

Returning to the twin objectives established by the CPK, it becomes clear that policy decisions were based on particular productivity calculations. Foremost was the proposed increase in rice production, an objective that was pivotal to the CPK's overall strategy of state building and—by extension—the state's ability to foster life in Democratic Kampuchea. It was determined by the CPK that Democratic Kampuchea would need to *triple* rice productivity, to a national average yield of three tons per hectare per year. Only by attaining such a surplus could the CPK raise sufficient revenues to obtain necessary goods and commodities from abroad, notably ammunition. The strategy for increased rice production was predicated on the introduction of more "rational" and "efficient" agricultural techniques. Thus, the CPK classified rice fields into two categories: those harvested once a year and those harvested twice. Calculations provided by the CPK indicate that in 1977, there would be an anticipated 2.4 million hectares of land suitable for rice production; of these, 1.4 million hectares could sustain a single harvest per year; the remaining would be conducive to two harvests. Over the next four years, according to Pol Pot, the land devoted to single harvests would remain constant, while the amount of

6. Khmer Rouge cadre harvesting rice. Courtesy of the Documentation Center of Cambodia Archives.

double-cropped lands would progressively increase from 200,000 hectares in 1977 to 500,000 in 1980. However, it was determined that all new agricultural lands would generate two harvests per year.[47]

The comparative advantage of different administrative zones was also stressed. Party members, for example, noted that the Northern Zone and Northwest Zone were "more favorable in terms of rice fields" and therefore required "more people," that is, labor. The Northwest, in particular, was highlighted for its favorable conditions, including fertile soils, a flat topography, an existing labor force, and some machinery and tools. However, to fully exploit the zone's potential, another three or four hundred thousand workers were needed, possibly even a half million. Significantly, the report indicated that if an insufficient workforce remained, they must "resort to using machinery." Additional effort must also be made to diversify crops in the Northwest in order to "improve people's living conditions throughout the country" and to "find new capital for purchasing materials to be used in building the country and diversifying agricultural and industrial production." In direct reference to labor capacity, the report explains that if workers with "less ability" are deployed, time and effort would be lost. It was important, therefore, that they "fight in the right place where it is effective."[48]

Food Rations and Relative Surpluses

The expansion of lands devoted to rice production and the attempt to overcome "objective" problems constituted efforts to generate absolute surpluses.[49] To these material practices, however, the CPK added an exploitative practice that, in effect, was a means of attaining relative surpluses.

To fully articulate the accumulation of surplus capital, it is necessary to delve further into the process of commodity exchange. Marx argued that commodities are not exchanged according to their degree of usefulness; instead, there is a quantitative relation that appears in all commodities that facilitates their exchange. This common denominator, Marx concluded, was not money (itself a representation of value) but instead labor power. Such an argument, which is an extension of the writings of Adam Smith and David Ricardo, in particular, is crucial in that it establishes a foundation by which "work" is evaluated within capitalism. This is illustrated in Marx's well-known form: "Commodity–Money–Commodity," or simply C–M–C. The first transformation, C–M, represents the conversion of a commodity into money (that is, the act of selling), while the second transformation, M–C represents the conversion of money into a commodity (the act of buying). Hence, this single process is two-sided: from one pole, that of the commodity owner, it is a sale; from the other pole, that of the money owner, it is a purchase.[50]

Following the simple model of circulation, C–M–C, commodities are exchanged (sold) for money; that money is then used to purchase additional commodities. On the surface, this would seem to account for both the policies proposed and the practices carried out by the Khmer Rouge. Rice, as a commodity, was shipped to myriad destinations, including China, Yugoslavia, Madagascar, and Hong Kong. To give but one example, between January and September 1978, the CPK exported 29,758 tons of rice, valued at nearly US$6 million, to China.[51] In return, Democratic Kampuchea imported tons of other commodities, including machine parts and medicine. Schematically, rice is converted into money (M); this money is then used to purchase additional commodities, including (C). In practice, this exchange would exist virtually; the CPK would in effect obtain "credit" or a "balance" from China for future purchases. At this level, no material transfer of printed money would take place.[52] International trade, therefore, could continue without the reintroduction of currency *within* Democratic Kampuchea.

However, to leave the CPK's economy at this surface level is unsatisfactory, for it risks losing sight of the specific mechanisms introduced to generate *surplus* capital and, by extension, to fully understand the *economic rationale* for the introduction of food rations. One is tempted, for example, to conclude that "surplus" capital was simply derived from increased rice production, that the "surplus" identified by the CPK was not "surplus" from a Marxist standpoint but merely additional rice appropriated from the Cambodian civilians and exported to foreign countries. This, in fact, is the most conventional account of the mass starvation experienced within Democratic Kampuchea. Contra previous accounts, I maintain that the CPK explicitly sought to generate surplus value, as opposed to simple surplus (that is, excess quantities), through a system of production for exchange. Workers in Democratic Kampuchea were oppressed through violent means, but they were also exploited in the Marxist sense of the term.

Under systems of production for exchange (for example, capitalism), surplus value is derived from the exploitation of labor. This constitutes a second form of circulation: M–C–M, the transformation of money into commodities (M–C), and the reconversion of commodities into money (C–M). Whereas the first circulation results in the exchange of commodities (mediated through money), the second circulation entails the exchange of money for money (mediated through commodities). And here, Marx finds the crucial component of capitalism in that commodity exchange would be pointless if identical quantities of money were simply exchanged. As David Harvey writes, "M–C–M only makes sense if it results in an increment of value," this being surplus value.[53] For this reason, it is more proper to rewrite the circuit as M–C–M', with M' designating the added value. Surplus value is thus the defining feature of capitalism and would—on the surface—appear to bear no resemblance to the economics practiced by the Khmer Rouge. Appearances, of course, are deceiving.

Within systems of production for exchange, surplus value is generated through the exploitation of workers. More specifically, exploitation is derived not from the commodification of individual men and women, but instead from their capacity to labor. Furthermore, when capitalists purchase labor power, that is, hire workers, they do so on two conditions: first, that the laborer works under the control of the capitalist and, second, that the product is the property of the capitalist and not that of the worker/producer. Obviously, workers were not "hired" by the CPK; workers did not "freely" engage in productive activities. However, in an ironic twist, workers under the Khmer Rouge were "free" in the sardonic sense implied by Marx. This is a theme I develop in greater depth in chapter 6. For now, suffice it to say that the products produced by laborers in Democratic Kampuchea did not belong to the workers, but instead were appropriated by the CPK.

To fully appreciate the generation of surplus value, it is necessary, Marx writes, to leave the noisy sphere of exchange and to step into the "the hidden abode of production."[54] Marx's comments are in reference to the commodity fetish in capitalism, whereby the surface appearance of commodity exchange appears as a "free" exchange between the capitalist and the wageworker. It is the plainly obvious purchase of wage labor by the capitalist in exchange for a fair's day work that hides the real source of exploitation. Turning to Democratic Kampuchea, likewise, the obvious forced nature of work masks the underlying economic rationale of communal labor, food rations, and famine.

In the "hidden abode" of production, capitalists combine the means of production (for example, machinery and raw materials) with labor power (purchased on the labor market) in order to transform materials into commodities for exchange. The exchange value of the commodity, consequently, is composed of two parts: constant capital and variable capital. Constant capital is past labor—Marx terms this "dead labor"—already congealed in commodities that are used as means of production in a current labor process. The machines in a factory, plows in agriculture: these are themselves former commodities that were produced, distributed, and sold. Variable capital, conversely, is "living labor." As Marx explains, variable capital is added in the process of production and is thus the source of surplus value (that is, profit).

Surplus value is generated through the exploitation of labor capacity and assumes two basic forms: absolute surplus value and relative surplus value. First, Marx argued that the value of labor power (wages) is equal not to what a worker can produce (for example, a shirt) but instead to the labor time necessary to make up what it costs to keep the laborer and his or her family alive. To illustrate, laborers may produce enough value in six hours' work to offset their daily living expenses. Capitalists, however, purchase labor power for a full day's work, say, eight hours. The remaining two hours, Marx argues, appear as absolute surplus labor time, that is, the work time beyond the time it takes to make enough commodities to pay back the value of labor power (that is, wages) and also to account for the costs of the means of production necessary (for example, factories and machines).

The prolongation of the working day is foundational to capitalism and, by extension, to any system of production for exchange.[55] Within Democratic Kampuchea, initially, the CPK devised a means to generate *absolute* surplus value. Increased rice surpluses, for example, were to be obtained through the use of forced labor and the extension of the working day. In the CPK's Four-Year Plan, workers were to be allocated "three rest days per month," which would translate into "one rest day in every ten." Over the course of the year, laborers would receive "between ten and fifteen days, according to remoteness of location, for rest, visiting, and study." However, even "off-days" were to be productive: "Resting at home is nominated and arranged as time for tending small gardens, cleaning up, hygiene, and light study of culture and politics." During the day, all Khmer citizens worked according to rigid timetables; production quotas were likewise assigned. Chhay Phan, a Khmer Rouge cadre, was in charge of a work "platoon" at the Trapeang Thma Dam in the Northwest Zone. She recalls that the workday went from 4:00 a.m. to 11:00 a.m. and, after a brief lunch, continued from 2:00 p.m. to 5:00 p.m. Men, women, and even children were required to excavate three and a half cubic meters of dirt per day in the building of the canal.[56]

Long working hours and high quotas coupled with insufficient rations led to widespread exhaustion and death. For the CPK, these losses were inconsequential; all labor was considered "surplus" and therefore expendable. This is clearly illustrated from the minutes of a Standing Committee meeting held on March 8, 1976, in which reports were presented by zone secretaries and deputy secretaries on the living conditions in different regions of the North Zone. It was reported, for example, that there were "many sick people" and "outbreaks of chickenpox and cholera." The possibility of food shortages was also apparent. Yet the Standing Committee explained that "we think much about the livelihood of the people, but expenditures for material purchases to solve the livelihood of the people are limited because we must purchase many other things as well, and our funds are few." The Standing Committee also recognized that come August and September, there would most likely be many food shortages and that those shortages would impact the "health and labor strength" of the workers. However, it was concluded that "as for rice, it should be two cans or a little more."[57] This amount, following the committee, constituted an appropriate "minimum" or "living wage." In other words, the possibility of starvation and loss of life was significant only to the extent that labor productivity would suffer. Beyond that, what mattered was the continued accumulation of capital through rice production.

Limitations to the working day, coupled with the potential decline in labor productivity, restricted the absolute surplus value that could be accumulated. The CPK identified this problem and, ironically, resolved it dialectically by a deepening of capitalist logic: the generation of relative surplus value. This requires an explanation of *socially necessary labor time* in that for Marx, it was not "necessary" labor time that defined labor power's value; rather, it was *socially necessary* labor time. Here, the expression "socially necessary" means "the quantity of labor necessary under the average conditions of labor productivity existing in a given country at a given time."[58] Thus, socially necessary labor time, as "the labor-time required to produce any use-value under the conditions of production normal for a given society and with the average degree of skill and intensity of labor prevalent in that society," transfers the level of argument from any individual capitalist to society as a whole.[59] This is possible because, as

Ben Fine and Alfredo Saad-Filho explain, "production of relative surplus value depends critically upon all capitalists, since none alone produces a significant proportion of the commodities required for the reproduction of the working class."[60]

An increase in average production increases the average number of commodities produced per unit of time; it thereby decreases the amount of socially necessary labor time required for the production of a single commodity and, hence, the value of each commodity.[61] In other words, whereas absolute surplus value is related to the *length* of the working day, relative surplus value is related to the *intensity* of the working day. Greater efficiencies of scale lessen the costs of production, thereby facilitating greater profits. With an increase in the productivity of labor—through refinements in the division of labor, the introduction of machinery, or even the threat of death—the value of labor power falls, and the portion of the working day necessary for the reproduction of that value will be shortened. Capital thus "has an immanent drive, and a constant tendency, towards increasing the productivity of labor, in order to cheapen commodities and, by cheapening commodities, to cheapen the worker himself."[62]

In Democratic Kampuchea there were obviously no capitalists, no wages, and no private property. Consequently, in the absence of private competition among capitalists *within* Democratic Kampuchea, how could socially necessary labor time materialize and, by extension, relative surplus value come about? The answer, I suggest, lies in the particular form of state capitalism adopted by the CPK. Recall that the value (not the price) of a commodity is fixed by the socially necessary labor time required to produce any use value under the conditions of production normal for a given society and with the average degree of skill and intensity of labor prevalent in that society.[63] Under developed systems of capitalist exchange, such as in the United States, capitalists may invest capital into machinery that requires less labor time than the average conditions, thereby gaining extra surplus value (that is, a hyperprofit). This is a form of relative surplus value at the level of the individual capitalist; it is also ephemeral, in that other capitalists will adopt the same machinery. At the societal level, as more and more capitalists invest in the new technology, the hyperprofit for the innovative capitalist vanishes.

It is important therefore to distinguish between relative surplus value as a class phenomenon as opposed to an individual phenomenon. At the societal level, class competition among capitalists provides the catalyst for an overall reduction in the socially necessary labor time required for commodity production. As goods and services become cheaper, the amount of wages necessary for reproduction diminishes. This is the basis of relative surplus value and would appear to have been nonexistent in Democratic Kampuchea. There was, however, the calculated administration of food rations as a means of garnering additional surpluses. The CPK, for example, determined in its Four-Year Plan that production levels of rice, specifically, would increase continually from 1977 to 1980.[64] In the Southwest Zone, by way of illustration, rice production was to increase from 1,140,000 tons in 1977 to 1,440,000 in 1980. During this same period, however, the CPK determined that the amount of rice necessary for consumption (that is, rice as wage) would remain constant. Thus, returning to the Southwest Zone, the CPK calculated that for each year between 1977 and 1980, laborers would require a constant 470,000 tons of rice *for reproduction*. In 1977, consequently, 46 percent of rice went into reproduction, while by 1980 an estimated 33 percent would be required. In other words, an artificial reduction in socially necessary labor time was imposed by the CPK. While capitalist competition was therefore removed, the *effects* of competition were built into the overall production estimates. As David Harvey writes, historically many state-organized strategies have been utilized to intervene in the value of labor power.[65] Agricultural production within Democratic Kampuchea, I maintain, is one such illustration.

Now, what I wish to consider further is the idea that the "food ration" contains its own internal contradictions, for the food ration as constituted by the CPK entailed both a "use value" and an "exchange value." On the one hand, food rations marked the CPK's attempt to "make life" in an immediate sense, a supposed guarantee of equal access on an individual basis to one of life's basic necessities: food. On the other hand, the imposition of food rations was an attempt to "make life" for society as a whole, given that agricultural surpluses would be used to acquire other necessities for the party and the revolution. Ironically, a communal system predicated on collectivized labor ensures a standardization of labor. The

Khmer Rouge—through the elimination of "individual" producers and owners—was effectively able to impose its own determination of socially necessary labor time.

How, then, did the CPK foster the accumulation of *relative* surplus value in the absence of currency? It was accomplished by the substitution of food rations for wages. Money, of course, is simply a representation of value. In and of itself, whether in paper or metal form, money has no intrinsic value beyond the material of which is it made. Money's *real* value is derived from that given it by social convention; it is agreed to have equivalence in value to assorted commodities and services. Accordingly, the mere abolition of currency does not negate the underlying social relations that give money its purchase. This is illustrated by comments recorded during a meeting of the CPK Standing Committee on May 30, 1976: "Growing rice is not only about supporting yourselves. You have to produce more yields."[66] In other words, rice was viewed as a commodity; its importance was its exchange value and not its use value. Increased yields were necessary not to feed more people, but rather because this is where the accumulation of capital would emerge.

In practical terms, relative surplus value is the difference between the living costs of labor power—the minimum amount necessary for bare survival—and the exchange value created by this labor power. In fully developed capitalist societies, the living costs of labor power are understood as "minimum wages." Under the Khmer Rouge, following the abolition of currency, wages were not paid. Instead, food rations assumed the role of "minimum wages." This is most fully articulated in—but not limited to—the CPK's Four-Year Plan. In this plan the CPK proposed that from 1977 onward, "The [food] ration for the people will average . . . 312 kilograms of rice per person per year throughout the country." This amount translates to roughly 0.85 kilograms per day. More specifically, a fourfold system was devised to distribute food rations based on the type of workforce. Those workers classified in the "number 1 system" (*robob*) would be allocated three cans of rice per day; those in the "number 2 system," two and a half cans; number 3, two cans; and number 4, one and a half cans. The "cans" used for measurement were most often Nestlé's condensed-milk cans; each can contained approximately 200 grams of rice.[67] Restated in Marxian terms, the living cost of labor power under the CPK was (on average) two cans of rice per day; the surplus value was any amount of rice produced above and beyond this minimum living wage.

Capitalist logic dictates that greater profits (that is, surplus value) are accrued by reductions in socially necessary labor time. In other words, a reduction in the amount of labor time necessary for the workers' reproduction is positively related to an increase in the amount of value generated. This, as Ernest Mandel concludes, "is the basis for all Marxist economic theory in general" and (ironically) was the basis of Marx's critique of capitalism.[68] By way of illustration, in the Four-Year Plan, the CPK determined that the average amount of rice production would increase from 245,000 tons in 1977 to 462,000 tons in 1980; this would, according to their estimates, result in a gain of US$121 million over the four-year period. To meet these objectives, workers were to remain vigilant in their revolutionary zeal and, with "proper" consciousness, increase productivity. Crucially, the amount of rations to be allocated for worker consumption was to remain at 320,000 tons per annum. In other words, it was assumed that as productivity increased and workers became more efficient, there was no need to increase the amount of food rations allocated. In this manner, reductions in socially necessary labor time contributed to an ever-increasing surplus value derived from the export of rice.

When the Khmer Rouge eliminated currency, therefore, they did not sunder the basic form of economic exchange: farmers produced rice, rice was collected by government officials, and rice was exported to garner capital. When money was eliminated, the Khmer Rouge simply continued an earlier practice, namely, the use of rice as a form of exchange. However, whereas traditionally rice was used for barter or trade, under the CPK rice was more completely subsumed into the productive sphere. Rice was commodified in the full Marxian sense of the term. As Jason Read explains, there is a "fundamental difference between the commodity form at the emergence of capital and the commodity form in its maturity—a difference between the isolated commodities exchanged on the markets of mercantile capitalism and the planned and designed commodities of contemporary capitalism." Read states that the capitalist mode of production does not preserve its presuppositions (for example, preexisting and small-scale market activities and craft production) but transforms them. This is what Marx meant by the transition from formal to real subsumption—the restructuring of social relations according to the demands of capitalist valorization.[69]

Rhetorically, the Khmer Rouge sought to remake society, to erase all vestiges of previous modes of production. In practice, however, the CPK did anything but this. In fact, a picture emerges whereby preexisting technical and social organizations of production were not eliminated but instead transformed more explicitly along the lines of a capitalist mode of production. Defined by Marx as a process of "formal subsumption," this initial transformation constitutes a process whereby commodity production and wage labor are more fully imposed on society. This, according to Marx, corresponds to the extraction of "absolute surplus value."

Following Marx, the production of relative surplus value "presupposes that the working day is already divided into two parts, necessary labor and surplus labor. In order to prolong the surplus labor, the necessary labor is shortened by methods for producing the equivalent of the wage labor in a shorter time."[70] In Democratic Kampuchea, productivity was projected to increase yearly, yet, as illustrated in the party's Four-Year Plan, food rations were to remain constant. This indicates that for the CPK, under a supposedly communal society bereft of private ownership, the living wage would be fixed. There was, in other words, no justifiable reason to increase the food ration, for everyone was to receive and "enjoy" an equivalency in foodstuffs. Communist rhetoric, in short, provided the moral authority of Khmer Rouge macroeconomics and, by extension, occasioned the transition to the real subsumption of society.

Over time, an elaborate division of labor and corresponding system of food rations developed throughout Democratic Kampuchea. Laborers were classified as either *kemlang ping* (full strength) or *kemlang ksaoy* (weak strength), with the former consisting mostly of adults and the latter consisting of small children and the elderly. Those designated as full strength were further classified into two subgroups: *kemlang* 1, which consisted of young, able-bodied, single men and women who composed mobile work brigades (*kong chhlat*), and *kemlang* 2, composed of married, able-bodied men and women who were divided by sex but generally worked closer to the village. The heaviest tasks were generally reserved for *kemlang* 1 persons. These work teams were segregated by sex; males belonged to *kong boroh* and females to *kong neary*. These brigades were set to work primarily on land clearance, the digging of canals and reservoirs, and the construction of dams and dikes. As the name implies, people assigned to mobile work brigades often lived outside of villages, in temporary work camps also segregated by sex. *Kemlang* 2 workers generally worked closer to their villages, performing such tasks as local woodcutting (for building materials or fuel), preparation and cultivation of agricultural fields, and maintenance of irrigation schemes. These tasks were also, but not always, segregated by sex; women, for example, reaped the rice, while threshing was performed by the men.[71] Last, the "weak strength" laborers (*kemlang* 3) were tasked with lighter tasks. Elderly workers were grouped into work teams known generically as *senah chun*; male groups were termed *senah chun boroh* and female groups *senah chun neary*. Duties for members of *senah chun* groups included sewing, gardening, collecting small pieces of wood, and care for children. Depending on the conditions and the attitudes of the cooperative chief, some elderly workers might be required to labor in the rice fields or engage in other more strenuous work. Children under fourteen years of age were assigned to work groups known as *kong komar*, with boys and girls separated into *kong komara* and *kong khomarei*, respectively. Children were responsible for watching after cows and water buffalo, light digging in gardens and fields, collecting firewood, and gathering cow dung for fertilizer.[72]

An embryonic distributive justice is evident in the distribution of food rations established by the CPK: those people performing the heaviest manual labor, in principle, were to receive the highest rations. The lightest tasks, performed by the elderly or the sick, received the smallest rations. Pregnant women, or women who had just given birth, were to be allotted higher rations. Consequently, the CPK was able to calculate work quotas, such as the amount of soil to be excavated, the amount of forest to be cleared, or the acreage of fields to be planted and harvested. Often, these quotas were calculated collectively, based on the work group in question. A work team of fifteen "full-strength" women, for example, may be assigned to reap one hectare of rice per day.[73]

7. Khmer Rouge cadre threshing rice. Courtesy of the Documentation Center of Cambodia Archives.

For each administrative zone, separate calculations were also computed to determine the balance between surplus production and food rations. In the Western Zone, for example, a senior party official—most likely Pol Pot—explained how such calculations would be determined: "If the Zone has 600,000 people, they must eat 150,000 tons of [rice]. But we want more than this in order to locate much additional oil, to get ever more rice mills, threshing machines, water pumps, and means of transportation, both as an auxiliary manual force and to give strength to our forces of production. So we must not get just 150,000 tons of [rice]. We must get 300,000, 400,000, 500,000 tons just to break even and be able to build socialism."[74]

Administrative calculations of food rations for each zone, in turn, were aggregated to establish national quotas, forming the cornerstone of the CPK's overall economic policy. As detailed in the party's Four-Year Plan, a target of 5.5 million tons of rice was established for 1977 for the entire country, with each zone responsible for a set proportion. By extension, the

8. Khmer Rouge women's unit collecting rice. Courtesy of the Documentation Center of Cambodia Archives.

CPK determined that an equivalency of 3.2 million tons was required to be expended as capital (for example, food rations, seeds, and "welfare"). Of the estimated 2.3 million tons of "surplus" rice, 1.3 million tons were to be exported; it is unclear as to distribution of the remaining 1 million tons. Based on an exchange rate of US$200 per ton of rice, the CPK concluded that they would earn—in 1977—more than US$277 million. Subsequently, a ratio of 7:3 was established, whereby 70 percent of surplus was to be spent for the "base" in order to build the zones, regions, and other units, while the remaining 30 percent was set aside for the state to defend and build the country. Last, separate calculations were determined to allocate the distribution of expenditures, categorized by national reconstruction, defense of bases, and livelihood.

Despite attempts by the CPK to standardize the quantities of labor to be performed (and by academics who uncritically parrot such figures), in practice there was no uniform quota system. As Charles Twining correctly identifies, whoever was in charge of a group of workers (for instance, one of the cooperative's team chiefs or the head of the village committee) determined the hours to be worked or, alternatively, how much work had to be performed in a day: so many meters of irrigation canal to be dug or so much rice field to be cultivated.[75] An illustration of these accountings is provided by Chhum Seng, a former company chief of the Khmer Rouge.[76] Between 1975 and 1979, Chhum worked on various projects, including the construction of Prey Moan Dam, the Preah Neth Preah Dam, the Trapeang Thmar Dam, and a cotton farm. His primary role was the supervision of one hundred workers, divided into three units. These units were based on expected (average) productivity: those workers who were expected to excavate four to five cubic meters per day, those excavating three cubic meters per day, and those excavating less than three cubic meters per day. Based on assignment to various work teams, food rations were distributed accordingly, with these amounts based on a determination of socially necessary labor time: those who labored "more productively" and performed more "strenuous" tasks received (in principle) greater rations.

Both absolute and relative surplus values were, in theory, to be generated through the establishment of food rations. It is important to emphasize that, under communism (in general), the products of surplus labor are received collectively by the same workers.[77] Within Democratic Kampuchea, designated state officials—persons other than the producers—appropriated the products of worker labor. One readily sees in this the class structure of an exploitative economic system of exchange. Private property was abolished, but crucially, the people remained separated from the means of production; they owned neither land nor tools. Workers also did not collectively appropriate their own surplus production, nor did they distribute it according to collective need; rather, state functionaries appropriated the surplus and exchanged it for commodities on the global market.

The "Nature" of the Khmer Rouge

Such a system of economic exchange was necessary for the CPK for reasons beyond the generation of surplus value; indeed, it was through the transformation of physical nature—the cultivation of rice, for example—that a "correct" political consciousness was to be cultivated. Here, we see clearly the dialectic reasoning behind the CPK's social organization of production and the subsequent ideological foundation of building social-ism within Democratic Kampuchea.

Neil Smith, in his reading of Marx, identifies a fundamental distinc-tion between *production in general* and *production for exchange*. As Smith writes, "With production for exchange, the relation with nature is no lon-ger exclusively a use-value relation; use-values are not produced for direct use but for exchange." This is crucial, for as Smith concludes, "With pro-duction for exchange rather than direct use, there arises first the possibil-ity and then the necessity for alienation of the individual."[78] A particular form of nature transformed, in other words, works to estrange, or alienate, humans from their human nature.

Marx's theory of alienation is most fully developed in the posthu-mously published *Economic and Philosophic Manuscripts of 1844*. Here, Marx presents alienation as comprising four broad relations that cover the whole of human existence: the worker's relationship to his or her productive activity, product, other people, and the species-being, that is, humanity.[79] First, according to Marx, alienation exists when the laboring activities are *external* to the worker. Those workers assigned to assembly lines, for example, exist as mere appendages to the surrounding machin-ery; they do not control their own productive activities but rather exist at the beck and call of those who own the means of production. Under such conditions, workers become alienated from the *object* of their productive activity; this is because the commodities produced are owned not by the worker but rather, again, by those who own the means of production. However, if the worker does not own his or her own products, who does? The answer is: someone else. This leads to a third form of alienation, namely, the alienation of people from other people. Last, Marx held that under systems of exchange production, workers become alienated from human nature itself.

A *Marxist conception of nature* therefore holds that it is through the deliberate transformation of what we take as physical nature that human-ity assumes its own essential nature, that consciousness emerges dialec-tically between the concrete activities undertaken by humans and the materialities of the objective, material world. Given such a position, for Marx communism was necessary to overcome the process of alienation endemic to capitalism. Under systems of production for exchange, men and women—but humanity as a whole—were precluded from developing their own consciousness. As Bertell Ollman concludes, "The human species is deprived of its reality, of what it requires to manifest itself as the human species."[80] It was for this reason that Marx believed that communism—as a collective, nonindividuated form of production—was necessary to overcome the alienated life that typified capitalism. It was for this reason, also, that the Khmer Rouge sought to "build socialism" in the rice fields of Democratic Kampuchea.

The Standard Total View would hold that "nature" for the Khmer Rouge was something to be mastered in order to produce a socialist utopia. Such a vulgar position is held, in part, by the Khmer Rouge slogans "Let us be master of the water, master of the nature" and "Let us not be defeated by nature." Consequently, so the story goes, it was necessary for every work site to become "a fiery battlefield."[81] The CPK's line of reasoning was apparently simple: "We fight in the field of agriculture because we have agricultural resources. We'll move to other fields when the agricultural battle is finished." Following this conception of nature—as something to be mastered—Daniel Bultmann therefore concludes that for the CPK, "the aim was to build an environment defeating nature and operating purely in line with socialist functions, inhabited by pure socialist people, using pure revolutionary methods. This ideal socialist space aimed to operate beyond natural conditions, geographic specifics and environmental diversity."[82]

There is an element of accuracy in this position. The transformation of nature was pitched as a crucial element in the policies of the CPK and the planned transformation of Khmer society. However, this position risks losing sight of several key elements that deepen our understanding of both CPK ideology and material practice. Embedded within Khmer Rouge agricultural policy was a dialectic relationship between the natural environment and human nature. Simply put, and in response to Bultmann's conclusion, we need to ask: How were "pure socialist people" to be developed? The answer, I maintain, stems from the Marxist unity of nature that holds that the production of consciousness is an integral part of the production of material life.

The CPK conception of nature was complex. Nature was largely premised as some*thing* external; nature was something to be used or overcome; it was a barrier to progress but also laden with possibilities. In their attempt to transform physical nature as a means of securing capital, the CPK leadership sought to transform human nature. Consequently, men, women, and children were deployed to wage war on nature—but with a "purposeful will"—not as spiders or bees, for it was through their specific laboring activities that socialism was to be built. Here, though, the CPK adopted a caricature of a Marxist conception of nature, namely, one in which economic relations were considered to be preeminent. This accounts for their belief that political consciousness would follow economic production.[83] It was not therefore that people under the Khmer Rouge were blank sheets of paper or clumps of clay to be molded by ideology; rather, it was through labor itself, the cultivation of rice fields, that "right minds" and "right attitudes" were to be cultivated. At this level, therefore, physical nature and human nature were united. The transformation of Democratic Kampuchea's natural environment would, according to the CPK, result in a transformation of consciousness; in turn, a proper political consciousness would lead to additional transformations of the country's natural resources. And it was through this dialectical unity, according to the Khmer Rouge, that any production quota could be achieved.

The implications of nature so conceived proved quite fatal. If production quotas were unmet, the theoretical conclusion to be drawn was that a proper level of consciousness had not been achieved. Bultmann is correct in his assessment that "the leadership suspected sabotage within its own ranks" and that "the occurrence of shortcomings in the actual implementation of the Four-Year Plan were directly linked to a resistance against the sovereign power behind the plan."[84] However, such a brutal conclusion conforms readily to the "socialist" economy envisioned but not implemented by the CPK. Collective production was, in theory, to overcome individuality and lead to the proper consciousness.[85]

A document from 1976 vividly illustrates the CPK's belief in the transformative nature of collective labor. In this fifty-eight-page report, dated December 20, 1976, it is noted that the "problem of individualism still

9. Khmer Rouge children learning about harvesting. Courtesy of the Documentation Center of Cambodia Archives.

exists." This problem remains, allegedly, because there are "contradictions between collectivism and individualism," and "traitors" continue to "create antagonistic contractions." Consequently, "in comparative terms, political consciousness lags behind the other aspects" of the revolution. The report explains that an expanded collectivism throughout society is required and that collectivism must proceed at all administrative levels. This requires a "rejection of old relations of production" and the transformation to "collective relations of production."[86] Tellingly, however, the report not only bemoans the lack of political consciousness, but also reaffirms the necessity of generating surplus through the continuation of subsistence wages (that is, minimum food rations).

Conclusion

The CPK understood political consciousness as being related to a particular production of nature and, specifically, laboring activities that transform nature into use values. Arguably, the CPK also understood—from a Marxist standpoint—that communism, in principle, would lead to the elimination of oppression, exploitation, and alienation that are perceived as being endemic to capitalism. However, they failed to recognize that the system they imposed was neither socialist nor communist; rather, the peculiar economy established by the CPK was nothing less than an exploitative system of production for exchange. This impacted their approach both to "physical" nature (as something to be mastered, dominated, and perverted to a particular exchange value) and also to "human" nature.

Living within a system of production for exchange, those who labored in Cambodia's fields became alienated from labor itself, the products of their labor, other persons, and humanity as a whole. Work under the Khmer Rouge was something external to those who labored. Instead of cultivating a "pure socialist" consciousness, the Khmer Rouge produced the opposite: compulsory, collectivized labor within a production-for-exchange system was *estranged, alienated labor.* This in turn imparted a tragic, fatal irony: the commodities produced (for example, rice) were the substances of life, yet production was principally not for consumption but instead for exchange. Workers were to serve the revolution; more abstractly, however, workers were to exist only as producers of exchange value. The natural existence of humanity within Democratic Kampuchea was negated *not* because the CPK initiated a socialist/communist revolution; rather, humanity was negated precisely because such a revolution did not occur.

5

Manufacturing Indifference

"Spare them, no profit; remove them, no loss." The terseness of this widely evoked phrase of the Khmer Rouge calls to mind images of swift punishment, of an unyielding authority that quickly passes judgment on life or death. For Henri Locard, the slogan "suggests the clearing of a field, to uproot all poisonous weeds, before sowing the good seed." This, according to Locard, implies the need to start anew and underscores the argument that the Khmer Rouge sought to create a "pure" utopian society. Thus, drawing mostly on slogans and Khmer Rouge rhetoric, many commentators—myself included—have argued that the Communist Party of Kampuchea sought to create a "pure" society; doing so entailed the elimination of both external and internal enemies, as well as those who purportedly did not conform to the rigid dictates of the CPK. Miguel Cunha and colleagues, for example, conclude that CPK "leaders saw their country as a paragon of virtue. In fact, the new [Democratic Kampuchea] would be an example to the entire world: purity turned real. In this case, purity was built around categories: the new people, bourgeois, were the impure, and base people, the agrarian class, were depicted as the pure." Elsewhere, these authors explain that the "Khmer Rouge utopia would be one in which the evils and miseries of Khmer feudalism had vanished, to be replaced by peace, harmony and happiness by subordinating the individual to the collective; reckoning a-historically, and de-contextualizing human beings so that the collective will is total and controls individuals in detail, unavoidably using violence and power to keep everything under control and to ward off foreign influences."[1]

There is no doubt the Khmer Rouge used a litany of dehumanizing terms, such as *microbes*, *parasites*, and *worms*, in reference to perceived enemies, including anyone thought to be associated with capitalism, feudalism, the previous Lon Nol government, foreign governments, April 17 people, and so on. Likewise, countless aphorisms, contained in slogans, songs, and magazines, spoke to these undesirable elements. One slogan, for example, warned, "The winnowing basket separates the wheat from the chaff," a not so subtle reference that Angkar would weed out undesirable elements.[2]

Alexander Hinton is correct in his conclusion that for the Khmer Rouge, these groupings were constructed as evil and required purification from Democratic Kampuchea.[3] At this juncture, I want to contribute to Hinton's key insights and to consider how dehumanizing practices align with the CPK's form of state capitalism. My title for this chapter is thus in homage to Hinton's chapter titled "Manufacturing Difference." Hinton draws heavily on Buddhist theory in an attempt to understand how and why the Khmer Rouge manufactured a "difference" that provided justification for torture, execution, and murder. Here, I complement Hinton's work by drawing on Marxist economics to propose that Khmer Rouge attitudes of the dehumanized Other were based not only on *difference* but also on *indifference*.

Following Marx, ideology is dialectically related to economic production, to the extent that "men [sic] are the producers of their conceptions, ideas, etc., that is, real, active men, as they are conditioned by a definite development of their productive forces."[4] Consequently, it is worthwhile to consider to what extent the Khmer Rouge's dehumanizing ideology is connected to their embryonic social organization of production. In other words, by applying a Marxist critique to CPK ideology, what insights might be gained that may flesh out the social classifications forwarded by the Khmer Rouge?

In the *Grundrisse*, Marx writes, "Indifference towards specific labors corresponds to a form of society in which individuals can with ease transfer from one labor to another, and where the specific kind is a matter of chance for them, hence of indifference." Here, Marx highlights an abstract form of labor, a form that is vitally necessary for determinations of socially necessary labor. Marx explains, "Indifference towards any specific kind of labor presupposes a very developed totality of real kinds of labor, of which no single one is any longer predominant."[5] Under systems of production for exchange, for example, it is essential that equivalencies be established to facilitate commodity exchange, such as how many bushels of corn are equivalent to yards of cloth. Likewise, it is necessary to establish equivalencies among workers.

Marx critiqued the homogenization of labor under capitalism; it formed a core component of his desire to promote communism, whereby workers would be freed from exploitative relations and be able to develop their creative potential. The CPK, however, and in contradistinction to Marx, attempted to achieve a total state of conformity, as seen most visibly but not exclusively in their attempt to regiment what people wore and how they groomed their hair. The Khmer Rouge also, apart from the imposition of age and gender divisions of labor, set out to establish a supposed equivalency among workers. This too countered Marx, who explained that when labor becomes the means of creating wealth in general, labor has thus "ceased to be organically linked with particular individuals in any specific form."[6]

In chapter 4 I concluded that, living within a system of production for exchange, those who labored in Cambodia's fields became alienated. Work under the Khmer Rouge became external to individual existence, as men, women, and children became mere components of a larger, faceless machine known only as Angkar. Instead of cultivating a "pure" socialist consciousness, I argue, the CPK produced just the opposite: compulsory collectivized labor within a production-for-exchange system of state capitalism. Thus, the slogan "Spare them, no profit; remove them, no loss" acquires a different interpretation, one that places emphasis on the economics—the profitability—of life. The slogan also speaks to a pervasive indifference, and it is this indifference, I believe, that underscores the CPK's promotion of equivalences (as opposed to equality) and its imposition of structures of violence. However, to the indifference of life itself on behalf of the CPK, we must also consider those actions and inactions of the international community, for in contrast to the Standard Total View, it is untenable to consider CPK policies isolated from their broader transnational context.

Valuing Life

In making this argument, it is necessary to return to Marx's discussion of simple commodity exchange. The exchange between labor and capital, where workers are forced by their very survival needs to seek employment, is readily and routinely portrayed as a fair exchange between two equal partners.[7] Of course, such a portrayal—of a fair exchange of a *day's labor for a day's wage*—is anything but fair. No "surplus value" is added to commodities during the process of circulation but instead originates in the process of production: the difference between necessary labor time and surplus labor time. It is incumbent upon capitalists, as such, to keep wages as low as possible—an observation made both by Adam Smith and by Marx. Marx, for example, explained that the "lowest and the only necessary wage-rate is that providing for the subsistence of the worker for the duration of his [*sic*] work and as much more as is necessary for him to support a family and for the race of laborers not to die out."[8]

That said, capitalists cannot (usually) work their laborers to death or impose conditions that would prevent their living—a topic I address in the next chapter. Here, we need consider only that the health and fitness of the working class—the "making of life"—are often a matter of considerable state interest.[9] This is a point clarified by Tania Murray Li: "Make live interventions become urgent when people can no longer sustain their own lives through direct access to the means of production, or access to a living wage."[10] Ironically, and contradictorily, it frequently becomes necessary for both the "state" and the individual capitalist to limit the exploitation and degradation of the living worker, if only to facilitate the generation of further surplus value.

How, though, might this exchange operate if it were truly "open" and unregulated? Robert Albritton provides a particularly apt summary of life and death in the capitalist labor market: "A completely commodified labour market would be managed completely by the wage rate, which in turn is a result of the supply of and demand for workers. A large supply of workers relative to demand will lead to lower and lower wage rates. If this situation continues, wages will eventually fall below bare physical subsistence and workers will die off, until their supply shrinks enough to once again push wages to a level at or above subsistence." In other words, a pure, completely commodified capitalist labor market would necessarily operate on the basis of *letting die* a certain proportion of workers. In theory, the inability to survive within the labor market would operate as a biological regulatory mechanism, not unlike ecosystems. Of course, given the vagaries of capitalism, it is not always profitable to have excess labor die off. At times, when capital is rapidly expanding, additional workers are required immediately. Capitalists cannot wait for additional workers to be born, raised, trained, and inserted into the labor market. Consequently, this is one reason (among others) it is advantageous to capitalism to have a reserve supply of labor waiting in the wings. As David Harvey notes, the existence of a surplus population permits capitalists to superexploit their workers without regard for their health or well-being; consequently, a surplus population affects whether the capitalist has to care about the health, well-being, and life expectancy of the labor force.[11] This is also why there exist (selectively) "make live" interventions. However, to make live is to sustain not the life of the laborer *as an individual* but instead to sustain the capacity of the laboring class *as a population*. It is, in other words, to socially reproduce the system as a whole.

How does this relate to Democratic Kampuchea? Thus far, I have argued that the CPK initiated an economic system predicated upon production for exchange. Superficially, we begin to see that Democratic Kampuchea appears very much like a completely commodified society, as described by Albritton, a society whereupon all life was dependent on the food ration imposed by a minority ruling class, where all opportunities to obtain the basic material necessities of life were violently restricted, and where massive loss of life occurred. To be sure, Democratic Kampuchea did *not* function as a completely commodified labor market, yet we can make the argument that as food rations diminished and people began to die off in large numbers, the CPK did (as I discuss later) consider various ways to intervene. Significantly, when regional labor shortages did arise because of massive starvation (or purges), the CPK initiated large-scale transfers of workers to provide needed labor. Indeed, documents of the Khmer Rouge indicate that from 1977 onward, approximately five hundred thousand people (laborers) were transferred from the East to the Northwest Zone.[12]

To properly understand how the CPK valued life, it is necessary to do so from the standpoint of how value is conceived according to dominant social relations of production. Following Marx, "The presupposition of exchange value, as the objective basis of the whole of the system of production, already in itself implies compulsion over the individual, since his immediate product is not a product for him, but only becomes such in the social process, and since it must take on this general but nevertheless external form; and that the individual has an existence only as a producer of exchange value, hence that the whole negation of his natural existence is already implied; that he is therefore entirely determined by society."[13] In this complex statement, Marx puts forward a number of claims. Within a system of production for exchange, commodities are produced not to address any particular use value, but rather to satisfy the accumulation of capital. Workers within such a system are viewed from a strict utilitarian vantage point; they exist simply to produce for others. The overall indifference to use value is transposed onto the working class. At this point, work "is not just defended on grounds of economic necessity and social duty; it is widely understood as an individual moral practice and collective ethical obligation."[14]

The CPK approached the labor process accordingly. In their assessment of economic progress in 1976, the CPK concluded that "the strength of the labor force is rather feeble. . . . Thus this year we must make arrangements and persuade people to follow the Party's Plan, and to rest according to the Party's Plan. In a month, three days off is sufficient for health." Within Democratic Kampuchea, men and women, collectively, were seen as having a moral obligation to fulfill their duty to accumulate surplus. It was only through the combined efforts of society, according to the CPK, that national objectives could be met. This would, naturally, entail a sacrifice and hardship for the workers. The report continues, "If people work without stopping, their health will suffer." This statement is vital, for it highlights the awareness of the party center to the horrific conditions experienced by the Cambodian people. And while the report does make passing reference to improving conditions—"We must also find a way to let people rest at certain times so as to maintain their health"—the overall tenor of the report is clear. Toward the conclusion of the report, it is noted,

"The most important thing is to nourish viewpoint and stance, politics, consciousness and [to perform] tasks as assigned by the Party."[15]

In Democratic Kampuchea, geography mattered. As Anthony Barnett summarizes, "When we look more closely we can see that life in one zone or region could differ significantly from another in one crucial respect: that of life itself, or death." He continues, "The enforced confiscation of food from the producers in the countryside, and the 'collectivized' rationing of its distribution, placed an arbitrary power of life and death in the hands of the authorities on the spot. Similarly, their powers of arbitrary execution could be exercised with greater or lesser zeal or with none at all. There would be zonal differences in the utilization of such power, and within each zone in turn there would be regional differences. But nowhere, it seems, was this power not placed in the hands of the cadre on the spot." As such, Michael Vickery concludes that "the different conditions could not all have been directly determined by central policy."[16]

However, the salience of regional differentiation should not divert attention away from the broader national-level policies enacted—and attitudes engendered—by the CPK. Following Barnett, the existence of marked differences in the implementation of policy in different parts of Cambodia, at different times, does not disprove that the central authorities were imposing their rule. Indeed, throughout Democratic Kampuchea, the CPK established a degree of direction over the lives of the population of utmost severity.[17] And while the upper echelons did not directly order each execution or necessarily withhold needed food and medical supplies, it was the overall tenor of national policy within a governance structure of democratic centralism that created the conditions under which local cadre made decisions. Consequently, one needs to articulate more fully the gestalt of CPK policy. More precisely, therefore, to fully understand the value of life under the Khmer Rouge, it is necessary to explore more concretely the *making of life* by the CPK.

Such a task immediately rings discordant with the Standard Total View, for it is widely assumed that the Khmer Rouge simply unleashed violence "to eliminate those unworthy of utopia, those whose past commitments threaten[ed] the creation of conditions for a cleansed peace that those whose worth [had] been proven would enjoy."[18] However, the mass violence that occurred was not only about taking lives; it was also about establishing those structural conditions that, for some groups (for example, base people and Khmer Rouge cadre), made life while for others (April 17 people) disallowed life. In other words, life under the Khmer Rouge *had value*. This value, however, was determined based on the needs of the party and, by extension, on the need to build political consciousness and to generate surplus value in the form of commodities.

The Practice of Medicine under the Khmer Rouge

Health care is one of the clearest and most visible expressions of a society's attitude to the value of life, for it is within the context of deciding who is to receive health care, and what types of treatments and medicines are available, that one sees most clearly the calculated management of life and death.

On the eve of the genocide, Cambodia exhibited two coexisting medical traditions. On the one hand, traditional forms of medicine were widely practiced, while, on the other hand, Western-based "modern" medicinal practices were also available. Cambodia's indigenous (or precolonial) medical tradition was (and remains) based on the *kru khmae* (meaning "Khmer [style] teacher"). Unlike Western medical practice, the indigenous healing process in Cambodia consists of a "diagnosis dialogue." In tandem, the *kru khmae* and the patient coproduce a body of knowledge regarding the latter's health; this knowledge contains physical, social, and cosmological aspects. As such, the traditional practice of medicine in Khmer society is socially, psychologically, and spiritually therapeutic. Of equal importance is that the entire process of diagnosis and therapy must be based on a consensus between the *kru*, the patient, his or her relatives, and the spirits.[19]

The arrival of French colonialism brought with it a Western-based medical practice. Initially, these practices were overseen by the French military and focused on curative (surgical) aspects and some preventative practices. As civilian authorities assumed principal responsibility for the health of its colony, medical practices shifted. Preventive health care, in particular, assumed center stage. French colonial officials were concerned primarily to prevent the spread of infectious diseases, such as cholera, smallpox, and the plague. Consequently, substantial investments (both financial and scholarly) were placed on developing "tropical" medicines, specifically vaccinations that would foster the health of French residents in the colony. With limited scope, these preventative practices were extended to the indigenous Cambodians. This was done not so much out of altruism, but rather because it was rational. France's economic interests in Cambodia, certainly, but throughout all of Indochina hinged on rice production. It was therefore in the financial interests of the colonial authorities to maintain a productive, viable labor force.

Throughout the period of occupation, indigenous medical practices were viewed mostly with indifference by French authorities. In effect, as long as traditional practices did not negatively impact French policies and practices—such as the vaccination program—they were tolerated. Consequently, the majority of the Khmer were able to maintain their traditional way of life with respect to health. One notable exception was that the Khmer were generally receptive to French "relief" medicines, as these typically resembled indigenous herbal remedies. Surgery, however, was almost universally rejected by the local Khmer.[20]

Following independence in 1953, Western-based medicines were actively promoted through the establishment of medical hospitals, clinics, educational facilities, and pharmaceutical companies. Between 1955 and 1969, for example, the number of hospitals and district clinics rose from 16 to 69, and the number of commune dispensaries increased from 103 to 587. Specifically, in 1959 the French opened l'Hôpital Calmette in Phnom Penh—a state-of-the-art research hospital; this was followed with the opening of the Khmer-Soviet Friendship Hospital (l'Hôpital de l'Amitié Khméro-Soviétique, or "Russian" Hospital) in 1960. Medical training also became more widespread. L'École des Officiers de Santé (a medical school established in 1946) became in 1953 the Royal School of Medicine (l'École Royale de Medicine); this institution later became the Faculty of Medicine. And, last, domestic production of pharmaceuticals began in 1963 with the establishment of the Pharmacie d'Approvision Khmère.[21] In short, by 1975 there was a distinct geography to the two medical systems throughout Cambodia. Most Western-based clinics, hospitals, and educational facilities were concentrated in Phnom Penh, while the vast majority of Cambodia's population continued to rely on indigenous health practices.

The arrival of the Khmer Rouge brought about substantial changes to the practice of health care. However, it is erroneous to assert that the practice of medicine was completely eliminated by the Khmer Rouge. The Khmer Rouge did appear to view the medical profession as an instrument of the bourgeois ruling class. And similar to the elimination of former soldiers and government officials, the Khmer Rouge purged many of these men and women. Consequently, doctors, nurses, and others who were educated in Western-style medicine were killed. According to some estimates, by 1979 fewer than fifty medical doctors who had practiced medicine before 1975 remained alive. However, the CPK also recruited and trained its own medical personal.[22] Thus, young girls—mostly between twelve and fifteen years of age—were recruited from the "base" people living in the provinces. In addition, many other girls actively left home and volunteered to train as nurses or other medical personnel.[23]

According to Sokhym Em, the revolution was "obliged to abolish all hospitals and their staff left by previous regimes with a view to establishing hospitals of a new style with a socialist character—revolutionary pureness and cleanliness." Here we see what appears to be an effort to maintain a purified society, untainted by Western influence. However, this practice is also consistent with Lenin's argument in *State and Revolution* that jobs are largely *exchangeable* under capitalism. Lenin explains, "Capitalist culture has created large-scale production, factories, railways, the postal service, telephones, etc., and on this basis the great majority of functions of the old 'state power' have become so simplified and can be reduced to such simple operations of registration, filing and checking that they can be easily performed by every literate person."[24] On the assumption that members of the CPK internalized this argument, this provides a plausible explanation as to why the Khmer Rouge believed that anyone, regardless of training, could work as a doctor, nurse, or other profession. It is noteworthy that documents related to the expansion of health care are conspicuously silent on the topic of skills acquisition.[25] Apart from reference to training provided by the Chinese, the CPK considered formal educational systems to be bourgeois; learning was to be experiential.[26] Thus, the

CPK determined that "technical studies emerge from work and practice. Practice in turn teaches us technology." By way of comparison, this report explains that "people who pilot our helicopters can't read a great deal. But by cultivating good political consciousness, we all can learn swiftly and we can exceed the plan's requirements. Formerly to be a pilot required a high school education—twelve to fourteen years. Nowadays, it's clear that political consciousness is the decisive factor."[27]

To become a filing clerk, helicopter pilot, nurse, or doctor: for the CPK, training was the same; a proper political consciousness, combined with revolutionary will and hands-on experience, was all that was required. The tasks were simple; it was simply a matter of correct attitude. Accordingly, medical training was hurried and rudimentary. Their training lasting at most a matter of weeks, "nurses" were taught how to give injections and administer pills and other medicines. Because most of the trainees could not read, they were instructed how to "recognize" the words printed on the bottles.[28] These medical personnel were known as *pet padevat*, or "revolutionary medics."[29]

Traditional but also Western medicines and pharmaceuticals were available throughout Democratic Kampuchea. This statement stands in stark contrast to the Standard Total View that generally posits the complete absence of such commodities. David Chandler, for example, writes that the Khmer Rouge rejected Western-style medicine and refused to import medicine.[30] This is not correct. Indeed, copious documents testify to the importation of medicines and other supplies from China, Thailand, South Korea, and other countries during the Khmer Rouge regime.[31] These documents, moreover, indicate that Western medicines, in particular, were warehoused both in Phnom Penh and in zone-level warehouses.[32] To highlight but one example, in December 1976 a shipment arrived from China that contained nine tons of penicillin; four tons of nivaquine, quinine, and chloroquine; and one ton of vitamins. Moreover, the Khmer Rouge accepted "gifts" from abroad, such as US$12,000 worth of antimalarial drugs delivered in 1976 by the American Friends Service Committee, with Washington's approval, via China.

The Khmer Rouge also established a series of factories to "produce" their own medicines and pharmaceuticals.[33] At least four pharmaceutical factories are known to have been in operation in Phnom Penh, designated as "P1," "P3," "P4," and "P6." The factory known as "P1" produced traditional medicines, while the other three produced penicillin, serum, setropharine, and vitamins B1, B6, and B12.[34] The efficacy of these medicines and pharmaceuticals was, not surprisingly, of dubious quality. One type of medicine produced was based on indigenous practices, and, indeed, local *kru* were recruited to oversee production. These medicines were used to "cure" fever, headache, stomachaches, and fainting. Chinese advisers often provided guidance in the manufacture of indigenous medicines. Raw materials included plant roots, tree bark, sap, and other "natural" compounds. Young girls would mix these materials together and shape them into small "pills," which became widely known as "rabbit-dropping medicine" because of its appearance—and effectiveness.[35]

A hierarchical system of hospitals, clinics, and other health facilities was established throughout Democratic Kampuchea. At this point, unlike the detailed understandings of the Nazi medical program, the precise coordinates and arrangement of the Khmer system remain poorly understood. It is known, for example, that the two principal hospitals in Phnom Penh—although initially evacuated and ransacked—were later put into operation: the Russian Hospital (renamed the 17 April Hospital) and the Calmette Hospital. Outside of the capital city, provincial hospitals existed; these generally had a few fully trained doctors, some Chinese advisers, and "decent" medicinal supplies. Conditions deteriorated as one proceeded down the hierarchy. At the district level, health clinics were rarely staffed by trained medicinal practitioners, and medicines consisted mostly of domestically produced pharmaceuticals—the "rabbit-dropping medicine." The lowest level consisted of *munti pet* (infirmaries or small clinics). In typical fashion, the Khmer Rouge simply appropriated suitable buildings, such as *wats* and other religious sites, to serve as infirmaries.[36] These would be staffed by *pet padevat* and were poorly supplied at best.

The Khmer Rouge did also permit the practice of indigenous healers—the *kru khmae*. However, the ability of the *kru* to conduct their services was severely limited. While allowing the *kru khmae* to distribute traditional medicines, the Khmer Rouge forbade them from performing the spiritual component of health care; likewise, *kru* were not allowed to use mantras or offerings, and the family's role in health care was prohibited.[37]

Both traditional and Western-based medicinal practices were thus available within Democratic Kampuchea. The crucial point, as Jan Ovesen and Ing-Britt Trankell correctly note, is that proper hospitals, adequately trained doctors and nurses, and effective pharmaceuticals were not for everyone.[38] During its reign, the Khmer Rouge constructed—and normalized—many different populations that were subjected to differential treatment: a calculated management of life through the provision of health care. Some populations were ethnically defined. The Khmer Rouge, for example, targeted all persons who were perceived as racially distinct, including the Viet-Khmer, the Sino-Khmer, and the Muslim Cham. Other marginalized populations were based on previous occupation (for example, soldiers and officials of the previous government). Most prevalent, of course, was the political distinction between "new" and "base" people.

Both the Calmette and the Russian Hospitals were reserved primarily for the highest Khmer Rouge leadership—the *Angkar loeu*.[39] In the Russian Hospital, for example, CPK leaders would stay in private rooms with attached bathrooms, they would be assisted by personal servants and received choice (and adequate) food, and they were treated with imported medicines administered by Chinese doctors.[40] And while conditions were decidedly worse at the provincial- and district-level facilities, none compared with the malpractice of medicine found at the *munti pet*. Here, the *pet padevat* both learned and practiced health care—often with tragic results.

Young girls, barely into their teens, were largely responsible for diagnosis and treatment at the *munti pet*. Beyond certain obvious symptoms of ailment or illness—fevers, body aches, diarrhea, and open wounds—these medics could do nothing. They administered rabbit-dropping medicines (when available); they gave injections of any liquids available—coconut milk, chicken soup. Predictably, the administration of improper medicines caused many patients to suffer adverse reactions or die.[41] But this too was consistent with CPK policy. As Pol Pot explained in a 1978 interview, "We have to establish a research team to do research and conduct experiments on traditional drugs. Even though we do not have proper formulas, we can still produce them. We are practicing self-reliance in medicine."[42]

Productive Life under the Khmer Rouge

Is it possible to square the CPK's system of health care (an element of the superstructure) with the CPK's system of production for exchange? I maintain that it is. Moreover, this understanding is crucial for our reconstruction of Democratic Kampuchea and also for our determination of the political philosophy of the CPK.

Given that "the commodity form reifies and objectifies social relations by subsuming them to a commodity-economic logic," it follows that the accumulation of wealth for its own sake will be determinate of a particular market logic.[43] This logic, I maintain, is characterized by a value system predicated on *indifference*. In other words, rather than focusing on "difference" as the basis of societal inequalities, it is necessary to engage in the capitalist logic of indifference.

It matters little if the capitalist produces rice or timber or textiles; whichever offers the best opportunity for capital accumulation will, in principle, be produced. Marx refers to this tendency as "indifference to use value." Faced with a seemingly indifferent choice, how then are decisions made? Within capitalism, all else being equal, the choice is actually straightforward. Capitalists *prefer* to produce those commodities that will generate profits. Marx explains that "capital withdraws from a sphere with a low rate of profit and wends its way to others that yield higher profit." If it becomes too costly (because, say, of declining profits) to produce one commodity, the capitalist may attempt to produce something else entirely. Albritton concludes that exchange value must always be connected to a use value wanted by someone, but value as capital strives to be indifferent to use value in the sense that it would always prefer to focus single-mindedly on maximizing quantity in the form of profit. In order to behave according to the imperatives of capitalist rationality (that is, market logics), capital must always be opportunistic (that is, indifferent to use values).[44]

What is most important in this "trade-off" of products is that the concept "indifference to use value" contains within it its own inner contradictions, namely, a unity of opposites between "indifference" and "preference." Restated, systemic to the concept "indifference" is the concept "preference." Thus, while capitalists may be indifferent to any particular commodity produced, producers under a system of production for exchange will prefer to produce those commodities that have the greatest possibility of realizing surplus value. Consequently, as societies, including that of Democratic Kampuchea, become ever more subsumed to the market logics of commodity exchange, societal values exhibit a general preference toward those practices that generate surplus value; a commodified society therefore is one that expresses the dominant value of *indifference* and a corresponding *preference* based on those elements that are deemed most valuable. Production under commodity exchange is first and foremost a profit-driven activity; it is not needs based. This "hidden" objective has profound implications, for given that "the commodity form reifies and objectifies social relations by subsuming them to a commodity-economic logic," it follows that the accumulation of capital will be determinate of a particular market logic.[45] This logic, I maintain, is characterized by a value system predicated on *indifference*.

As societies become ever more subsumed to the market logics of production for exchange, societal values exhibit a general preference toward those practices that generate surplus value. Work, for the CPK, was viewed dialectically. The CPK presumed that (correct) political consciousness emanated from (correct) economic tasks. As stated in a 1976 report, "Our students aren't merely students. They are productive workers [that] come to study subjects to serve production so that they can work together."[46] By extension, those workers with proper consciousness would better serve the revolution and the state through improved work habits. This was translated into idolatry of productive workers and, by extension, an indifference to those deemed nonproductive. In short, those *productive* workers who were capable of tending fields, digging irrigation canals, or transporting rice were preferred over any other activity that was deemed nonproductive. This, more than social, political, or ethnic status, was the crucial distinction made in the treatment of people in Democratic Kampuchea.

Considerable misunderstandings are found vis-à-vis Marx's discussion of "productive" and "nonproductive" work; this is important because it reveals a key theoretical error on behalf of the CPK. For many readers, Marx supposedly downplays the role of those activities that take place outside the formal production process; that work performed in other (non-wage) venues, such as household work, is nonproductive (or, alternatively, unproductive). This is not what Marx is saying, although I suggest that this is what the CPK understood. Instead, Marx is letting readers know that if we consider production only from the point of view of the capitalist, we see that only certain types of labor (that is, employment or work) are productive, that only those activities that generate exchange value are themselves valuable. This of course is not Marx's position; it is the position, he writes, of the capitalist. Such a misunderstanding has a tremendous bearing both on general critiques of Marx and, more specifically, on the incorporation of Marxist theory into CPK policy and practice.

Given this apparent *contradiction*, it is worthwhile to reconsider the broadest objectives of the CPK's communist revolution: to build socialism and to defend the country. This is an oft-repeated phrase that contains its own internal contradiction, namely, a disconnect between productive and nonproductive labor. I maintain that the CPK attempted to resolve this contradiction—of the necessity of supporting soldiers and other non-productive workers who were nevertheless vital for the security and maintenance of society—dialectically. For the CPK, all soldiers were to work as farmers, and all farmers were to serve as soldiers. A common saying, for example, held: "With a rifle in one hand, we will remain vigilant to fulfill the task of defending the country, the Revolutionary Angkar and the people; with the other hand we will fulfill the task of building the country." Likewise, the Four-Year Plan explains, "We fight in the field of agriculture because we have agricultural resources. We'll move to other fields when the agricultural battle is finished."[47] The militaristic metaphors are obvious and have been well discussed.[48] Rice fields were viewed as battlefields; farmers were soldiers marching to do battle with nature. However, we should not lose sight of the fact that the CPK forwarded a unity of opposites, a dialectic synthesis of productive and nonproductive workers as embodied by the soldier-farmer.

Through an engagement of productive and nonproductive labor, it is possible to view the mass violence unleashed by the CPK as being deadly ironic. The specific policies imposed—displacement and dispossession, imposed food rations, and self-sufficiency in medical care—were done so in an attempt to *make life*. Accordingly, the deaths from exposure, starvation, and disease were not unintended side effects of poor research, poor planning, or poor implementation, but rather the necessary consequence of the CPK's distinct imperative to increase surplus capital and, by extension, a pervasive indifference to life individually. Hence, "The goal of our collectivism," a CPK report explains, "is to raise the living standards of the people quickly and rapidly. . . . But an important point which must be discussed in a systematic way is whether we are to improve the people's living standards in the direction of individualism or in the direction of collectivism." The report concludes that "our plan is to raise the living standards of the people quickly, in the direction of collectivism."[49] As detailed in chapter 4, this implied a focus on creating those conditions that reduced socially necessary labor time as opposed to promoting conditions that improved individual lives. Life under the Khmer Rouge was valued on a preference for one's capacity to labor and, consequently, to generate value at the level of the collective. This is seen, for example, in numerous slogans forwarded by the Khmer Rouge: "Angkar only favors those who are indefatigable"; "The slothful are spineless, the sluggish are lazy"; and "We absolutely must remove the lazy; it is useless to keep them, else they will cause trouble. We have to send them to hell." As such, the reorganized space economy, and the draconian security apparatus, subjugated life to the threat of death, an expression of what Mbembe terms *necropower*: "the generalized instrumentalization of human existence and the material destruction of human bodies and populations."[50] The CPK implemented these policies not out of insanity or impulsive cruelty, but because such policies were *rational* to the imperatives of a system of production for exchange.[51]

Disallowing Life under the Khmer Rouge

To make the claim that the CPK disallowed life through an attempt to make life challenges the traditional dichotomy of direct and structural violence. It also brings into question the moral partition between "killing" and "letting die." For many bioethicists and philosophers, the act of killing is considered morally worse than letting die. Such a presumption hinges on our understanding of agency: to "kill" is considered an action, whereas "letting die" is perceived as an omission, or lack of action. This moral partition, likewise, is premised on a distinction between "negative" and "positive" duties. And while these differ by culture, in general we can identify the existence of duties not to harm others, which require restraint; these are termed negative duties. We also have positive duties, whereupon we have duties (some might say obligations) to help others.

The dichotomy between "positive" and "negative" duties, as well as between "killing" and "letting die," significantly informs international law and, specifically, the prospect of prosecuting individuals for human-rights abuses. Simply put, international tribunals and war-crime trials focus attention on forms of *direct* violence (that is, extrajudicial executions, war rape, and torture); these are actions for which an "individual" may be found guilty and where the intent was specifically to harm others. The failure to provide positive duties, such as the provision of adequate medical care or even food, is generally not viewed (legally) as a crime against humanity; this holds even if those "inactions" lead to the death of hundreds of thousands of people.

According to Will Cartwright, a plausible account of the difference between "killing" and "letting die" may be that one kills someone if one initiates a causal sequence that ends in one's death, whereas one lets another die if one allows an already existing causal sequence to culminate in that person's death.[52] In effect, Cartwright is addressing the broader context, or conditions, that may result in death. From this perspective, however, states (should) have a moral and legal responsibility for the creation of conditions that lead to starvation, malnutrition, or exposure to pollutants.

Within the context of the Cambodian genocide, we may, on the one hand, argue that those social and environmental conditions that led to famine, disease, exhaustion, and exposure to the elements were the direct result of specific practices undertaken by the Khmer Rouge. The collectivization of agriculture, the extreme rationing of foods, the mandatory dawn-to-dusk work hours: these were the conditions that made death possible. However, on the other hand, we must also recognize that these policies did *not* materialize out of thin air. Rather, these were draconian actions put forward by the CPK as part of a postconflict reconstruction program. The Khmer Rouge inherited a country mired in poverty and misery. Years of armed conflict and indiscriminate bombing coupled with unequal trade relations, corrupt and inefficient institutions, and a traumatized population would prove daunting problems for any government. This is not to deny culpability on the part of the CPK; their policies certainly augmented the grave conditions facing Cambodia's populace. However, unlike the Standard Total View that renders all deaths to those actions and inactions that took place between 1975 and 1979, an equal responsibility lies elsewhere, notably those policies put forward by the United States and China.

An argument predicated on conditionality—that of structural violence—is necessary but insufficient. Indeed, a defendant of the Khmer Rouge *might* argue that the deaths resultant from these conditions were unfortunate but unintended. Instead, those practices—the collectivization of agriculture, the establishment of labor camps—were enacted *to foster life.* Consider, for example, the CPK's Four-Year Plan for 1977–80, developed between July 21 and August 2, 1976. Although never published, and apparently not widely implemented, the document provides insight into the key policies and practices envisioned by the Standing Committee of the CPK. Thus, a stated objective of the CPK was to "produce rice for food to raise the standard of living of the people" and "to obtain capital" for the purchase of imports.[53] However, according to the document, the CPK recognized several immediate limitations, such as the lack of existing infrastructure to facilitate increased rice production. These *structural* limitations were used to justify the establishment of labor camps— to build needed canals, reservoirs, and irrigation pumps—and to initiate food quotas.

However, lurking beneath a focus on unequal structures is a more difficult question: What role does "intentionality" play in structural violence? For Johan Galtung, direct violence occurs when there is an *identifiable* actor who commits an act of violence. Structural violence, conversely, occurs when no such actor is identifiable. Galtung elaborates that "whereas in the first case [direct violence] these consequences can be traced back to concrete persons or actors, in the second case this is *no longer meaningful*. There may not be any person who directly harms another person in the structure. The violence is built into the structure and shows up as unequal power and consequently unequal life chances."[54]

Galtung's conceptualization of structural violence has been influential but, as a whole, remains knotty. Indeed, Akhil Gupta allows that structural violence, conceptually, is both necessary and problematic. In part, this consternation arises from Galtung's original focus on outcomes rather than processes. Gupta elaborates that for Galtung, violence was present when outcomes (or conditions of living) were unequal. Thus, structural violence is found when groups of people are denied access to food, water, and shelter; structural violence is also found whenever groups of people are excluded from particular forms of recognition and representation, including but not limited to citizenship rights, rights before the law, and rights to education.[55]

Within the context of the structures of violence, therefore, intentionality remains a slippery concept for two reasons. First, to argue, morally, that a failure to act is intentional, one must satisfy three conditions: ability, opportunity, and awareness. In Democratic Kampuchea, the CPK leadership had the ability to save lives—to prevent deaths. This is evidenced, for example, by the reestablishment of hospitals, by the presence of Western-based medicines, and by the presence of skilled doctors from China. However, the CPK leadership refrained from providing *equal* access to these services. In a starkly calculated management of life, the Khmer Rouge determined who was allowed to live and whose lives were disallowed to the point of death. The hierarchical construction of populations by the CPK established the conditions whereby top-ranking Khmer Rouge leaders (often) had access to lifesaving techniques and practices, rank-and-file members ("base" people) had less access, and those classified as "new" people, or "April 17" people, had access, at best, to inferior medicines and medical treatment. And in an ironic twist, the sick and the injured were often viewed as the *least deserving* of medical care. Henri Locard discusses how the Khmer Rouge viewed the "sick" and the "disabled" as impediments to the revolution, to the state. According to Locard, "The

10. Ieng Thirith (*in center of photograph wearing glasses*) visiting a forced-labor camp. Courtesy of the Documentation Center of Cambodia Archives.

sick could not be anything other than malingerers, because they could or would not work, and therefore, were sabotaging the revolution." The following slogans capture these sentiments: "The sick are victims of their own imagination" and "We must wipe out those who imagine they are ill, and expel them from society!" Locard explains that all Cambodians "heard these rebukes shouted at them with violence and unusual harshness every time they had a fever or fell ill."[56] In short, for the vast majority of the people of Democratic Kampuchea, by denying access to available medicines and medical techniques, the CPK leadership disallowed life to the point of death. The life that was disallowed was fundamentally life conceived as unproductive.

Here again we must consider the opportunity to intervene by those governments outside of Cambodia. Despite the tired cries of "never again," the international community has an undistinguished track record when it comes to humanitarian aid in light of ongoing genocides. Between 1975 and 1979, American officials were aware of the deplorable conditions in place in Democratic Kampuchea; these officials were aware of the famine—brought about, in part, by their own bombing campaign; they were aware also of reports of widespread executions. Yet for Cold War geopolitics, American officials elected to *support* the Khmer Rouge, in a vain hope that they would function as a counterbalance to a communist Vietnam. For example, from 1977 through 1980, President Jimmy Carter and his national security adviser, Zbigniew Brzezinski, supported the Khmer Rouge either directly or, through the Chinese, indirectly. This support, moreover, was not based on ignorance of Khmer Rouge atrocities; indeed, according to Kenton Clymer, officials both within and apart from the Carter administration were well aware of the vicious nature of the Khmer Rouge. Representative Stephan Solarz (D-NY) went on record stating that what was happening in Cambodia was "one of the most monstrous crimes in the history of the human race," while both Richard Holbrooke, assistant secretary of state for East Asian and Pacific affairs, and Charles Twining, Foreign Service officer, testified about the flagrant human-rights violations that were occurring in Democratic Kampuchea, including the systemic execution of tens or even hundreds of thousands of Cambodians.[57] Moreover, in 1977 the US Embassy based in Thailand clarified the horrific conditions throughout Democratic Kampuchea. According to this telegram—declassified only in 2009—US intelligence officers were well aware of various resistance movements currently under way to overthrow the Khmer Rouge. These resistance fighters, however, were "desperately short of funds, medicines, and ammunition." Indeed, so dire was the situation that "without foreign support," they were "struggling more for their own survival than actively resisting Khmer Rouge rule in Cambodia." Moreover, according to the telegram, resistance leaders "described rising [death] tolls from disease, malnutrition and famine" and that "the population of Cambodia may have been reduced by more than half."[58] Consequently, we must also, contra the Standard Total View, reconcile two million deaths with a grave inaction on behalf of the international community to intervene when given the opportunity.[59]

A second condition rests on the idea of opportunity: Is it logically possible that a person has the opportunity to prevent death? Take an obvious geographic example. A doctor living in Los Angeles may have the ability—the skills—to save the life of a person suffering a heart attack in New York but not, because of the spatial separation, have an opportunity to do so. Within Democratic Kampuchea, as the work conducted by Sokhym Em, Laura Vilim, Jan Ovesen, and Ing-Britt Trankell, among others, has documented, the CPK leaders had the opportunity to provide better medical care. Furthermore, these leaders had the opportunity to rethink and thus improve the deplorable working and living conditions discussed above. That they failed to do so was not so much an attempt to purify society as it was a trade-off between the provision of health care and the generation of surplus value. By extension, members of the international community had the opportunity to intervene, but again Cold War politics prohibited any direct action that might have saved lives.

Awareness constitutes the final condition: Did the CPK leadership—or, of course, members of the international community—know of the conditions? Were they aware that their policies and practices were resulting in widespread morbidity and mortality? I contend that CPK policies must be recognized and understood as *rational administrative decisions calculated and executed with full knowledge and awareness of the consequences.* Moreover, officials in China, the United States, and even Thailand were very much aware of conditions in Democratic Kampuchea. With respect to the first, to suggest otherwise is to argue either that the CPK did not maintain complete administrative oversight over agriculture or that the CPK was unaware of the fatal conditions that resulted from these policies. Here, the extensive records of rice production, the geographically specific decisions made for each district and subdistrict, and the system of weekly reports from all rice-producing areas argue convincingly for a government in complete control. Furthermore, DeFalco finds that the evidence "strongly suggests that the upper echelons of the CPK government expropriated and exported mass quantities of rice throughout the DK period with clear knowledge that this rice was coming at the expense of civilians." In a speech delivered on April 17, 1978, marking the third anniversary of the Khmer Rouge victory, Khieu Samphan, president of the Presidium of the

State of Democratic Kampuchea, announced that the CPK "decided to export more rice than the previous year so that [Democratic Kampuchea] can accumulate more capital for national construction." Likewise, documentary evidence reveals that top members of the CPK were aware of these conditions yet pursued different courses of action. In meeting minutes from March 8, 1976, cadre acknowledged "the problems of many sick people in the work sites, a loss of 40 percent of the labor force," yet concluded that "expenditures for material purchases to solve the livelihood of the people are limited because we must purchase many other things as well." In the end, the committee reiterated the two-can-per-day food ration.[60] The solution to the problem was greater "revolutionary zeal" among the workers, and those cadre not meeting expectations were, by the CPK's definition, traitors to both the state and the revolution.[61]

With respect to the international community, we have seen how officials in the United States, as one example, were aware of the deplorable conditions in Democratic Kampuchea. However, these circumstances were either ignored or recast to support larger Cold War politics. Moreover, American officials were aware of the devastation caused by their armed interventions from 1965 onward, of the destruction this caused to the country's economy—to say nothing of the deaths and injuries that resulted directly from these actions. To ignore these actions and inactions is to reproduce a certain form of the Standard Total View. To account for the deaths resultant from exhaustion, disease, and famine without adequate engagement with the role of US bombing or postwar complicity of the Khmer Rouge is both inaccurate and inadequate. The men, women, and children of Cambodia suffered greatly at the hands of the CPK. These deaths resulted from an entrenched indifference to life itself. Sadly, these deaths can and should also be attributable to an indifference exhibited by the international community.

Conclusion

In Democratic Kampuchea, all life was precarious; this does not equate with the presupposition, however, that all were reduced to a homogenous bare life. We know, for example, that the Khmer Rouge sought to implement (and brutally enforce) a total subjugation of body and mind; concrete individualism was reduced to an abstract collectivism. Societal members were to lead simple productive lives based on "equality" and "self-sacrifice." People's actions were no longer based on individual profit or self-fulfillment; instead, a selfless dedication to the collective health of the party was promoted. In the process, classes were to be eliminated. In practice, however, the Khmer Rouge unwittingly replaced old social divisions with new ones. Pointedly, the differences between "base" and "new" people were masked—fetishized—by superficial practices of equality. Of course, the Khmer Rouge compelled all people to dress alike; men and women were to wear black peasant clothes; hairstyles likewise were regimented.[62] Of more significance is that these concrete practices marked a transformation from qualitative differences, differences that were internally related to the revolution itself, into a quantitative sameness. Laborers were to serve the party and, by extension, the revolution. It was the *capacity* to labor—not the laborer—that was of importance. Life-or-death decisions hinged on whether any given body was perceived as having "use value": the ability to produce for the party. Indeed, it was this preference that accounted for the apparent indifference of the Khmer Rouge toward sickness, health, and life itself.

Beyond this, however, the massive loss of life in Cambodia was accompanied by an indifference exhibited by the international community: an indifference to the plight of Cambodians by the Vietnamese during the revolution, by the United States in its illegal and indiscriminate bombing between 1965 and 1973, and by both China and the United States in their covert support of the Khmer Rouge between 1975 and 1979. The CPK should not be absolved of creating those conditions that led directly to upwards of two million deaths; neither should the rest of the world.

6

Abolishment and Reproduction

Did the Communist Party of Kampuchea implement specific policies to destroy the traditional family structure of Cambodia? This, as Kalyanee Mam asks, remains a central question and one that has tremendous bearing on our examination of the social organization of production in Democratic Kampuchea. Prior to the Khmer Rouge coming to power, the extended family was the center of economic and cultural life, as families worked together as a unit, responsible for both household production and consumption.[1] Marriages were arranged—but importantly, this signified a more inclusive union of more than just the bride and the groom: marriages constituted the coming together of families. It was customary for mothers and elder women in the village to play key roles in arranging marriages; it was common also that an elderly religious man (*achar*) be consulted to determine both the compatibility of the potential couple as well as the timing of the wedding.

Within Khmer society, matrilocal marital residence was customary. Young married couples would frequently stay with or near the bride's mother; the groom—often from a neighboring village—would continue to work his family's land as well as his wife's land. Spatially, this arrangement served both social and economic functions. On the one hand, the newly married couple would be able to provide for the woman's parents in their old age. The grandparents could also help raise the children. On the other hand, this arrangement helped in the provision of labor.[2]

The nuclear family, despite the proximity of extended family members, was typically the basic unit of economic production and consumption in Khmer society. Husbands were often viewed as retaining authority over wives and children, although women were not without their own rights and privileges. Both women and men, for example, could inherit land and hold title, and both women and men contributed to agricultural and other income-generating activities. Gendered divisions of labor were (and remain) apparent, however, as men would typically plow the fields, transport goods, and maintain localized irrigation schemes, while women would prepare seed rice, sow and transplant seedlings, and harvest the crops. Women were also responsible primarily for the cultivation of vegetable gardens and the raising of livestock.[3]

Gender relationships, traditional or otherwise, in Cambodia should not be considered as fixed systems.[4] Indeed, a diversity of social relationships and experiences is reflected throughout the country. Religious differences, notably between the Buddhist Khmer and the Muslim Cham, account for much of the variation; so too do geographical and historical factors enter into the equation. Attitudes and expectations toward gender, for example, are manifested differently in urban areas than in the countryside; likewise, those areas influenced more or less by French colonial practices exhibit differences with respect to proper behavior.[5]

Under the Khmer Rouge, traditional family life was altered, although scholars disagree over both the scale and the scope of transformation and, given the type of change, the underlying motivation. Ratana Huy, for example, contends that the CPK instilled a revolutionary ideology and "showed disapproval for the conventional marriage, regarding it as imperialist, feudalist, and capitalist." May Ebihara agrees, affirming that "in its attempt to control various aspects of life and to transfer authority and loyalty from local foci to the central state, Democratic Kampuchea undermined the solidarity of what was perhaps the most important grass-roots social unit: the family." Also in agreement are Patrick Heuveline and Bunnak Poch, who state that the Khmer Rouge's "attempt to radically transform Cambodian society included a frontal attack on the family, which it saw as the core institution of social reproduction."[6]

Arguably, the practice of "forced marriages" has been held as prima facie evidence of the CPK's attempt to radically disrupt traditional family life. And under the Khmer Rouge, marriages were indeed arranged, and such arrangements were generally made in consideration of class position. Thus, "base" people were permitted only to marry other "base" people, "new" people permitted only to marry "new" people. According to Huy, "Marriages were arranged between members of the same social class because new couples were thought to have the same level of class anger."[7] It is also accurate that many couples "met" their partner only on the day of the wedding and that weddings were frequently conducted en masse.[8] Finally, many survivors testify that following their arranged marriages, they were quickly separated (possibly after one or two nights to "procreate") and returned to their work teams.

Do these practices support the argument that the CPK sought explicitly to destroy traditional family life and, if so, provide any indication as to the motivation for such an attempt? Michael Vickery challenges these conclusions, noting, "One theme of early anti-DK propaganda was 'destruction of the family,' and it is still an integral part of the [Standard Total View]." According to Vickery, CPK policy toward the family was by and large neutral, although some evidence suggests that a primary goal was an increase in population. He elaborates that "since sexual relations outside marriage were prohibited by one of the strictest regulations of all, it is obvious that policy was to encourage the formation and maintenance of at least nuclear family units of husband, wife, and children." Neha Jain supports this conclusion, explaining that the "Khmer Rouge vision of marriage had less to do with forging an emotional bond between the couple; rather, it was intended as a method of obtaining control over people's sexuality and ensuring more workers for the revolution."[9] Certainly, the apparent pronatal practice of allowing newly married couples the opportunity to procreate prior to returning to age- and sex-segregated labor camps provides some support to this argument.

The so-called practice of forced marriages has also been called into question. Peg LeVine cautions that "it is not helpful when the phrase 'forced marriages' is a throwaway line." For LeVine, "public assumptions about the Khmer Rouge weddings as *uniformly forced* have been unyielding." Her scholarship and also that conducted through the Documentation Center of Cambodia provide evidence that CPK attitudes and policy toward the family are decidedly more complex. Huy finds that Khmer Rouge cadre—usually of good standing—and base people were given the right to reject a marriage when they were not satisfied and the right to

11. A Khmer Rouge wedding. Courtesy of the Documentation Center of Cambodia Archives.

propose to Angkar to marry someone. For example, Kou Siem, a former Khmer Rouge cadre, asked and received permission to marry another Khmer Rouge cadre. Phann Chanta, also a former Khmer Rouge cadre, explains that she rejected Angkar's proposal to marry at least twice before agreeing to wed another cadre.[10]

These findings, albeit anecdotally, indicate that the CPK did not unambiguously or uniformly attempt to destroy traditional family structures. Rather, marriage and hence family formation and experience were class defined; in other words, the institution of the family was dialectically related to the overall social organization of production initiated by the CPK. Khmer Rouge cadre and other persons considered loyal and trustworthy were allowed relatively greater freedoms in both their decisions regarding marriage partners and the ability to continue to live as a "nuclear" family; those on the other end of the political spectrum, the "new" people, had minimal choice at best.

If, following LeVine, we conclude that it was *not* CPK policy to "break down 'all' social order," how are we to proceed? I maintain that any examination of a so-called communist organization must employ a Marxist critique. Consequently, it is appropriate to approach the Khmer Rouge "family" not in isolation, but rather as part of a totality of the overall mode of production. To this end, Marx declares that "every social process of production is at the same time a process of reproduction."[11] In other words, no production is possible unless it ensures reproduction of the material conditions of production.[12] However, as Friedrich Engels elaborates, "The determining factor in history is, in the last resort, the production and reproduction of immediate life. But this . . . is of a twofold character. On the one hand, the production of the means of subsistence, of food, clothing and shelter and the tools requisite therefore; on the other, the production of human beings themselves, the propagation of the species." This in turn calls into question the role of "the family" and, more specifically, the social relations between men and women. As Heather Brown explains, "Men and women always exist and interact within concrete circumstances mediated by definite social relations."[13] To articulate the "family" as conceived and transformed by the CPK, a theoretical and empirical examination of social reproduction as a political economic practice is therefore required.

From chapter 4 we understand that the exchange value of a commodity is determined in part by the quantity of labor socially necessary for its production. Logic dictates, therefore, that greater profits are accrued by reductions in socially necessary labor time. As Ernest Mandel explains, "This is the basis for all Marxist economic theory in general"—but it was the basis of Marx's critique of capitalism.[14] In an ironic twist, the Marxist economic principles adopted by the CPK were those that Marx chastised. Indeed, we readily see that the fundamental divergence between Marxist political philosophy and CPK practice is *surplus appropriation without compensation*.

Within capitalism, the owner of the means of production purchases the labor power of the worker; this is masked by the supposedly free exchange of work for wages. However, throughout the production process, the owner appropriates the entire product of that worker. Thus, following Marx, "the very necessity of first transforming individual products or activities into exchange value, into money, so that they obtain and demonstrate their social power in this objective form, proves two things: (1) that individuals now produce only for society and in society; (2) that production is not directly social, is not 'the offspring of association,' which distributes labor internally. Individuals are subsumed under social production; social production exists outside them as their fate; but social production is not subsumed under individuals, manageable by them as their common wealth."[15] At this point, we readily see that the Khmer Rouge did not "purchase" labor power as we understand this process in the formal, capitalist labor market. We do, however, see that workers were dispossessed by extraeconomic means—literally at the barrel of a gun. Only in this manner were workers "free" to participate in the revolution. Workers were expected to work for Angkar and, in return, were compensated by what the CPK promoted as a fair ration. Subsequently, all production (rice especially) was appropriated by an elite ruling class—the CPK. A certain portion was returned, collectively, to the workers in the form of consumption, a proportion was set aside for the following season's planting (constant capital), and a third proportion—the bulk of all products—was exported in exchange for capital. Workers had no decision-making authority over the appropriation and reallocation of their production, nor did the workers have any decision-making power over the distribution of surplus value generated by exchange. All authority was monopolized by the ruling class, which, in this case, was embodied by certain members of the CPK.

Such an economic system has a tremendous bearing on matters of reproduction. Following Marx, reproduction is neither synonymous with nor reducible to biological procreation. Rather, the term refers to myriad interlocking social *relations*, including but not limited to biological reproduction, class reproduction, and modal reproduction.

A Marxist Critique of the Family

Michèle Barrett finds that "the 'family,' in popular ideology and in a vast amount of historical and intellectual work, is posed as self-evidently the same whether we speak of it in feudal, slave or capitalist societies." She continues, "Even to conceptualize '*the* family' is to concede the existence of an institution that, in whatever historical context it is found, is essentially and naturally there."[16] A similar critique could be made of scholarship addressing the Cambodian "family" both before and after 1975.[17] This bears upon subsequent discussions of the family under the Khmer Rouge, for the simple fact that familial relations are malleable; thus, while some institutions remain dominant for long periods of time, all institutions—including that of marriage—are subject to change. Vickery is correct, I believe, in his assertion that the CPK's overall objective was not the "destruction of the family"; I disagree, however, in his suggestion that Khmer Rouge policy was either neutral toward the family or pronatal in orientation.

The influence of selected concepts developed by Marx, Engels, and Lenin—in particular—is apparent in the policies forwarded by the CPK. However, I have challenged any interpretation that the CPK either understood perfectly these concepts or was consistent in their application. There is nothing in the documentary evidence—beyond hubris and hyperbole in the rhetoric of CPK spokespersons—to indicate a "radical" or "extreme" use of concepts loosely cobbled together under the appellation of "Marxism." Is it possible, however, to reconfigure CPK practice in an attempt to define their overall attitude toward the family? I believe so, but first we must dispel any essentialist notion of the "family."

For both Marx and Engels, the family under capitalism was inherently and irrevocably oppressive and exploitative. Viewed accordingly, the family was but a microcosm of capitalism writ large; the family emerged as an institution of the ruling class, one that was predicated on private ownership, wage employment, and the legalities of inheritance. Their argument is based on the observation that dominant economic systems, such as feudalism or merchant capitalism, would be manifest both on the landscape and in the various constitutions of home and family. In precapitalist, agrarian societies, for example, both productive and reproductive[18] work was carried out within the household or family. The rhythms of work were regulated by need, and the amount of labor used in production was equivalent to the amount of labor needed for reproduction. There was, however, no "universal" family; social arrangements reflected local customs and different geographical and historical contexts. The *family*, for example, might include both immediate and extended kin, servants, apprentices, and even slaves. Indeed, as Stuart Aitken explains, the "Latin root of the word 'family' is *famulus*, or servant." Aitken continues that when *family* was first used in English in the fifteenth century, it was derived from *familia*, in reference to the domestic servants who lived and worked in the home. Only rarely was *familia* used for the entire household. It was not until the middle of the seventeenth century that the term narrowed to include only groups of related people.[19]

Depending on the society in question, therefore, the household (or "family") was composed of both kin and nonkin members. There was a customary division of labor, with women largely responsible for reproductive tasks (that is, the processing and preparation of food, housecleaning, gathering firewood, fetching water, tending to the fields) and men mostly engaged in harvesting.[20] There was considerable variation among these relations, however, and they did not always imply a hierarchy in importance. In most precapitalist societies, work arrangements were mostly based on the satisfaction of immediate needs. Under other systems, such as feudalism, families typically produced some goods as commodities or as recompense to their feudal lord.[21]

These socioeconomic relations and practices underwent a significant transformation throughout Europe between the fourteenth and sixteenth centuries, transformations that would significantly impact the structure and meaning of both "home" and "family." Although subject to debate, there is a growing consensus that the transition from feudalism, through merchant capitalism, to industrial capitalism in Europe was the result of a "phase of economic, demographic and political 'crisis' [that] brought about the combination of steady population growth, modest technological improvements and limited amounts of usable land."[22]

Under the evolving system of merchant capitalism, the widespread introduction of money and of wage labor ushered in crucial changes in labor arrangements. Consequently, there emerged a reallocation of work effort between women and men and among family members in household production and reproduction. Three key transformations stand out among all others: the separation of the producers from their means of production and subsistence, the formation of a social class that has a monopoly of the means of production (that is, the capitalist class), and the transformation of human labor power into a commodity. Combined, these changes would have a profound effect on the household as a unit of production and consumption. As productive tasks shifted from the needs of the household to those of the market, the household per se no longer had access to the means of production. Familial needs, including the provision of foodstuffs and (increasingly) clothing, were provided through an exchange of labor power for wages. In turn, work for wages became distinct from work in the household.[23]

There emerged a gradual but notable separation between "work" spaces and "living" spaces, a *spatial* separation that carried with it important *social* dimensions. As Peter Saunders and Peter Williams write, men and women, children and adults, enjoyed different capacities for action and encountered different constraints on their actions within the home and beyond.[24] Women, for example, continued to work in the home, engaged in such activities as child care and food preparation; however, these "jobs" came to be defined as being qualitatively different from *men's work*.[25] Consequently, as Aitken concludes, women's work became invisible and spatially isolated from the public sphere. It was also during this transition that the idea of the "family" underwent an important ideological shift. By the late seventeenth century, according to Aitken, as the control of the means of production moved away from the private sphere, servants were no longer considered part of the family.[26]

In time, the division of family labor began to assume a new spatial dimension, one in which (most) women and children were confined to the domestic sphere, separated physically and ideologically from men's activities in the public sphere.[27] As explained by Mona Domosh and Joni Seager, the development of these "separate" spheres served very particular purposes, among which was the reproduction of capitalism itself.[28] As more and more components of social reproductive tasks, including education, health, and manufacturing (for example, food processing and cloth making), were transferred away from the household, the home became recognized as a separate place in which the labor force could be indoctrinated with the appropriate values and attitudes of discipline and service.[29]

A reconfigured spatiality of everyday life translated into a gendered ideology of *familialism*. As Elizabeth Eviota explains, this ideology centered on "the extension of women's procreative functions to women's responsibility for the home" and included such constructs as feminine nurturance, masculine protection, maternalism, self-sacrifice, and emotional and financial security.[30] Accordingly, the home *under capitalism* became a place of patriarchal control and discipline. First, embedded within capitalism are the control and appropriation of women's labor. Whether as wives or daughters, women's access to the products, benefits, and (at times) income has been decidedly unequal. Women, for example, were increasingly excluded from the better-paying industrial occupations, as men recognized the dangers of competition from female labor.[31] Indeed, as Aitken explains, women in the public sphere were viewed as threats to the newly constituted modern family as well as society as a whole. By the end of the nineteenth century, in fact, the presence of women in the public sphere was increasingly seen as unnatural and even dangerous.[32] A second form of control hinges on women's childbearing abilities. Thus, women are represented as "crucial economic assets who hold the key to future labor power and male heirs." And last, male prerogative extends into the control over women's desires and affections. Social bonding, including the regulation of sexuality and care, plays an important role in gender formation, necessary to discipline unruly desires and behaviors and the role of enforcement. To be sure, as Andrew Sayer and Richard Walker note, women have throughout history been overwhelmingly consigned to child rearing, household upkeep, and family nurturance; however, under capitalism, the cultural artifact of home and work, the private and the public, became particularly acute.[33]

A particular ideology emerged, dialectically related to the dominant mode of production, an ideology that presupposed a *heteropatriarchal* social system. The family was the means by which labor was reproduced; consequently, the family came to be identified almost purely in terms of biological reproduction. Heterosexuality was the unquestioned norm. It was widely understood and promoted that the natural purpose of sexuality was for reproduction and that sexual identity was linked inextricably to the individual's role in the reproductive family.[34] Marriage as an institution was thus predicated on procreation, and the family was to ensure a proper upbringing based on strictly defined gendered and aged roles. The husband-father figure came to be identified as both primary provider and disciplinarian; the wife-mother, consequently, was seen as both subservient and complementary in that she was the fundamental caretaker and spiritual center.[35]

In *The German Ideology*, Marx and Engels conclude that "the production of life, both of one's own in labor and of fresh life in procreation, now appears as a twofold relation: on the one hand as a natural, on the other as a social relation—social in the sense that it denotes the co-operation of several individuals, no matter under what conditions, in what manner and to what end."[36] This would have a profound impact on the development and practice of Marxist political philosophy. On the one hand, the idea of the family as a mutable social form corresponding to a given mode of production was a significant advance over prevailing notions of the family as a natural, fixed entity.[37] On the other hand, it was Marx's tendency to reduce the family to an effect of relations of production such that many Marxists concluded that the family could—and should—be abolished.[38] It is this latter repercussion that warrants further attention.

The social organization of the "family" is conditioned by the general development of society; only certain family structures can occur according to particular modes of production.[39] Under capitalism, Marx and Engels argued, a particular family structure emerged that was characterized by the exploitation and oppression of women. This argument would spark considerable debate, especially among feminists, regarding the intersections of class and gender oppression—a debate that continues to the present day.[40] For my present purposes, I focus on the implications of this argument as developed specifically by Lenin.

Lenin, as we saw in chapter 3, understands the bureaucracy and the standing army as "parasites" on the body of bourgeois society. Consequently, a successful revolution requires not the *replacement* of these institutions but their wholesale destruction. Heretofore, Lenin explains in *The State and Revolution*, "All the revolutions which have occurred up to now have helped to perfect the state machine, whereas it must be smashed, broken."[41] This, we may surmise, seemingly provided justification for the Khmer Rouge to, first, smash those members who occupied positions of the former Lon Nol government and military and, second, to not replicate these institutions (especially the government) but instead to develop their own unique form of government—one that supposedly had no precedent, including China, the Soviet Union, or Vietnam.

It is tempting, but premature, to conclude that the CPK, following Lenin, sought to smash the traditional Khmer family. Khmer Rouge slogans, for example, advised, "Let us all live as one huge new family and think only of the interest of the collective." Similarly, the Khmer Rouge counseled men, women, and children, "Give up all personal belongings: renounce your father, your mother, all your family" and "Renounce immediate family ties, the hearth's pot, and adopt the big pot, the big family, the immense family; have an extremely high revolutionary consciousness!" For scholars such as Elizabeth Becker, these attitudes lend credence to the argument that "nearly all directives of the Khmer Rouge led somehow toward the dissolution of the family." By way of evidence, Becker singles out the abolition of the use of the family name. Party members, for example, devised their own names, usually monosyllabic.[42] Becker also explains that the various class divisions created by the Khmer Rouge (for example, "new" and "base" people, full rights or candidate members) were an attempt to eliminate the family as any meaningful unit of society.[43]

Care should be taken not to confuse correlation with causation. Though such practices may have led to the dissolution of *some* familial arrangements, it does not follow that the imposition of class structures— itself anathema to most Marxist political philosophy!—was designed to abolish the family. Caution is also required for the simple fact that—based on our above discussion—the family was not completely abolished under the Khmer Rouge. Instead, in line with Becker's correct identification of a *class-structured* organization, high-ranking members of society could choose marriage partners, live as nuclear or even extended families, and even continue to own private property in the form of houses. If there was any attempt to dissolve or abolish the family, it was directed predominantly if not exclusively to those occupying the lowest ranks of society.

That being said, the CPK did attempt to *transform* the traditional Khmer family. First, propaganda indicates that the Khmer Rouge were receptive to the arguments forwarded by Marx, Engels, and Lenin (among others) that the oppression of women would be eliminated following a socialist revolution. A Khmer Rouge song entitled "We Are New Revolutionary Women" reads:

> The revolutionary light is glittering like sunrays from all directions throughout the beloved nation. It is really far-out and terrific.
>
> We are women, who used to have no honor and lived meaningless lives. Now we have a chance to see the light and enjoy freedom of movement.
>
> We are equal to men and can become as famous. Angkar upgrades and guides us. Our name is as a fragrance.
>
> We seem to have been reincarnated and comprehend the political context. We have a genuine stance and good morality.
>
> Our ears are able to hear, while our eyes can see things very clear. We are able to listen and read without confusion and also we can observe and carry out brainstorming activities.
>
> We are in loyal solidarity with men in all fields of work. We can be medical practitioners, workers, soldiers, and are absolutely involved in agricultural production.
>
> Our existence is brilliant. We can master all work with the stance of self-mastery. We always take responsibility and practice brave attacks for the sake of the revolution.
>
> We suffer pains in all parts of our body and have constant wrath against contemptible imperialists who had oppressed us for decades. We endured utmost hardship.
>
> There can be no comparison between the weight and size of the Himalayan Mountains and the revolution's virtue in freeing women from suffering.
>
> Thus, we are committed to sacrificing flesh, blood and life for building a new [affluent] society and defending the nation without hesitation.[44]

The song is informative for many reasons. In its totality, it argues that women's oppression is directly associated with imperialism and that Khmer women have endured innumerable hardships for generations. In the aftermath of revolution, however, women are reborn; they are no longer deaf and blind to their oppression. Women, under the guidance of Angkar, are equal to men in all facets of life, most notably, though, in the fields of employment.

The CPK wanted to present their new society as one free from class and gender oppression. As codified in various documents, including the Constitution of Democratic Kampuchea, gender equality was to be the law of the land. Women were active in the revolutionary movement, and women could (in principle) assume prominent political positions.[45] Agricultural collectives were also portrayed as a means of promoting equality and freeing women from oppression. The socialization of household labor, for example, liberated women from "nonproductive" housework, thereby permitting women (as the song indicates) to be in loyal solidarity with men in all fields of work. Indeed, as specified in a 1976 report, "Mothers must not get too entangled with their children; there should be time (for the mothers) to go and work."[46] In this way, the Khmer Rouge actually replicated gendered patterns of oppression so widely critiqued by Marxists, namely, the "opportunity" for women to enter into an exploitative system of production for exchange. Consequently, once "freed" from the demands of housework, women were compelled to labor in the fields and factories of Democratic Kampuchea, subject to the same minimum food rations enjoyed by their male counterparts.

In practice, gender inequalities and sexual violence remained stalwart features of society under the Khmer Rouge. To begin, the Khmer Rouge enforced a strict stance on extramarital affairs—a position diametrically opposed to Marxist-inspired Soviet doctrine, which advocated free love.[47] However, in Democratic Kampuchea, sex outside of marriage was forbidden, as was polygamy. These attitudes, however, must also be placed in their proper historical context. Traditionally, women in Khmer society were expected to be "dutiful daughters," through their help in the household but also through their chaste sexuality.[48] As Judy Ledgerwood explains, this requires that "girls must be virgins when they marry. . . . To lose [this aspect of life] is not just to lose gender identity but to lose Khmer-ness itself." Consequently, "those not living up to these expectations are considered 'broken' (*kouc*): physically because of their loss of virginity, and socially because of their improper behavior."[49] This suggests that CPK policy was not, contra some interpretations, that far out of line with conventional attitudes toward sexuality.

The prohibition against "moral offenses" put forward by the CPK was not enforced as a means of abolishing the family—as some commentators write—for it enshrined the traditional bond between husband and wife as the only permissible relationship under which two people could have sex. Indeed, pregnancy outside of marriage was likewise a moral offense, frequently punishable by death. Rape was also a feature of Khmer Rouge society, despite public and official admonitions against such acts. Both Nakagawa Kasumi and Trudy Jacobsen document that supposed gender-positive declarations forwarded by the CPK in effect placed women in greater danger. Given that rape was punishable by death, those cadre (and especially prison guards) would more likely resort to killing the women following rape rather than risk being accused of their crimes.[50]

The CPK promoted, but did not enact, a society of gendered equality. More pressing, a class-based system was instituted whereby family form and function were determined by one's personal relationship to the overall social organization of production. It is therefore not possible to pigeon-hole CPK policy as a radical or extreme form of any preexisting system. To this end, the rhetoric of the Khmer Rouge matches with reality: they were implementing a society that was in many respects unprecedented. However, we are still left with the question of how the CPK's vision of the family squared with their attempt to reproduce workers, class relations, and the production system as a whole.

Social Reproduction under the Khmer Rouge

Recall the long-standing argument that the CPK attempted to abolish the family. Mam argues that the Khmer Rouge used three methods to separate family members as a means to fracture the family structure: deportation, execution, and the collectivization of work and living.[51] As to the first two methods, there is no documentation of which I am aware that demonstrates the CPK explicitly and deliberately separated families during the various evacuations, deportations, and forced-labor transfers as part of a national policy. That such separation happened is not in dispute, nor is the traumatic experience of physical separation to be discounted in the lives of those who endured these conditions. Likewise, there is no demonstrative evidence that executions were employed as a means of intentionally separating families. Indeed, building on Alexander Hinton's discussion of disproportionate revenge, and the evidence that frequently all family members were executed when, say, the father was "guilty" of crimes, one may actually argue the inverse: because of the continuation of the extended family, execution was a method of destroying families in their entirety, as opposed to fracturing families.

Mam's argument that the collectivization of work and living arrangements as a systematic and deliberate policy aimed at undermining the traditional family structure would, on the surface, appear to carry more weight. However, her conclusion that "these irrational policies prove that collective dining was enforced not because of a lack of food, but because the regime feared that allowing families to produce their own food would encourage family interests and distract loyalty from *Angkar*" is problematic.[52] If these policies were enacted *merely* to redirect loyalty from one's family toward Angkar, then perhaps we might argue that the policies were irrational. However, from a *material* standpoint, the policies acquire a different meaning, for the basic objective of the CPK was simultaneously to "build socialism" and to reproduce the CPK's still-evolving mode of production. The system initiated by the Khmer Rouge was predicated on adequate supplies of labor, the maintenance of the separation of workers from alternative means of subsistence, and the continued accumulation of surplus value. If, on the whole, sufficient numbers of workers were able to obtain an adequate means of subsistence beyond that provided by the ruling party, the system would fail. Loyalty was demanded of workers not to assuage fragile egos among the ranking echelon; rather, loyalty was necessary to wage permanent revolution and to reproduce an embryonic economic structure based on a system of production for exchange.

The processes of reproduction and production must be understood as dialectic instead of dichotomous. This means that production (for example, the production of commodities by factory workers) cannot take place without *social reproduction*.[53] Marx, for example, writes that if the worker's "appearance in the [formal labor] market is to be continuous, and the continuous transformation of money into capital assumes this, the seller of labor power must perpetuate himself."[54] Social reproduction, in other words, is a necessary component of any mode of production. It is a component, though, that operates on multiple interlocking levels. First, reproduction entails the day-to-day continuance of any given worker. The main rationale for a minimum wage, as a case in point, is to ensure the daily survival of the worker, to enable the worker to live (and work) from one day to the next. Of course, given the constant wear and tear of the worker, and the biological fact that humans are mortal, capital requires a second form of reproduction, namely, the generational replacement of one worker with another. In principle, the minimum (or "living") wage is to cover both individual and generational replacement—a topic that has long been debated and contested. Third, reproduction occurs at a class level. Capitalism requires that the *class* of laborers perpetuates itself; here, it does not matter if any individual laborer (or his or her children) sells his or her labor power, as long as some*one* can replace the first worker. Finally, reproduction must exist at the level of the mode of production; that is, the system itself must be reproduced.

It is incorrect to view these four forms of social reproduction as exclusive or isolated; rather, they are both internally and dialectically related. Moreover, reproduction is something more than mere repetition insofar as it presupposes certain relationships to remain in place. Under systems of production for exchange, for example, Rosa Luxemburg explains that reproduction "depends on purely social considerations: only those goods are produced which can with certainty be expected to sell, and not merely to sell, but to sell at the customary profit. Thus profit becomes an end in itself, the decisive factor which determines not only production but also reproduction."[55] Applying this to Democratic Kampuchea, the predominant *economic* concern of the CPK would have been the continued export of agricultural commodities, namely, rice, and the ability to substitute for imports. Two examples will suffice.

During a meeting held on May 8, 1976, members of the Ministry of Commerce discussed both the export of rice and the import of other commodities. Unnamed officials noted that greater volumes of rice could be exported in 1977, although the "international market" demanded high-quality rice, which meant that their rice was "less expensive." It was also reported that current production levels of latex rubber surpassed two thousand tons, but the quality was also low and so could not be exported. It was concluded, therefore, that it was not possible, at the time, to sell rubber in exchange for currency. The report continued that production levels of fish and timber were too small to be viable economic prospects. This in turn gave added weight both to increased production of rice and to the expansion and improvement of rubber plantations. Turning to the other side of the equation, the report details that imports of cotton and jute were anticipated to decrease in the coming year, since efforts were under way to increase domestic production of these commodities. In conclusion, the report affirmed that to "solve [the] currency issue," it was necessary to increase productivity; economic problems were not to be solved by "taking loan[s] from the West or Eastern Europe." In doing so, Democratic Kampuchea would "lose [its] self-reliant stance."[56]

On May 30, 1976, members of the Standing Committee met to discuss "soldiers' agricultural work."[57] Pol Pot opened the meeting by announcing three main duties of soldiers: to defend the country, build the country, and perform agricultural labor. Throughout the meeting, it was clear that these duties were not separate, but rather internally related. According to Pol Pot, defense of the country remained the "core duty" of all soldiers; here, defense included not only the physical security of the country, but also the protection of "party and state officials." The internal deployment of troops therefore had to be cognizant of these different missions. Next, Pol Pot explained that troops built the country through farm activities. It was not the responsibility of the party, however, to support these troops; rather, they had to be self-reliant. Pol Pot identified some regional variation: he noted that troops around Phnom Penh had been superb in their activities, although in rural areas success was not as strong, "because most of them [the troops] were women." Regardless of these differences, Pol Pot stressed that troops must "produce surplus in order to support themselves yearly." In other words, all troops, male and female, were to receive thirteen *thang* of rice; however, they were to produce a "surplus amount" of at least 20 percent of overall demand in case something (for example, flood or drought) happened. This was crucial, according to Pol Pot, because a core duty of the troops was to build the country through the distribution of rice to the state. Pol Pot concluded that growing rice was not only about supporting the soldiers themselves, because as soldiers and workers of the party, they had a greater responsibility. Last, Pol Pot called attention to the *agricultural line*. Whereas rice production was viewed as a crucial component of building the country, the agricultural line referred to a host of structural conditions deemed vital to agriculture in general. Thus, Pol Pot directed attention toward the "natural" conditions of soil and water availability; attention also focused on the necessity to improve irrigation systems and install water pumps. These efforts, in turn, were dependent upon the continual availability of cement, iron, oil, and electric generators.[58]

Combined, these two documents testify to the interconnectedness of production and consumption understood by key members of the CPK—including Pol Pot. Ironically, however, these documents also indicate that the system of production established by the Khmer Rouge was anything but communism as understood, certainly, by Marx and, indeed, by most theoreticians of Marx's work. Let us follow Marx, as it were, into the fields of commodity exchange.

Under systems of production for exchange, the capital advanced by the owners of the means of production is divided into two parts: the first part represents the expenses of the means of production (for example, factories, machines, raw materials), while the second part is spent on wages. The former is called *constant capital*, while the latter is termed *variable capital*. This gives rise to an additional value (surplus value), which is realized upon completion of the circuit M–C–M' (as discussed in chapter 4). The various components (that is, constant capital, variable capital, and surplus value) may be formulated as: $c + v + s$, where c is constant capital, v is variable capital, and s is surplus value.[59]

As illustrated in the minute meetings of May 8, 1976, Pol Pot understood the fundamental dilemma faced by all capitalists: "For the capitalist producer the manufacture of commodities is not an end in itself, it is only a means to the appropriation of surplus value."[60] Pol Pot recognized that poor-quality rice and rubber would not be competitive on the global market; accordingly, the reproduction of Democratic Kampuchea's economy was placed in jeopardy. Simply put, once a commodity has been produced, surplus value must be realized; it must be converted into monetary form—but this occurs only if sold. In other words, if commodities are produced *but not sold*, then it does not constitute realized capital. Warehoused commodities become useless. Yet, for the Khmer Rouge, it was not an option to redistribute stored goods, notably rice, to the starving masses because to do so would have further jeopardized their economic system. I will expand on this notion later. Here, it needs to be stressed that the CPK initiated a system predicated upon production for exchange and *not* for personal consumption. Furthermore, it was the CPK—but mostly a few key members of the Standing Committee—that made decisions related to quotas and rations (that is, wages). Finally, Pol Pot's awareness both of global demands for high-quality rice and rubber and that the commodities produced by competing states surpassed the quality of Democratic Kampuchea indicates that Democratic Kampuchea was *not* isolated from the rest of the world and that all contacts were not—and never were intended to be—severed completely. Were Democratic Kampuchea *purely* isolated, and had it sundered all international relations, the CPK would not have been in a position to realize its surplus value. This was clearly a concern for Pol Pot and like-minded officials.

To more fully make the case, consider Marx's notion of expanded reproduction. The aim and incentive of a system of production for exchange are "not a surplus value pure and simple, to be appropriated in any desired quantity, but a surplus value ever growing into larger quantities, surplus value *ad infinitum*."[61] In other words, to reduce capitalism to the formula M–C–M' is insufficient. Left on its own, this formula merely states that money (M) is extended to purchase constant capital and variable capital in order to produce a commodity (C); this commodity is exchanged (sold), and in the process surplus value (M') is realized. This is the basis of Marx's labor theory of value, and in chapter 4 I detailed how the CPK's economy was structured around the obtainment of absolute and relative surpluses. Here, I continue this argument, for the formula M–C–M' is insufficient because it lacks follow-up. To accumulate additional surplus value, a certain portion of M' must be reinvested. The general formula for enlarged *re*production is thus: $c + v + [s/x] + s'$. Here s/x refers to the capitalized part of the surplus value appropriated in an earlier period; thus, a certain portion (x) of the surplus value (s) obtained through an initial sale is set aside for reinvestment in constant capital (c) or variable capital (v); x refers to this amount.[62]

In other words, upon completion of the initial sale, a capitalist will reinvest some profit back into his or her factory, machines, and other means of production (that is, constant capital); likewise, the capitalist will also continue to pay wages to laborers (that is, variable capital). Throughout the second and third volumes of *Capital*, Marx devotes considerable attention to the complexities of expanded reproduction. How, for example, does one account for the wear and tear of constant capital? Machines break down, and it is not necessarily straightforward how repair costs over, say, a ten-year life span of a machine should be accounted for in the above formula. This level of detail need not detain us in consideration of expanded reproduction within Democratic Kampuchea. There is, however, one additional component that must first be addressed.

In order for surplus value to be realized, commodities must be purchased. This is generally understood as taking place in the so-called market. For simplicity's sake, we can distinguish between foreign markets and domestic markets. As indicated above, the CPK was well aware of its precarious position within the foreign market. Trade with key allies, including China, North Korea, Yugoslavia, and Thailand, to name a few, remained viable. Domestically, the CPK banned market exchange. Their reasoning, purportedly, was to eliminate class distinctions and hence exploitation. In practice, as we have seen, the CPK instituted a countrywide class division whereby they, as ruling class, retained the means of production and controlled all distribution and allocation of goods produced. For those who labored in Democratic Kampuchea, this decision would prove tragic.

Domestic markets are crucial for capitalism, in that workers are *both* producers and consumers. This in fact is a well-known contradiction among Marxists and non-Marxists alike. On the one hand, capitalists seek to keep wages as low as possible; in accordance with the labor theory of value, this translates into higher profits. On the other hand, workers—as consumers—are necessary for the realization of value; commodities must be purchased. If wages are too low, workers are less able to purchase commodities. In capitalist societies, therefore, a balance is sought whereby workers are paid a sufficient amount—in order that markets continue to function—but not too much, thereby cutting into profits. Recall also from chapter 5 that capitalists normally do not set in place conditions that prevent workers from living; minimum wages are imposed that, ideally, allow workers to continue to live, have sufficient funds to replace the next generation of workers, and still purchase commodities.

This contradiction, of workers being both producers and consumers, is related to a second and no less significant contradiction, one that pivots also on the unity of production and consumption. Marx identifies two forms of "worker's consumption": *individual consumption* and *productive consumption*. What Marx proposes is to understand both production and consumption as dialectically related and to acknowledge that "production" and "consumption" both represent unities of opposites found in reproduction. For example, consider a worker who sells her labor power to a factory owner, the capitalist. During the production process, the worker converts existing materials (for example, cloth and thread) into other goods (for example, shirts); this is what Marx means by "reanimating" past labor. In the process, the capitalist is *consuming* the labor capacity of the worker; in so doing, the capitalist is then able to realize surplus value when the commodities are sold. It is this *productive consumption* that permits the capitalist and capitalism to be reproduced. Conversely, the worker—who is denied any alternative means of subsistence—must purchase (consume) goods obtained in the market in order to survive. This is *individual consumption*. To be denied access to the means of production is also to be denied access to the means of subsistence. Not only are workers "free" to sell their labor; they are also "free" to purchase commodities in order to live.

Marx explains that the minimum price paid, whether "paid" as wages or "provided" as food rations, is that of "the means of subsistence that is customarily held to be essential in a given state of society to enable the worker to exert his [sic] labor power with the necessary degree of strength, health, vitality, etc. and to perpetuate himself by producing replacements for himself." In other words, concrete wages are determined abstractly, calculated on the basis of market logics that determine the least costs necessary to keep workers and the next generation of workers alive. This tendency, however, is hidden within the workings of the formal wage-labor market. The "wage" appears as something that results from an equal exchange between employer and employee. As the saying goes, workers receive a "fair day's wage for a fair day's work." Marx details that this is anything but the case. In a well-known—but particularly apt—section of *Capital*, Marx writes, "Capital has one sole driving force, the drive to valorize itself, to create surplus value, to make its constant part, the means of production, absorb the greatest possible amount of surplus labor. Capital is dead labor which, vampire-like, lives only by sucking living labor, and lives the more, the more labor it sucks. The time during which the worker works is the time during which the capitalist consumes the labor power he has bought from him."[63]

What happened in Democratic Kampuchea was that the CPK, through the elimination of currency and substitution of money with food rations, established an inherently fragile system of production for exchange that was doomed to fail. Simply put, in Democratic Kampuchea, workers were no longer consumers in the sense of being able to realize surplus value. With no money, they were in no position to purchase commodities. Indicative of their overall approach to development based on import substitution, the CPK accepted the view that an unfettered participation in the free market would not solve their economic problems. This argument holds that the competitive global market, long dominated by colonial powers, was itself an instrument of those powers. But CPK policy was neither fish nor fowl. On the one hand, the CPK participated, selectively, in the global economy—primarily through the export of rice but also rubber, timber, and a few other commodities. On the other hand, to shelter the domestic economy from the vagaries of the global economy, the

CPK eliminated currency, wages, and all systems of economic exchange. These latter policies were initiated most likely in an attempt to eliminate once and for all the inherent contradictions in capitalism (for example, the crisis of overaccumulation) and the attendant problems of inflation and declining rates of profit. This proved to be an impossible feat.

As such, the accumulation of surplus capital—something the Khmer Rouge leaders were so acutely aware of—was severely limited. Not only could profits be obtained solely through international exchange, any "increase" in wages, that is, higher food rations, would literally eat into any potential profit. As Pol Pot noted in a committee meeting on May 30, 1976, workers were required to produce additional amounts of rice beyond what was provided by the party for their own consumption, and regardless of productivity levels, nothing was to prevent the party from first appropriating its own share to exchange on the foreign market.

We can see this graphically. The formula $v + s$ expresses the function of living labor under capitalism, or rather its double function: first, to restore the wages, or the variable capital, and, second, to create surplus value for the capitalist.[64] Thus, if a capitalist pays wages to workers, this is not "money" being given to the workers. Rather, it signifies an exchange in value form of variable capital, whereby it is used to purchase labor power. In Democratic Kampuchea, rice, as the material representation of value (that is, money), was invested in workers in exchange for labor.[65] In this case, workers were compelled to literally consume this form of variable capital. There was no opportunity for investment beyond that necessary to stave off hunger.

This draconian form of exchange conforms to the overall social organization of production set in place by the CPK and highlights the *selected* dissolution of families. For those workers consigned to work in agricultural collectives and other work sites, no one individual was responsible for the biological reproduction of society. Consequently, food rations could be imposed that—in principle—would maintain the life of the worker and *nothing else.* Food rations quite literally were "living wages." All other costs of social reproduction for these workers would be borne collectively; previously "nonproductive" workers, such as the elderly, would assume the maintenance of raising the very young. This, as Mam and Jain correctly identify, guaranteed that mothers could be fully incorporated into the "productive" economic system.[66]

Within capitalism, therefore, it is not simply that some are denied access to the means of production; it is also that some are denied access to the means of subsistence. It is this vulnerability, this precariousness, which reproduces capitalism and, I argue, reproduced the social organization of production in Democratic Kampuchea. As Marx explains, "Individual consumption provides, on the one hand, the means for the workers' maintenance and reproduction; on the other hand, by the constant annihilation of the means of subsistence, it provides for their continued re-appearance on the labor-market." Marx concludes that "the Roman slave was held by chains; the wage-laborer is bound to his owner by invisible threads. The appearance of independence is maintained . . . by the legal fiction of a contract."[67]

In Democratic Kampuchea, independence and self-mastery were given appearance through slogans of revolutionary zeal. The constitution held that workers were equal, public pronouncements and published materials declared that exploitation and oppression were eliminated following the abolition of money and markets, and cadre from top to bottom impressed upon workers that sacrifice was a form of loyalty and honor. Of course, just as the free market is a myth, so too was the nonmarket in Democratic Kampuchea. Work was an obligation—it was not, as Marx yearned—an opportunity for creative and individual fulfillment. It was an obligation, a duty, a responsibility. One could choose not to participate, but those who did would suffer grave consequences.

Conclusion

Throughout his writings, Marx wrote at length of the specter of premature death, of the radical inequalities of life experienced by those men, women, and children consigned to factory work. In response to the dismal working conditions endured by England's factory workers of the late nineteenth century, for example, Marx writes, "[Capital's] answer to the outcry about the physical and mental degradation, the premature death, the torture of over-work, is this: Should that pain trouble us, since it increases our pleasure (profit)?" Foreshadowing our contemporary engagement with the precariousness of life, Marx declares, "Capital . . . takes no account of the health and the length of the worker, unless society forces it to do so."[68]

The comments of Marx significantly inform my reconstruction of the sociospatial organization of Democratic Kampuchea and, by extension, the political philosophy of the Communist Party of Kampuchea. Marx's comments, however, also point to another, equally disturbing, feature of the Khmer Rouge. It is not simply a matter of who lives, who dies, and who decides; it is also a matter of *who profits?* In other words, not only did the CPK initiate an exploitative and oppressive system of production for exchange, a mode of production whereby surplus value was appropriated by economic and extraeconomic means by a ruling class that did not directly produce value, but the CPK also established a system that was designed to garner surplus profit through the deaths of countless men, women, and children.

To what extent, however, can we conclude that the CPK functioned as a ruling class or was simply trying to survive, both in its attempt to reconstruct a devastated economy in the aftermath of armed conflict and as a vanguard that never enjoyed widespread support?[69] On the one hand, the CPK assumed control over a country marked by a shattered economy. Years of war left the countryside in ruins, with fields either bombed or abandoned, livestock killed, and farmers having fled for refuge in the cities. Factories and plantations were destroyed or functioned at a diminished level; consequently, exports of rice and rubber were seriously curtailed. To this was added the lack of imported foodstuffs and medicines, barred from entry largely through US policies that reflected a concern more with the political image of American presidents than with the sick and starving people of Cambodia.

Once in power, the CPK refused foreign aid—what little there was to receive—and introduced a suite of policies that largely followed the precepts of import-substitution industrialization. Minimal attention, though, was devoted to the ways in which domestic production could be restarted—a problem compounded by the damaged infrastructure inherited by the CPK. Maps, surveys, and planning reports were requested, and some materialized. In scope and content, however, these were woefully deficient, indicative of inept or untrained cadre who nevertheless displayed a proper political consciousness and revolutionary will. The primary area in which considerable thought *appears* to have been devoted is in the voluminous data surrounding rice production and food rations. Here, unlike the brief assessments of "energy" problems or "health" problems, CPK officials were exceptionally precise in their calculations. This, I suggest, distinguishes CPK policy at the national level, for it highlights a preeminent concern with capital accumulation. Indeed, it becomes apparent that the CPK leadership was willing to forestall all other activities—education, industry, health—until a necessary surplus was generated.

7

Dead Labor

Walking among Graves

Some forty miles south of Phnom Penh, Cambodia's modern capital, nestled among the rolling hills of Kampot Province, sits an altogether unremarkable earthen structure. Spanning nearly seven and a half miles in length, nine miles high, and twelve miles wide, what remains of the Koh Sla Dam seems at peace among the short grass and scrub, its flanks crisscrossed by narrow footpaths connecting the stilt houses that dot the scene. The villagers who tend the rice fields and fish in the surrounding ponds anchor Koh Sla, the seemingly timeless landscape of rural Cambodia. But the tranquil repose of this earthwork in such an idyllic setting conceals a darker past. Under the vegetation that covers its canted bulk—beneath the sediment of intervening years—lingers a geography of starvation, disease, exposure, and execution. Nine thousand men, women, and children perished here, killed or left to die at the hands of the Khmer Rouge.

During the Cambodian Civil War (1970–75), as parts of the country were "liberated" by the Communist Party of Kampuchea, villagers were gradually subsumed into various work brigades. In 1973 planning began for the Koh Sla Dam, a massive weir located in the vicinity of the village of Sre Lieu. To provide labor, thousands of Cambodians were forcibly relocated to the site; conditions were deplorable and mortality was high.

Construction was slow, and, through 1975, Khmer Rouge officials redoubled their efforts. Additional work brigades were deployed to the site, and work continued through 1977. Laborers continued to suffer. Malaria and cholera were rampant, and many others died from injury or execution.[1] Srey Neth was assigned to bury members of her unit who died. She recalls, "I was forbidden [by the Khmer Rouge] from telling others about the number of deaths." She explains that "sometimes they [the Khmer Rouge] woke me up in the middle of the night and order me to take bodies to be buried. . . . The number of bodies I buried ranged from two to six per night."[2] Nget Chanthy was only sixteen years old when she was forced to labor at the site. Her duties included the clearing of forests and the movement of dirt to build the earthen weir. Food was inadequate, and people worked in constant fear of punishment by the Khmer Rouge.[3] Sickness—construed as "idleness"—was often considered a traitorous offense, punishable by death.

Samon Prum writes firsthand of the death associated with the Koh Sla Dam.[4] Throughout the reign of the CPK, Samon lost more than thirteen family members, including his grandfather, father, three brothers, a sister, and numerous aunts, uncles, and cousins. He recalls the continuous propaganda of the Khmer Rouge, of how Angkar would provide all the necessities of a fruitful, prosperous life. Exactly who—or what—constituted Angkar was unclear. What was most important for Samon Prum was that Angkar promised that people would have enough to eat.

There was, however, no food security. Samon Prum and millions of other Cambodians were restricted to insufficient food rations—often a watery rice gruel—that formed a cornerstone of CPK policy. It was through the rationing of food, but especially rice, that the Khmer Rouge sought to build socialism. In practice, however, this policy led to widespread malnutrition and susceptibility to disease. In the case of Heat, Samon's cousin, it led to an early death. Heat was seventeen years old when she was assigned to a woman's mobile unit at Koh Sla. One day, Samon recalls, Heat "was very hungry, so she picked an ear of corn and cooked it. Before the corn was ready to eat, the unit chief caught her and gathered people around for a meeting. The unit chief tied her arms in back of her, grabbed the hot corn from the fire, and put it into her mouth, burning her. He then declared that Heat had betrayed *Angkar* and the cooperative. Everybody at the meeting was threatened to not follow in her footsteps."[5] Although Heat was not executed for her "crime," she would later become seriously ill and die of starvation-related causes.

The mass graves at Koh Sla today stand as silent testimony to the violence that engulfed Democratic Kampuchea.[6] The recollections of Srey Neth and Prum Samon likewise bear witness, but in different ways, to the production of mass graves. On the one hand, Srey Neth's job was literally to produce mass graves, to transform "nature" into an object, a grave, while, on the other hand, Prum Samon's story provides insight into the laborers who were buried in the graves dug by Srey Neth. Combined, their narratives speak to the social organization of production of the Khmer Rouge.

Karl Marx, in his critique of capitalism, conceived of "dead labor" as labor power, the expended energy, that is embodied within a *thing*, whether that thing is a machine, a factory, or even a piece of fruit. For Marx, the term *dead labor* was used metaphorically, to call attention to the previous activities that went into the making of some*thing*, for the "product of labor is labor which has been congealed in an object, which has become material." Don Mitchell, however, asks geographers to consider the concept in other than metaphorical terms. For example, Mitchell considers a piece of fruit, a strawberry, and notes how the surface appearance of the strawberry "says nothing of the labor that makes it."[7] However, as a commodity, the strawberry embodies the social relations of its own production, such as the labor involved in cultivating the fields, the planting and harvesting of the crops, and the distribution of the berries. In short, commodities—such as the strawberry—"stabilize" social relations; they are "dead labor, work ossified and made concrete."[8]

Extending this argument, Mitchell calls attention to the violence that surrounds the production process. More precisely, he highlights the exploitative and oppressive working conditions of farmworkers, the dangers of prolonged exposure to pesticides and insecticides, and the dangerous migratory journey to the fields themselves. Indeed, the labor that is embodied in commodities—the living labor that reanimates dead labor— is frequently injured or killed in the labor process. In other words, living laborers, through the transformation of dead labor, may become (quite literally) dead laborers. Mitchell forces us, therefore, to think of the dead laborers that lay buried beneath the ground. I acknowledge Mitchell's lead and consider, on the one hand, how killing fields were *produced* by living labor and, on the other hand, how mass graves literally contain dead laborers. Mass graves, so conceived, are contradictory pivots upon which the living are transformed into the dead and where the dead transform the living. It is my argument that mass graves are not simply the material manifestation of *direct* violence, but instead provide insight into the constitution of *structures* of violence through the social organization of production.

On achieving military victory, the Khmer Rouge attempted to "build socialism" through forced labor. Societal members were to lead simple productive lives based on "equality" and "self-sacrifice." People's actions were no longer based on individual profit or self-fulfillment; instead, a selfless dedication to the collective well-being of the party was promoted. In theory, classes were to be eliminated. In reality, however, the CPK replaced previous social divisions with new ones, including that between "base" people and "new" people.

Regardless of formal or informal classification, all laborers in Democratic Kampuchea were, ultimately, reduced to that of a "surplus population": an army of reserve labor that existed at the discretion of the state, a population that could be made to reanimate "dead labor" when necessary or eliminated when not. Laborers were to serve the state and, by extension, the revolution. It was the *capacity* to labor—not the laborer—that was of importance. Life-or-death decisions hinged on whether any given body was perceived as having "use value": the ability to produce for the state. Ultimately, the transformation of Cambodia's population into "surplus population" was predicated on the necessity to generate *surplus profit*.

The CPK leadership identified that increased agricultural productivity was critical to the establishment of a "self-sufficient" Democratic Kampuchea. As Marx recognized, a certain amount of accumulation of capital is a necessary precondition for subsequent economic growth.[9] Consequently, it was necessary for every work site to become "a fiery battlefield." The CPK's line of reasoning was simple: "We fight in the field of agriculture because we have agricultural resources. We'll move to other fields when the agricultural battle is finished."[10] In other words, to *reanimate* the past dead labor stored within the fields, it was required, as Marx writes, that "living labor must seize on these things, awaken them from the dead, change them from merely possible into real and effective use values." Simply put, "The labor process is purposeful activity aimed at the production of use values. It is an appropriation of what exists in nature for the requirements of man."[11] Members of Democratic Kampuchea, consequently, were to become "free" laborers—free in the sardonic Marxist sense of being dispossessed from the means of production and thus "free" to work and accumulate surplus through collectives. For the CPK, what was required was a massive mobilization of "freed" labor power to harness the natural qualities of Cambodia's resources and to metabolize these into *quantities for exchange.*

A rational administrative system was required to instantiate the accumulation of capital. Thus, following the abolition of currency, a food-ration system was required. This was not the only option available. Indeed, as Marx suggested, "With collective production, money capital is completely dispensed with. The society distributes labor power and means of production between the various branches of industry. There is no reason why the producers should not receive paper tokens permitting them to withdraw an amount corresponding to their labor time from the social consumption stocks. But these tokens are not money; they do not circulate."[12] Instead of money or tokens, the CPK converted their competitive advantage, rice, into a representation of value. Workers were to receive "calculated" amounts of rice as "payment" for services rendered.

Within Democratic Kampuchea, structures *of* violence were constituted through a reduction of the necessary conditions for survival, as the more communistic term *ration* was substituted for the more capitalist-sounding *wages.* Regardless of terminology, whether wage or ration, the end point was the same: laborers were denied access to the means of production, and through overwork and minimal means of sustenance, both profits and fatalities ensued; those who resisted, those who challenged these structures, were subject to direct violence in the form of imprisonment, torture, and execution. From the vantage point of the victim—where we witness the literal transformation of life into death—the qualitative and fatal differences between "structural" and "direct" violence become quantitatively identical. One was still dead, whether the cause was a bullet to the head or an empty stomach. And in Cambodia, both could become dead laborers buried in mass graves.

Throughout Democratic Kampuchea, all citizens were potentially equal in death—even those of the ruling CPK class; in this way, the production of mass graves served as a visual material cue to the transformation of qualitative difference—both of body and of violence—into quantitative exchanges. In other words, the anonymity of death as manifest in mass graves abolished difference and distinction. All were considered equal in death, and all manners of death were likewise equal. That such equality exists is internally related to the conception of life (and death) within Democratic Kampuchea. As surplus labor, workers were expected to exist solely for the party and the revolution; their existence was to animate constant capital (dead labor) to generate surplus for the party. If one was unable to produce, he or she was transformed into *being* dead labor.

The point I want to emphasize is that mass graves were and are deliberately produced; it is through this production that we may better understand the concrete practices that would constitute the Cambodian genocide. Retheorizing mass graves as *products of human labor power* provides insight into the social organization of production—but also the broader social formation—enacted by the CPK. The mass graves that were produced came about as by-products of other innumerable practices: the construction of irrigation canals, dams, and reservoirs; the elimination of persons deemed useless or threatening to the party and revolution; and the unequal access to adequate nutrition, medicine, and shelter. From these conditions, we can abstract that the Khmer Rouge sought to simultaneously "smash" the old order and to construct a new society. This new society was predicated on a rhetoric of equality, a communist ideal that promised class divisions would be rendered obsolete. In brutal irony, the physicality of mass graves *appears* to conform to this ideal, that the anonymous burials negated differences, that even in death all became equal. However, mass graves reveal more than they appear, for the *production* of mass graves—the sites where living labor is transformed into dead labor— demonstrates concretely how bodies were bureaucratically determined to be either economically useful or politically docile. Within Democratic Kampuchea, life was utilitarian. A person's worth was measured by his or her ability (and loyalty) to the party and revolution. And as politicized life, any life that ceased to have relevance—value—became expendable.

Beyond Democratic Kampuchea

The Cambodian genocide constitutes one of the twentieth century's worst episodes of mass violence. It is a mistake, however, to view this episode as separate, or apart, from broader geopolitical and geoeconomic transformations that have occurred over the past century. To this end, documentary evidence conclusively demonstrates that the CPK was not, nor ever intended to be, as completely isolated—to the point of autarky—as the Standard Total View suggests. Rather, it is necessary to reposition the CPK within both a more complex historiography of Cold War conflict *and* a postcolonial context. However bad we may view the CPK—and they were bad—we must also understand that they came into existence in an era of anticolonial and decolonization movements. Both their policies and their practices were incontrovertibly shaped by these events. Consequently, with respect to their overall political economy, the CPK rationalized limited international engagements as a means of maintaining sovereign control over their territory. Likewise, their promotion of self-mastery and self-reliance was a variation on an economic strategy of import-substitution industrialization. Likewise, we must also come to grips with the long-held view that Democratic Kampuchea was so isolated and so detached from the rest of the world that conditions were unknown at the time. To argue that Democratic Kampuchea was so completely isolated is to absolve the United States, China, and other governments from their culpability—in terms of both creating those conditions that led to the rise of the Khmer Rouge as well as maintaining the Khmer Rouge once in power.

The violence that beset Cambodia was very much part of the larger Cold War that brought about so much death and destruction to the peoples of Africa, Asia, and the Americas. The encroaching conflagration in Vietnam bled into Cambodia and helped foster the conditions necessary for the Khmer Rouge to come to power. And once in power, the CPK imposed a series of policies and programs made in the context of years of armed conflict and massive aerial bombardment. Relatedly, CPK policy and practice reflected the principles advocated by members of the Non-Aligned Movement. Itself a product of the Cold War, adherents to a "Third" way sought to promote strategies of economic development that would not merely replace one form of colonialism with another. The CPK was very much in line with the Non-Aligned Movement, and, accordingly, their attempt to rapidly increase agricultural production through the adoption of import-substitution policies must place the economic policies of Democratic Kampuchea alongside those of other "lesser developed" countries that achieved independence throughout the 1950s, 1960s, and 1970s.

Following Richard Wolff, the first key difference between capitalism and socialism deals with who owns the means of production: land, machines, factories, and so on. Under the many forms of capitalism, the distinguishing feature is that the means of production are privately owned; state capitalism, for example, refers to a society in which those who own the means of production are officials within the state apparatus. Production is organized such that workers, whether paid in wages, tokens, or rations, produce surpluses appropriated and distributed by those who own the means of production. In contrast, socialism is defined as a system in which productive property is socialized—becoming the property of the people as a whole—and is then administered by the state for the people as a whole; under communism, by extension, all property and all surplus are owned and controlled by the workers themselves.[13] In Democratic Kampuchea, workers labored and produced under the watchful eye of an elite class that ruled in the name of the state. The CPK effectively owned, controlled, and distributed at their discretion the productive resources and outputs of Democratic Kampuchea. This most basic relationship indicates that the system initiated by the CPK was a system of production for exchange; in the end, it constituted a variant of state capitalism.

I do not doubt that many members of the CPK genuinely believed that they embodied a vanguard that would bring about a society free of exploitation and oppression, that they implemented a host of rudimentary policies that, from their vantage point, would negate the unequal relations that typify feudalism and capitalism. Currency was abolished; personal private property was outlawed; superficial signs of individuality, such as hairstyle and clothing, were prohibited. But these are merely the surface appearances of unequal social relations, for the most important component—the defining aspect that Marx devoted so much attention—was not altered: class divisions within the social organization of production.

In other words, structurally, what happened in Democratic Kampuchea was not unique. What remains to be articulated is why, here and now, Democratic Kampuchea departed so significantly from other postcolonial states. Can we simply conclude that Pol Pot or perhaps a handful of other revolutionaries are responsible? My sense is that such an explanation is indeed too simplistic. A better path forward, I suggest, is to delve further into the structural contradictions enacted by the CPK. Within Democratic Kampuchea, the reconstructed economic system was perceived as being foundational to the concurrent political task of building socialism. As a system of production for exchange, however, whereby surpluses of food were confiscated and subsequently sold to China, the citizens of Democratic Kampuchea became more and more alienated. It is important to bear in mind that although the CPK did not enjoy widespread support or loyalty in April 1975, many people were willing to support them, given that they had endured years of American bombing and a not insignificant number wanted to restore Sihanouk to the throne. Rhetorically, the CPK promised paradise but delivered only horrors: starvation wages in the form of food rations, a disastrous health system, and indiscriminate killings. This disconnect, between promise and delivery, led to feelings among the populace that were perceived by the CPK as reactionary and therefore traitorous. The task of building socialism was not proceeding as rapidly or as fully as determined by CPK planning. Consequently, the CPK adopted more and more violent means to carry forward the revolution.

In the end, Democratic Kampuchea provides an invaluable lesson for those who study social revolutions and the political economics of development. We should not view the mass violence that transpired in Cambodia as a momentary period, a genocidal epoch that lasted three years, eight months, and twenty days. Rather, we must understand this period as part of an ongoing geographical and historical narrative that includes the political, economic, and military actions of, among others, the French, the Americans, the Vietnamese, the Chinese, and the Soviets. Without this larger perspective, it is not possible to satisfactorily understand why the Khmer Rouge did what they did. Most assuredly, the leadership of the CPK is guilty of crimes against humanity; so too, though, are the other governments that contributed to the development of CPK political and economic policy and practice.

Notes

Bibliography

Index

Notes

Preface

1. Michael Vickery, *Cambodia, 1975–1982*.

2. Karl Marx and Friedrich Engels, *The German Ideology: Including Theses on Feuer-bach and Introduction to the Critique of Political Economy*, 42; Communist Party of Kampuchea, "Report of Activities of the Party Center according to the General Political Tasks of 1976," 202.

3. See, for example, Alexander Hinton, *Why Did They Kill? Cambodia in the Shadow of Genocide*, 48 passim; and William W. Willmott, "Analytical Errors of the Kampuchean Communist Party."

4. David P. Chandler, "From 'Cambodge' to 'Kampuchea': State and Revolution in Cambodia, 1863–1979," "Revising the Past in Democratic Kampuchea: When Was the Birthday of the Party?," and "Seeing Red: Perceptions of Cambodian History in Democratic Kampuchea"; Ben Kiernan, *How Pol Pot Came to Power: A History of Communism in Kampuchea, 1930–1975* and "Origins of Khmer Communism"; Steve Heder, *Cambodian Communism and the Vietnamese Model: Imitation and Independence, 1930–1975*; Craig Etcheson, *The Rise and Demise of Democratic Kampuchea*; Serge Thion, "The Cambodian Idea of Revolution."

5. Henri Lefebvre, *The Production of Space*, 54.

6. See also Tony Cliff, *State Capitalism in Russia*; William Jerome and Adam Buick, "Soviet State Capitalism? The History of an Idea"; James Petras, "State Capitalism and the Third World"; Ben Turok, "Zambia's System of State Capitalism"; Mark N. Cooper, "State Capitalism, Class Structure, and Social Transformation in the Third World: The Case of Egypt"; Adam Buick and John Crump, *State Capitalism: The Wages System under New Management*; and Linda Matar, "Twilight of 'State Capitalism' in Formerly 'Socialist' Arab States."

7. Friedrich Engels, *Anti-Dühring: Herr Eugen Dühring's Revolution in Science*, 382; Karl Marx, *Capital: A Critique of Political Economy*, 2:177; Stephen Resnick and Richard Wolff, "State Capitalism in the USSR? A High-Stakes Debate," 48.

199

8. Stephen Resnick and Richard Wolff, "Between State and Private Capitalism: What Was Soviet 'Socialism'?," 10.

9. Vickery, *Cambodia, 1975–1982*, 40, 39.

10. Communist Party of Kampuchea, "The Party's Four-Year Plan to Build Socialism in All Fields, 1977–1980," 91.

11. Ibid.

12. Kiernan, *Pol Pot Regime*; Hinton, *Why Did They Kill?*

13. James A. Tyner and Stian Rice, "Cambodia's Political Economy of Violence: Space, Time, and Genocide under the Khmer Rouge, 1975–79," 85 passim.

14. David P. Chandler, *Brother Number One: A Political Biography of Pol Pot*, 3; Benjamin A. Valentino, *Final Solutions: Mass Killing and Genocide in the 20th Century*, 491, 493.

15. Marx and Engels, *German Ideology*, 61.

16. Michael Heinrich, *An Introduction to the Three Volumes of Karl Marx's "Capital*," 31.

17. David Harvey, *A Companion to Marx's "Capital*," 4.

1. A Critique of Khmer Rouge Political Economy

1. See, for example, Vickery, *Cambodia, 1975–1982*; Kiernan, *How Pol Pot Came to Power*; David Chandler, *The Tragedy of Cambodian History: Politics, War, and Revolution since 1945*; Kiernan, *Pol Pot Regime*; Hinton, *Why Did They Kill?*

2. There is no consensus as to whether the violence that transpired constitutes, in a legal sense, genocide. It is worth noting that of the three individuals prosecuted thus far (Kang Kech Ieu [alias Duch], Nuon Chea, and Khieu Samphan), none was found guilty of genocide.

3. Notable exceptions include Ben Kiernan and Michael Vickery. Kiernan, for example, acknowledges some influence of Marxism and Leninism, but privileges an explanation based on the racism and nationalism of members of the CPK. Vickery denies that the CPK was communist, arguing instead that the members were "petty-bourgeois radicals overcome by peasantist romanticism." See Kiernan, *Pol Pot Regime*, 26; and Vickery, *Cambodia, 1975–1982*, 306.

4. "Statement of the Communist Party of Kampuchea to the Communist Workers' Party of Denmark, July 1978," archived at the Documentation Center of Cambodia, Phnom Penh, http://www.d.dccam.org/Archives/Documents/DK_Policy; Scott Straus, "Organic Purity and the Role of Anthropology in Cambodia and Rwanda," 50.

5. Kate Frieson, "The Political Nature of Democratic Kampuchea"; Margaret Slocomb, "The Nature and Role of Ideology in the Modern Cambodian State"; Donald W. Beachler, "Arguing about Cambodia: Genocide and Political Interest."

6. Leo Cherne, "Cambodia—Auschwitz of Asia," 22. To be fair, Cherne was writing *before* the collapse of the Khmer Rouge and thus was without present-day archival materials; that being said, I doubt that his interpretation would differ that much.

7. Boraden Nhem, *The Khmer Rouge: Ideology, Militarism, and the Revolution That Consumed a Generation*, 43; James A. Tyner, *Genocide and the Geographical Imagination: Life and Death in Germany, China, and Cambodia*, 15.

8. John Milios, "Marxist Theory and Marxism as Mass Ideology: The Effects of the Collapse of 'Really Existing Socialism' on West European Marxism," 62, 64.

9. Matthew Edwards, "The Rise of the Khmer Rouge in Cambodia: Internal or External Origins?," 61; Miguel Pina e Cunha et al., "The Organization (Angkar) as a State of Exception: The Case of the S-21 Extermination Camp, Phnom Penh." It is worth noting at this point that S-21 was not an extermination camp; it was a security center and formed the apex of a hierarchical system of approximately two hundred centers. To be sure, detainees were tortured and many died; however, executions took place at a mass grave approximately nine miles distant. To employ the term *extermination camp*—with obvious references to places such as Sobibor and Treblinka—is disingenuous at best and detracts attention from the very different objectives of S-21 and those camps under Nazi rule.

10. Stewart Clegg, Miguel Pina e Cunha, and Arménio Rego, "The Theory and Practice of Utopia in a Total Institution: The Pineapple Panopticon," 1739; Karl D. Jackson, "Intellectual Origins of the Khmer Rouge," 241. Michael Vickery effectively dismantles Jackson's argument that the CPK was influenced by Fanon. See Vickery, *Cambodia, 1975–1982*, ix.

11. Charles H. Twining, "The Economy," 110; Clegg, Cunha, and Rego, "Theory and Practice of Utopia," 1739; Greg Procknow, "Human Resource Development in Democratic Kampuchea, 1975–1979," 371.

12. Nhem, *Khmer Rouge*, 54.

13. See, for example, discussions in Andrew Mertha, *Brothers in Arms: Chinese Aid to the Khmer Rouge, 1975–1979*.

14. Karl D. Jackson, "The Ideology of Total Revolution," 45; Randle C. DeFalco, "Justice and Starvation in Cambodia: The Khmer Rouge Famine," 52–53.

15. In attendance were Pol Pot, Nuon Chea, Ieng Sary, Son Sen, Khieu Samphan, and Koy Thuon; also present were Soeu Vasy, chairman of Political Office 870, and Phouk Chhoy, secretary of the Standing Committee. Following some brief remarks (unrecorded) by Ieng Sary and Koy Thuon, it was decided that a working group be formed. Ad hoc members included Koy Thuon (chief); Khieu Samphan (member); Ieng Sary, Vorn Vet, and Soeu Vasy (all advising members); and Phouk Chhoy (member and note taker). The tasks assigned to the working group were broad: to compile two lists, one of aid and another of items needed to be purchased. "Record of Minutes of Meeting of the Standing

Committee on March 13, 1976," Document No. D00691, archived at the Documentation Center of Cambodia, Phnom Penh.

16. See Mertha, *Brothers in Arms*, table 6.1. See also Kiernan, *Pol Pot Regime*.

17. "Minute Meetings of the Standing Committee, February 22, 1976," Document No. D00681; and "Minute Meetings of the Standing Committee, February 28, 1976," Document No. D00683, both archived at the Documentation Center of Cambodia, Phnom Penh.

18. "Cooperation with the Ministry of Commerce," Document No. D00698, archived at the Documentation Centre of Cambodia, Phnom Penh.

19. Mertha, *Brothers in Arms*, 127.

20. Ibid., 128.

21. Kristin S. Tassin, "'Lift Up Your Head, My Brother': Nationalism and the Genesis of the Non-Aligned Movement," 147.

22. "Minute Meetings," Document No. D00683.

23. Pol Pot, *Long Live the 17th Anniversary of the Communist Party of Kampuchea* (Phnom Penh: Ministry of Foreign Affairs, 1977), Document No. D30882, archived at the Documentation Center of Cambodia, Phnom Penh.

24. Michal Kalecki, *Essays on Developing Economies*.

25. "Minutes of the Meeting of the Standing Committee, December 2, 1975," Document No. D00678, archived at the Documentation Center of Cambodia, Phnom Penh.

26. Mertha, *Brothers in Arms*, 124.

27. "Minute Meetings," Document No. D00683.

28. Vickery, *Cambodia, 1975–1982*, 273.

29. Petras, "State Capitalism," 4.

30. "Minutes of the Standing Committee's Visit to Southwest Zone," Document No. L0001022, archived at the Documentation Center of Cambodia, Phnom Penh.

31. Richard Wolff, *Democracy at Work: A Cure for Capitalism*, 104; Stephen Resnick and Richard Wolff, *Class Theory and History: Capitalism and Communism in the U.S.S.R.*, 51.

32. See, for example, Resnick and Wolff, "State Capitalism in the USSR?" and "Between State and Private Capitalism."

33. Communist Party of Kampuchea, "Party's Four-Year Plan," 51, 110–12, 107; Marx and Engels, *German Ideology*, 37; Communist Party of Kampuchea, "Party's Four-Year Plan," 107.

34. Karl Marx, *A Contribution to the Critique of Political Economy*, 20.

35. Paul Paolucci, *Marx's Scientific Dialectics: A Methodological Treatise for a New Century*, 194. See also John Sommerville, "Marxist Ethics, Determinism, and Freedom."

36. Marx and Engels, *German Ideology*, 38.

37. Marx, *Contribution to the Critique*, 20–21 (emphasis added).

38. Richard Peet, "Materialism, Social Formation, and Socio-spatial Relations: An Essay in Marxist Geography," 149. See also Paolucci, *Marx's Scientific Dialectics*, 76–77.

39. Ron J. Horvath and Katherine D. Gibson, "Abstraction in Marx's Method," 15.

40. Richard Peet, *Global Capitalism: Theories of Societal Development*, 58.

41. Marx, *Capital*, 1:286; Peet, *Global Capitalism*, 59.

42. Marx, *Capital*, 1:290 (emphasis added).

43. Peet, *Global Capitalism*, 59.

44. Marx, *Capital*, 3:927–28.

45. Peet, "Materialism, Social Formation, and Socio-spatial Relations," 150.

46. Karl Marx, "The Poverty of Philosophy."

47. In principle, the CPK sought to impose a radical break from the past, a decidedly undialectical approach.

48. Paolucci, *Marx's Scientific Dialectics*, 90.

2. Revolution

1. Philip Short, *Pol Pot: Anatomy of a Nightmare*, 99–100.

2. Ibid., 107.

3. Chandler, "Revising the Past," 288. See also David P. Chandler, *Voices from S-21: Terror and History in Pol Pot's Secret Prison*, 58–60.

4. Quoted in Chandler, "Revising the Past," 289.

5. Marx, *Capital*, 1:548.

6. Marx's interpretation was materially grounded but not economically determinist—at least not in the sense later adopted by postmodernists. At the time of his writing, determination held a different, less rigid meaning. For Marx, instead, determinism was derived from his methodological approach of reading history backward. Think, for example, of your reading this book. This required that you obtained a copy of the book. However, it also required that I write the book. We can continue indefinitely, in a vain attempt to find an originary moment. The point is that all of these events had to happen in order for you to be presently reading this book. For Marx, these historical events—read backward—are considered determinants. They had to occur in order for the present to happen—the way it is happening. This unfolding is not to suggest, however, that a similar linear history will happen everywhere or anywhere else. It does suggest, similar to demographic forecasts, that if such conditions are found elsewhere, a similar outcome is likely.

7. Marx, *Contribution to the Critique*, 21.

8. Ibid.

9. David P. Chandler, *A History of Cambodia*.

10. Ibid., 140.

11. Within Indochina French colonial policy varied widely. In part, this variance stemmed from the territorially defined administration of Indochina. Vietnam was divided into three protectorates: Tonkin, Annam, and Cochin China, located in the northern, central, and southern regions, respectively. Cambodia and Laos were ruled as separate but integrated colonial entities.

12. Patrick Hearden, *The Tragedy of Vietnam: Causes and Consequences*, 8.

13. Jeffery M. Paige, *Agrarian Revolutions: Social Movements and Export Agriculture in the Underdeveloped World*, 283.

14. Ibid., 281–83; Hearden, *Tragedy of Vietnam*, 8.

15. Paige, *Agrarian Revolutions*, 305.

16. William J. Duiker, *The Communist Road to Power in Vietnam*, 8–9.

17. Robert D. Schulzinger, *A Time for War: The United States and Vietnam, 1941–1975*, 26.

18. Kent Helmers, "Rice in the Cambodian Economy: Past and Present," 2–3. Beyond these two systems, there were other productive arrangements, including larger holdings owned by ethnic Vietnamese and Chinese landowners.

19. Ibid., 2.

20. Chandler, *Tragedy of Cambodian History*, 108.

21. Margaret Slocomb, *The People's Republic of Kampuchea, 1979–1989: The Revolution after Pol Pot*, 2.

22. Heder, *Cambodian Communism*.

23. Gareth Porter, "Vietnamese Communist Policy toward Kampuchea, 1930–1970," 58.

24. Duiker, *Communist Road to Power*, 30–31.

25. Dmitry Mosyakov, "The Khmer Rouge and the Vietnamese Communists: A History of Their Relations as Told in the Soviet Archive," 45–46.

26. Heder, *Cambodian Communism*, 15.

27. Ibid., 14.

28. Chandler, *Brother Number One*, 31.

29. Heder, *Cambodian Communism*, 14. It is de rigueur to partition Cambodian communists into two groups. On the one hand, accordingly, there existed a group of men and women—variously described as the "Pol Pot clique" or the "Paris-educated" revolutionaries—who were adamantly opposed to working alongside the Vietnamese. Conversely, other revolutionaries were more receptive to working hand in hand with the Vietnamese. Such an artificial binary has, however, not withstood the growing documentary evidence. Steve Heder, in particular, has critiqued such a pat dichotomy, noting that the historiography of the communist movement in Cambodia is decidedly more complex. Indeed, Pol Pot, Nuon Chea, So Phim, and other leading Cambodian communists "were indoctrinated in and otherwise absorbed Vietnamese Communism starting in the early to mid-1950s, when they were members of the Vietnamese-led Indochinese

Communist Party" (2). And while Pol Pot and others, including Ieng Sary, Khieu Samphan, Hou Yuon, and Son Sen, did attend university in France and became involved in
the Khmer section of the French Communist Party, Heder argues that for many of these
revolutionaries, the ground had already been prepared. Indeed, with regard to Pol Pot,
Heder concludes that his earlier experiences with the Vietnamese were "more important
to his ideological formation than a brief sojourn as a vocational student in France" (ibid.).

30. Chandler, *Tragedy of Cambodian History*, 108.

31. Jonathan Neale, *A People's History of the Vietnam War*, 33.

32. Kiernan, "Origins of Khmer Communism," 175.

33. Heder, *Cambodian Communism*, 17–18.

34. Porter, "Vietnamese Communist Policy," 73.

35. Kiernan, *How Pol Pot Came to Power*, 191.

36. Pol Pot is referring to a secretive meeting held in the Phnom Penh rail yard during September 1960.

37. Pol Pot, *Long Live the 17th Anniversary of the Communist Party of Kampuchea*
(Phnom Penh: Ministry of Foreign Affairs, 1977), Document No. D30882, archived at
the Documentation Center of Cambodia, Phnom Penh.

38. Giorgio Agamben, *State of Exception*, 28.

39. Karl Marx and Friedrich Engels, *The Communist Manifesto* (emphasis added), 77.

40. Vladimir I. Lenin, *Essential Works of Lenin: "What Is to Be Done?" and Other
Writings*, 112.

41. Karl Marx and Friedrich Engels, *The German Ideology: Including Theses on
Feuerbach and Introduction to the Critique of Political Economy*, 67.

42. Pol Pot, *Long Live the 17th Anniversary*, 62.

43. In Khmer the word *angkar* is translated as "organization." As Steve Heder details,
angkar was used as early as the 1940s within the Cambodian communist movement. In
time, it would obtain more sinister connotations. See also Hinton, *Why Did They Kill?*

44. Lenin, *Essential Works*, 137, 143.

45. Heder, *Cambodian Communism*, 46.

46. Ibid., 49, 51.

47. Elizabeth Becker, *When the War Was Over: Cambodia and the Khmer Rouge
Revolution*, 81; Chandler, *Tragedy of Cambodian History*, 33.

48. The party was again renamed, in 1966, becoming the Pak Communist Kampuchea, or Communist Party of Kampuchea.

49. Kiernan, *How Pol Pot Came to Power*, 200–201. So Phim apparently challenged
Pol Pot for the post of secretary-general. He was later purged.

50. Kiernan, "Origins of Khmer Communism," 178.

51. Slocomb, *People's Republic of Kampuchea*, 10.

52. It was Sihanouk's belief that by allowing Vietnamese insurgents and armed
forces sanctuary and safe passage through eastern Cambodia, as well as access to the

deepwater port at Sihanoukville, the Vietnamese communists would be able to restrain their Cambodian counterparts.

53. Chandler, *Brother Number One*, 69–70.

54. Slocomb, *People's Republic of Kampuchea*, 10.

55. Ibid., 11. Numerous scholars have called attention to Pol Pot's visit to Beijing at this time, suggesting that it was during this period that Pol Pot "acquired" his understanding of Maoism and, by extension, his understanding of communism. At this point, a detailed empirical study of Pol Pot's visit is lacking, and so most interpretations are conjectural. It is my suspicion that Pol Pot did *not* spend much time learning about Marxism or even Maoism during his visit, as he was more concerned with the practicalities of interstate negotiations.

56. South Vietnam, alternatively known as the State of Vietnam and the Republic of Vietnam, was established following the Geneva Convention of 1954.

57. James A. Tyner, *America's Strategy in Southeast Asia: From the Cold War to the Terror War*, 94.

58. Hearden, *The Tragedy of Vietnam*, 67; Schulzinger, *Time for War*, 213.

59. Walter W. Rostow, *The Stages of Growth: A Non-communist Manifesto*, 107.

60. John Prados, *Vietnam: The History of an Unwinnable War, 1945–1975*, 94.

61. Schulzinger, *Time for War*, 213.

62. Kenton Clymer, *Troubled Relations: The United States and Cambodia since 1870*, 99–100.

63. Ibid., 99. Sihanouk's role and responsibility remain a source of contention. Clymer maintains that Sihanouk did not give his approval for military encroachment into Cambodia; he did, however, tolerate *limited* engagement. Sihanouk, for example, stomached certain demands of both the DRV and the United States to operate within Cambodia's borders. However, as Clymer explains, these were specific and limited arrangements, agreed to only in a desperate hope to keep the violence away from Cambodia and to retain his country's independence and neutrality.

64. Lenin, *Essential Works*, 74, 120.

65. Chandler, *A History of Cambodia*, 201.

66. Becker, *When the War Was Over*, 101, 103.

67. Short, *Pol Pot*, 167; Chandler, *Tragedy of Cambodian History*, 165. The uprising at Samlaut signaled both the weakening of Sihanouk's grip on the country and the limitations and contradictions of his policies. Believing, for example, that the rebellions were instigated by the Khmer Rouge, Sihanouk felt betrayed by the Vietnamese communists. For years Sihanouk had allowed Vietnamese insurgents free access to Cambodian territory; in return, the Khmer Rouge was to be kept in check. Following Samlaut, Sihanouk began to think that the DRV either could not or would not be able to control the Khmer Rouge. Ironically, the DRV had not betrayed Sihanouk. In fact, the DRV remained steadfast against any communist-led uprising in Cambodia.

68. Hinton, *Why Did They Kill?*, 53.

69. Pol Pot, *Long Live the 17th Anniversary.*

70. Hinton, *Why Did They Kill?*, 53–56. See also Willmott, "Analytical Errors."

71. Hinton, *Why Did They Kill?*, 56; Lenin, *Essential Works*, 299.

72. Geoffrey Warner, "Leaving Vietnam: Nixon, Kissinger and Ford, 1969–1975. Part One: January 1969–January 1972," 1489.

73. Operation Menu consisted of a series of six bombing campaigns, known as Breakfast, Lunch, Snack, Dinner, Supper, and Dessert. Each campaign targeted a specific base area located in the eastern provinces of Cambodia.

74. Ben Kiernan, "The American Bombardment of Kampuchea, 1969–1973"; William Shawcross, *Sideshow: Kissinger, Nixon, and the Destruction of Cambodia*; Taylor Owen and Ben Kiernan, "Bombs over Cambodia"; Brian Creech, "'The Rising Tide of War': Cambodian Bombings and the Discourses of American Military Power in *Time*"; Holly High, James R. Curran, and Gareth Robinson, "Electronic Records of the Air War over Southeast Asia: A Database Analysis"; and Ben Kiernan and Taylor Owen, "Making More Enemies than We Kill? Calculating U.S. Bomb Tonnages Dropped on Laos and Cambodia, and Weighing Their Implications."

75. Clymer, *Troubled Relations*, 96–101, 95.

76. See, for example, ibid.; and Shawcross, *Sideshow.*

77. Chandler, *A History of Cambodia*, 203.

78. Ibid., 208; Shawcross, *Sideshow*, 122; Clymer, *Troubled Relations*, 102.

79. Initially, China attempted to align itself with the Lon Nol government, if three conditions were met: permission for the Chinese to continue to supply the Vietnamese communists through Cambodian territory, authorization of Vietnamese communists to maintain their bases inside Cambodia, and Khmer support of the Vietnamese communists in government statements. In effect, the Chinese were willing to postpone the Cambodian revolution in order to help the Vietnamese revolution and to maintain a Chinese-Vietnamese front against the United States. The Lon Nol government, given its anti-Vietnamese and anticommunist hard-line stance, predictably refused the Chinese overture. It is also likely that Lon Nol assumed that the United States would not abandon a loyal ally in its proxy war against the communists.

80. Arnold Isaacs, *Without Honor: Defeat in Cambodia*, 199.

81. Donald Seekins, "Historical Setting," 43–44. Khmer Rouge members of GRUNK claimed that it was not a government in exile because Khieu Samphan and other officials remained in Cambodia. Publicly, neither Pol Pot, Ieng Sary, nor Nuon Chea was identified as a top leader—although political and military authority was firmly in their hands.

82. Richard M. Nixon, "Address to the Nation on the Situation in Southeast Asia," April 30, 1970, http://www.nixonlibrary.org.

83. Ibid.

84. Quoted in Kiernan, "American Bombardment," 5–6.

85. Shawcross, *Sideshow*, 294–95.

86. Isaacs, *Without Honor*, 218.

87. John Tully, *A Short History of Cambodia: From Empire to Survival*, 167.

88. Shawcross, *Sideshow*, 317; Henry Kamm, *Report from a Stricken Land*, 116.

89. Quoted in Kiernan, "American Bombardment," 13–14. See also Kiernan, *Pol Pot Regime*, 22.

90. Short, *Pol Pot*, 218.

91. Kiernan, "American Bombardment," 8, 20.

92. Ibid., 21.

93. Ibid., 22.

94. Ibid., 9.

95. Hinton, *Why Did They Kill?*, 57–58. For more on the Cambodian Civil War, see Wilfred Deac, *Road to the Killing Fields: The Cambodian War of 1970–1975*.

96. Anthony Barnett, "Democratic Kampuchea: A Highly Centralized Dictatorship," 214.

97. Clymer, *Troubled Relations*, 119.

98. Slocomb, *People's Republic of Kampuchea*, 18.

3. Reconstruction

1. Isaacs, *Without Honor*, 199. See also Noam Chomsky and Edward S. Herman, *After the Cataclysm: Postwar Indochina and the Reconstruction of Imperial Ideology*.

2. Isaacs, *Without Honor*, 209.

3. Ibid., 224.

4. Shawcross, *Sideshow*, 221; Isaacs, *Without Honor*, 208–10.

5. Shawcross, *Sideshow*, 222–23; Isaacs, *Without Honor*, 220.

6. Isaacs, *Without Honor*, 220.

7. Shawcross, *Sideshow*, 225; Isaacs, *Without Honor*, 209.

8. Shawcross, *Sideshow*, 348.

9. Ibid., 225.

10. Barnett, "Democratic Kampuchea," 214.

11. John J. Hamre and Gordon R. Sullivan, "Toward Postconflict Reconstruction," 89.

12. William Flavin, "Planning for Conflict Termination and Post-conflict Success."

13. Stephen Louw, "In the Shadows of the Pharaohs: The Militarization of Labour Debate and Classical Marxist Theory," 248–49.

14. Chandler, *Tragedy of Cambodian History*, 245. See also Kiernan, *How Pol Pot Came to Power*, 368.

15. Vatey Seng, *The Price We Paid: A Life Experience in the Khmer Rouge Regime, Cambodia*, 15, 16–17.

16. François Ponchaud, *Cambodia Year Zero*, 18.

17. Kevin McIntyre, "Geography as Destiny: Cities, Villages and Khmer Rouge Orientalism"; Karen J. Coates, *Cambodia Now: Life in the Wake of War*, 43.

18. Kiernan, *How Pol Pot Came to Power*, 371, 384.

19. Kiernan, *Pol Pot Regime*, 167.

20. Evsey D. Domar, "The Soviet Collective Farm as Producer Cooperative"; Michael E. Bradley, "Incentives and Labour Supply on Soviet Collective Farms"; Tse Ka-Kui, "Agricultural Collectivization and Socialist Construction: The Soviet Union and China"; Xin Meng, Nancy Qian, and Pierre Yared, "The Institutional Causes of China's Great Famine, 1959–1961."

21. Communist Party of Kampuchea, "Excerpted Report on the Leading Views of the Comrade Representing the Party Organization at a Zone Assembly," 25, 24.

22. Friedrich Engels, *The Origin of the Family, Private Property and the State*, 8.

23. Lenin, *Essential Works*, 290, 292 (emphasis in the original); Marx and Engels, *The Communist Manifesto*.

24. Lenin, *Essential Works*, 274.

25. Ibid., 290, 288.

26. Pol Pot, *Long Live the 17th Anniversary of the Communist Party of Kampuchea* (Phnom Penh: Ministry of Foreign Affairs, 1977), Document No. D30882, archived at the Documentation Center of Cambodia, Phnom Penh, 15, 17.

27. Quoted in Slocomb, *People's Republic of Kampuchea*, 21.

28. Thion, "Cambodian Idea of Revolution," 25.

29. "Minute Meetings of the Standing Committee, 9 January 1976," Document No. D00680, archived at the Documentation Center of Cambodia, Phnom Penh.

30. Document No. D55874, archived at the Documentation Center of Cambodia, Phnom Penh.

31. Brian R. Tomlinson, "What Was the Third World?," 309.

32. Tassin, "'Lift Up Your Head, My Brother,'" 148.

33. Roland Burke, "'The Compelling Dialogue of Freedom': Human Rights at the Bandung Conference," 948.

34. Tomlinson, "What Was the Third World?," 310.

35. Robert B. Potter et al., *Geographies of Development*, 22; A. W. Singham, "The Fifth Summit Conference of the Non-Aligned Movement," 5.

36. Document No. D55874.

37. Singham, "Fifth Summit Conference," 6–7.

38. Document No. D55874.

39. Ibid.

40. Ibid.

41. Ibid.

42. Ibid.

43. Christian Oesterheld, "Cambodian-Thai Relations during the Khmer Rouge Regime: Evidence from the East German Diplomatic Archives," 168.

44. Document No. D55874.

45. Ibid.

46. Pol Pot, *Long Live the 17th Anniversary*, 17.

47. Michael Waller, *Democratic Centralism: An Historical Commentary.*

48. Monty Johnstone, "Democratic Centralism," 135.

49. Stephen C. Angle, "Decent Democratic Centralism," 525.

50. Canchu Lin and Yueh-Ting Lee, "The Constitutive Rhetoric of Democratic Centralism: A Thematic Analysis of Mao's Discourse on Democracy," 151.

51. Quoted in Angle, "Decent Democratic Centralism," 525.

52. Jonathan London, "Viet Nam and the Making of Market-Leninism," 378.

53. Pol Pot, *Long Live the 17th Anniversary*, 59, 62.

54. Document No. D55874. It is noteworthy that Article 2 also specifies, "Articles for everyday use remain the personal property of the individual." This demonstrates that as of December 1975—at least in principle—individual private property was not yet abolished.

55. Ibid.; "Communist Party of Kampuchea: Statute," Document No. D00674, archived at the Documentation Center of Cambodia, Phnom Penh.

56. Membership fluctuated and normally consisted of upwards of thirty men and women. Apart from the Standing Committee members (who served on both committees), the Central Committee included Khieu Samphan, Koy Thuon, Ney Saran, and Ke Pok. The Central Committee also included a "Specialist Military Committee" that included Pol Pot, Nuon Chea, Son Sen, So Phim, and Ta Mok; Vorn Vet and Ke Pauk would later be added. See Office of the Co-Investigating Judges, *Closing Order*, 18.

57. Ibid., 17.

58. Document No. D55874; "Communist Party of Kampuchea: Statute," Document No. D00674. See also Office of the Co-Investigating Judges, *Closing Order*, 16.

59. "Communist Party of Kampuchea: Statute," Document No. D00674.

60. Ibid.; Office of the Co-Investigating Judges, *Closing Order*, 17.

61. Office of the Co-Investigating Judges, *Closing Order*, 17. Khieu Samphan (president of the State Presidium) was apparently not a formal member of the Standing Committee; however, evidence suggests that he actively contributed or assisted in their activities. See Office of the Co-Investigating Judges, *Closing Order*, 19.

62. The People's Representative Assembly met once, during a meeting held on April 11–13, 1976.

63. Documentary evidence indicates that the CPK Standing Committee decided as early as October 9, 1975, on these positions. See Office of the Co-Prosecutors, *Co-Prosecutors' Rule 66 Final Submission (Public Redacted Version)*, 51. For a thorough overview of these ministries, see Mertha, *Brothers in Arms*, 35–53.

64. Details of the establishment of these ministries are found in Document No. D21227, archived at the Documentation Center of Cambodia, Phnom Penh.

65. The respective ministers of these committees were Chey Soun, Cheng An, Koy Thuon, Ek Sophon, Mei Brang, and Ta Che. It is unclear how active any of these committees truly were; preliminary archival evidence suggests that the agriculture and commerce committees were most active. See ibid.

66. Nhem, *Khmer Rouge*, 46–47.

67. Mertha, *Brothers in Arms*, 24.

68. Lenin, *Essential Works*, 302.

69. Office of the Co-Investigating Judges, *Closing Order*, 20. Depending on the context, "870" may refer to the Standing Committee, Angkar, or even Pol Pot.

70. Ibid., 21.

71. The following is based on the extensive research in Boraden Nhem, *Khmer Rouge*, 29–32.

72. The third committee "member" may at times be simultaneously occupied by two or more people.

73. Mertha, *Brothers in Arms*, 30.

74. Nhem, *Khmer Rouge*, 30.

75. The Northeast, for example, was designated "108." In practice, numeric codes at the zonal level were rarely utilized.

76. Vickery, *Cambodia, 1975–1982*, 71–73.

77. Office of the Co-Prosecutors, *Co-Prosecutors' Rule 66*, 53.

78. Mertha, *Brothers in Arms*, 33.

79. The designation "group mother" was apparently used, regardless of the sex of the person in charge.

80. Herbert F. Schurmann, "Organizational Principles of the Chinese Communists," 52; James Tyner et al., "Phnom Penh during the Cambodian Genocide: A Case of Selective Urbicide."

81. London, "Viet Nam," 379.

82. Angle, "Decent Democratic Centralism," 525–26.

83. Communist Party of Kampuchea, "Report of Activities," 202, 203.

84. Internal factions among the CPK leadership would result in widespread purges.

85. Barnett, "Democratic Kampuchea," 215.

86. "Minutes of the Standing Committee's Visit to the Southwest Zone," Document No. L0001022, archived at the Documentation Center of Cambodia, Phnom Penh.

87. Lenin, *Essential Works*, 150; "Minutes of the Standing Committee's Visit," Document No. L0001022.

88. "Understand and Implement Political Line to Recruit People to Join the Front of People Democratic," Document No. D00676, archived at the Documentation Center of Cambodia, Phnom Penh.

89. Henri Locard, *Pol Pot's Little Red Book: The Sayings of Angkar*, 42. See also Hinton, *Why Did They Kill?*

90. Hinton, *Why Did They Kill?*, 81.

91. Communist Party of Kampuchea, "Decisions of the Central Committee on a Variety of Questions," 4–5; David P. Chandler, introduction to *Pol Pot Plans the Future: Confidential Leadership Documents from Democratic Kampuchea, 1976–1977*, edited by David Chandler, Ben Kiernan, and Chanta Boua, 1; Ponchaud, *Cambodia Year Zero*, 31.

92. Lenin, *Essential Works*, 285; Communist Party of Kampuchea, "Decisions of the Central Committee," 6.

93. Quoted in Ponchaud, *Cambodia Year Zero*, 27.

94. Quoted in ibid., 64, 65.

95. Quoted in ibid.

96. Lenin, *Essential Works*, 306.

4. Production

1. Francesca Bray, *The Rice Economies: Technology & Development in Asian Societies*, 13, 15.

2. Helmers, "Rice in the Cambodian Economy," 1.

3. With irrigation, of course, rice may be cultivated year-round.

4. Ibid., 2.

5. Henry J. Nesbitt and Chan Phaloeun, "Rice-Based Farming Systems," 31. See also E. L. Javier, "Rice Ecosystems and Varieties."

6. Nesbitt and Phaloeun, "Rice-Based Farming," 33.

7. Ibid.

8. The timing of sowing is also influenced by the photosensitivity of the rice seed. This refers to the relationship between rice variety and exposure to sunlight.

9. Javier, "Rice Ecosystems and Varieties," 44.

10. Ibid., 63.

11. Ibid., 75–76.

12. Historically, Vietnamese emperors had forbidden the export of rice. On the one hand, this prohibition was to provide some security against the possibility of famine, and, on the other hand, it was a means of retaining economic sovereignty through the avoidance of foreign alliances.

13. Paige, *Agrarian Revolutions*, 281.

14. Ibid., 305.

15. Helmers, "Rice in the Cambodian Economy," 2–3.

16. Ibid., 3; Chandler, *A History of Cambodia*.

17. Helmers, "Rice in the Cambodian Economy," 4.

18. Ibid., 4, 5.

19. Chandler, *Tragedy of Cambodian History*, 145.

20. Helmers, "Rice in the Cambodian Economy," 5.

21. Chandler, *A History of Cambodia*, 201.

22. Shawcross, *Sideshow.*

23. Bert Pijpers, *Kampuchea*, 5, 6.

24. Ibid., 8, 9.

25. It should be noted that no detailed study has attempted to calculate how much land was devoted to rice, maize, or tobacco under the Khmer Rouge; accordingly, such sweeping statements must be treated with caution.

26. Communist Party of Kampuchea, "Party's Four-Year Plan," 51.

27. Communist Party of Kampuchea, "Preliminary Explanation before Reading the Plan, by the Party Secretary," 133. To date, no empirical research has attempted to reconstruct with any level of specificity actual production levels throughout Democratic Kampuchea. At best, scholars parrot the unrealistic goal of three tons per hectare with little acknowledgment that at a national level, CPK documents identify that different areas will exhibit different yields.

28. Nhem, *Khmer Rouge*, 54; Communist Party of Kampuchea, "Preliminary Explanation," 134, 135.

29. Pijpers, *Kampuchea*, 9.

30. Ibid., 10.

31. David Biggs, *Quagmire: Nation-Building and Nature in the Mekong Delta.*

32. Pijpers, *Kampuchea*, 10–11 (emphasis added).

33. Communist Party of Kampuchea, "Party's Four-Year Plan," 51 (emphasis added).

34. Robert Albritton, *Economics Transformed: Discovering the Brilliance of Marx*, 26.

35. Marx, *Capital*, 1:140.

36. Michael Heinrich, *Introduction to Marx's "Capital,"* 58.

37. Marx, *Capital*, vol. 2.

38. Tony Smith, "The Underdevelopment of Development Literature: The Case of Dependency Theory"; Michael P. Todaro, *Economic Development in the Third World*; Henry J. Bruton, "A Reconsideration of Import Substitution"; Potter et al., *Geographies of Development.*

39. Todaro, *Economic Development*, 428.

40. Bruton, "Reconsideration of Import Substitution," 904.

41. "Cooperation with the Ministry of Commerce," Document No. D00698, archived at the Documentation Center of Cambodia, Phnom Penh.

42. Communist Party of Kampuchea, "Report of Activities," 200. This statement is important in that it reveals, on the one hand, a general indifference to use value; anything can be commodified. On the other hand, it highlights a broader indifference to life itself. If we reconsider the well-repeated slogan of the Khmer Rouge—"Spare them, no profit; remove them, no loss"—we gain a different understanding of CPK practice. The apparent

indifference to life expressed by the Khmer Rouge results not from some abstract callous-ness on behalf of the party center, but rather from a materialist rationale predicated on capital accumulation. The overarching concern of the CPK was to reorient all policies toward this singular goal. This theme is developed in greater detail in chapter 5.

43. Ibid.

44. Paul Knox and John Agnew, *The Geography of the World Economy*, 272.

45. Eric Sheppard, "Competition in Space and between Places," 178.

46. Communist Party of Kampuchea, "Excerpted Report," 27; Communist Party of Kampuchea, "Party's Four-Year Plan," 46, 51.

47. Communist Party of Kampuchea, "Preliminary Explanation before Reading the Plan, by the Party Secretary," 132.

48. Document No. L0001022, archived at the Documentation Center of Cambodia, Phnom Penh.

49. Pol Pot and the CPK identified a number of "objective" problems related to the production of rice, including but not limited to the availability of water for irrigation; access to necessary fertilizers, pesticides, and herbicides; and adequate numbers of agri-cultural tools. As for irrigation, the CPK launched massive work projects—employing forced labor—to construct a network of dikes, canals, and reservoirs. As for chemicals and tools, they were to be either manufactured within Democratic Kampuchea or purchased from abroad, again using revenues generated from the export of rice.

50. Marx, *Capital*, 1:203.

51. Document No. D23948, archived at the Documentation Center of Cambodia, Phnom Penh.

52. Such material-based money transactions did take place, especially when the Khmer Rouge traded with their Thai neighbors.

53. Harvey, *Companion to Marx's "Capital,"* 85.

54. Marx, *Capital*, 1:279.

55. Ibid., 645. It is for this reason that struggles over the length of the working day have been so contested.

56. Communist Party of Kampuchea, "Party's Four-Year Plan," 112; Chhay Phan, interviewed by Bunthan, June 15, 2011, archived at the Documentation Center of Cam-bodia, Phnom Penh.

57. "Minutes of the Meeting on Base Work, March 8, 1976," Document No. D00684, archived at the Documentation Center of Cambodia, Phnom Penh.

58. Ernest Mandel, *An Introduction to Marxist Economic Theory*, 30.

59. Marx, *Capital*, 1:129.

60. Benjamin Fine and Alfredo Saad-Filho, *Marx's "Capital,"* 38.

61. Moishe Postone, *Time, Labor, and Social Domination: A Reinterpretation of Marx's Critical Theory*, 193.

62. Marx, *Capital*, 1:436–37.

63. Ibid., 129.

64. Communist Party of Kampuchea, "Party's Four-Year Plan," tables 11, 14, 17, 20, 23.

65. Harvey, *Companion to Marx's "Capital,"* 165.

66. "Meeting Minutes of the Standing Committee on May 30, 1976," Document No. D00704, archived at the Documentation Center of Cambodia, Phnom Penh.

67. Communist Party of Kampuchea, "Party's Four-Year Plan," 51.

68. Mandel, *Marxist Economic Theory,* 31.

69. Jason Read, *Micro-politics of Capital: Marx and the Prehistory of the Present,* 105.

70. Marx, *Capital,* 1:645.

71. Twining, "The Economy," 127–28.

72. Kalyanee Mam, "The Endurance of the Cambodian Family under the Khmer Rouge Regime: An Oral History," 134–35.

73. Twining, "The Economy," 128.

74. Communist Party of Kampuchea, "Party's Four-Year Plan," table 60. See also Communist Party of Kampuchea, "Excerpted Report," 20.

75. Twining, "The Economy," 130.

76. Chhum Seng, interviewed by Vanthan Peou Dara, June 18, 2011, transcript archived at the Documentation Center of Cambodia, Phnom Penh.

77. See, for example, Resnick and Wolff, *Class Theory and History.*

78. Neil Smith, *Uneven Development: Nature, Capital, and the Production of Space,* 59, 63.

79. Bertell Ollman, *Alienation: Marx's Conception of Man in Capitalist Society,* 136.

80. Ibid., 151.

81. Locard, *Pol Pot's Little Red Book,* 246, 249, 227.

82. Communist Party of Kampuchea, "Party's Four-Year Plan," 48; Daniel Bultmann, "Irrigating a Socialist Utopia: Disciplinary Space and Population Control under the Khmer Rouge, 1975–1979," 48.

83. While it certainly holds that a person's consciousness is constituted by all of his or her social relationships and practices—and not just "economic" ones—I maintain that for the CPK, economic relations, as defined by agricultural work, were preeminent.

84. Bultmann, "Irrigating a Socialist Utopia," 49.

85. In an earlier draft of this manuscript, a reviewer astutely questioned: If collective production would overcome individuality, where did the consciousness come from that would enable "traitors" to sabotage the production process? This question is a key point, one worth pursing at greater length. Here, suffice it to say that the CPK was paranoid of foreign subversives that might introduce this consciousness into society: Vietnamese infiltrators, CIA-trained operatives, and so on. It was for this reason that the CPK periodically purged its members.

86. Communist Party of Kampuchea, "Report of Activities," 185, 186.

5. Manufacturing Indifference

1. Locard, *Pol Pot's Little Red Book*, 210; Cunha et al., "Organization (Angkar) as a State of Exception," 290; Clegg et al., "Theory and Practice of Utopia," 1738.

2. Locard, *Pol Pot's Little Red Book*, 182.

3. Hinton, *Why Did They Kill?*

4. Marx and Engels, *German Ideology*, 42.

5. Karl Marx, *Grundrisse: Foundations of the Critique of Political Economy*, 104.

6. Ibid.

7. Paul D'Amato, *The Meaning of Marxism*, 55.

8. Karl Marx, *Economic and Philosophic Manuscripts of 1844*, 20.

9. Marx, *Capital*, 1:348.

10. Tania Murray Li, "To Make Live or Let Die? Rural Dispossession and the Protection of Surplus Populations," 67.

11. Robert Albritton, *Let Them Eat Junk: How Capitalism Creates Hunger and Obesity*, 37; Harvey, *Companion to Marx's "Capital,"* 145–46.

12. Ministry of Culture and Fine Arts and the Documentation Center of Cambodia, *The Forced Transfer: The Second Evacuation of People during the Khmer Rouge Regime*.

13. Marx, *Grundrisse*, 247–48.

14. Kathi Weeks, *The Problem with Work: Feminism, Marxism, Antiwork Politics, and Postwork Imaginaries*, 10.

15. Communist Party of Kampuchea, "Report of Activities," 197, 211.

16. Barnett, "Democratic Kampuchea," 212, 216; Michael Vickery, "Democratic Kampuchea: Themes and Variations," 101.

17. Barnett, "Democratic Kampuchea," 216, 220.

18. Clegg et al., "Theory and Practice of Utopia," 1739.

19. Jan Ovesen and Ing-Britt Trankell, *Cambodians and Their Doctors: A Medical Anthropology of Colonial and Post-colonial Cambodia*, 9.

20. Ibid., 69.

21. Ibid., 79–81.

22. Many positions within the medical sector were filled by the daughters of high-ranking Khmer Rouge leaders. The four daughters of Ta Mok, for example, became nurses; likewise, all three of Ieng Thirith's children became "social affairs" cadre in Phnom Penh. See, for example, Sokhym Em, "Revolutionary Female Medical Staff in Tram Kak District," pt. 1, 25.

23. According to Sokhym Em, the motivation to volunteer varied. For some girls, it was a means of avoiding oppression by local authorities; for others, it was a way to avoid fighting on the battlefield. See ibid.

24. Sokhym Em, "Female Patients," 26; Lenin, *Essential Works*, 302.

25. See, for example, "Meeting about Works, Social Affairs and Health," June 10, 1976, Document No. D00707, archived at the Documentation Center of Cambodia, Phnom Penh.

26. James A. Tyner, Sokvisal Kimsroy, and Savina Sirik, "Nature, Poetry, and Public Pedagogy: The Poetic Geographies of the Khmer Rouge."

27. Communist Party of Kampuchea, "Preliminary Explanation," 160.

28. Em, "Revolutionary Female Medical Staff," pt. 2.

29. Ovesen and Trankell, *Cambodians and Their Doctors*, 91.

30. Chandler, *Tragedy of Cambodian History*, 249, 259.

31. See, for example, Documents D29694, D23720, D20473, and D21033, all archived at the Documentation Center of Cambodia, Phnom Penh.

32. Imported medicines and medical equipment, dental equipment and dental supplies, and pharmaceuticals were initially stored in warehouses in Phnom Penh and Sihanoukville before being distributed to various hospitals and clinics throughout the country. The most important distribution facility was apparently the "K2" warehouse, located in Phnom Penh.

33. Chinese advisers likewise oversaw the production of Western-based medicines and pharmaceuticals; these goods were produced with the raw materials imported from Thailand, Hong Kong, and elsewhere. The quality of these drugs varied widely; their distribution was selective. As with medicinal care overall, drugs were rationed throughout Democratic Kampuchea, with the Khmer Rouge calculating who was to receive which medicines.

34. Ovesen and Trankell, *Cambodians and Their Doctors*, 107

35. Sokhym Em, "Rabbit Dropping Medicine," 22.

36. Ovesen and Trankell, *Cambodians and Their Doctors*, 91.

37. Ibid., 92.

38. Ibid., 87.

39. The Russian Hospital was reserved for adults, while the Calmette Hospital was a children's hospital. Both served almost exclusively members of the CPK and other high-ranking political and military leaders.

40. Ibid., 102.

41. Em, "Female Patients," 26.

42. Laura Vilim, "'Keeping Them Alive, One Gets Nothing; Killing Them, One Loses Nothing': Prosecuting Khmer Rouge Medical Practices as Crimes against Humanity," n.p.

43. Albritton, *Economics Transformed*, 22.

44. Marx, *Capital*, 3:297; Albritton, *Economics Transformed*, 26.

45. Albritton, *Economics Transformed*, 22.

46. Communist Party of Kampuchea, "Preliminary Explanation," 160.

47. Locard, *Pol Pot's Little Red Book*, 227; Communist Party of Kampuchea, "Party's Four-Year Plan," 48.

48. See, for example, Locard, *Pol Pot's Little Red Book*.

49. Communist Party of Kampuchea, "Preliminary Explanation," 156.

50. Locard, *Pol Pot's Little Red Book*, 187–88; Achille Mbembe, "Necropolitics," 14.

51. This point is not to argue that rank-and-file cadre did not engage in cruelty for noneconomic rationales. See the extensive treatment on direct killing in Hinton, *Why Did They Kill?*

52. Will Cartwright, "Killing and Letting Die: A Defensible Distinction," 354.

53. David P. Chandler, "Introduction to Document III," 36, 41.

54. Johan Galtung, "Violence, Peace, and Peace Research," 170–71 (emphasis added).

55. Akhil Gupta, *Red Tape: Bureaucracy, Structural Violence, and Poverty in India*, 19–20.

56. Locard, *Pol Pot's Little Red Book*, 187–88. Locard explains that the reference to "imagination" is somewhat ambiguous (ibid.). In Khmer Rouge parlance, the term could mean "ideological frame of mind." Consequently, those individuals accused of malingering were behaving so because their minds were infected with the ideology of the old society; they were not pure of mind or heart. This point is made clear in the slogan "If you have the disease of the old society, take a dose of Lenin as medication."

57. Kenton Clymer, "Jimmy Carter, Human Rights, and Cambodia," 247, 251.

58. Bangkok Embassy Telegram 21997, "Cambodia—Conversations with the Resistance," September 29, 1977, http://nsarchive.gwu/NSAEBB/NSAEBB463.

59. For a more extensive discussion, see James A. Tyner, *Landscape, Memory, and Post-violence in Cambodia*.

60. Randle C. DeFalco, "Accounting for Famine at the Extraordinary Chambers in the Courts of Cambodia: The Crimes against Humanity of Extermination, Inhumane Acts and Persecution," 151–52; Document No. D21934, archived at the Documentation Center of Cambodia, Phnom Penh.

61. See, for example, Document Nos. D00707 and D02166, archived at the Documentation Center of Cambodia, Phnom Penh.

62. In actuality, there were many different "colored" clothes.

6. Abolishment and Reproduction

1. Kalyanee E. Mam, "An Oral History of Family Life under the Khmer Rouge," 2, 3. See also May Ebihara, "A Cambodian Village under the Khmer Rouge"; Siv Leng Chhor, "Destruction of Family Foundation in Kampuchea"; Ratana C. Huy, "Khmer Rouge Wedding"; Judy Ledgerwood and John Vijghen, "Decision-Making in Rural Khmer Villages"; Zal Karkaria, "Failure through Neglect: The Women's Policies of the Khmer

Rouge"; Patrick Heuveline and Bunnak Poch, "Do Marriages Forget Their Past? Marital Stability in Post–Khmer Rouge Cambodia"; Katherine Brickell, "Gender Relations in the Khmer 'Home': Post-conflict Perspectives"; Annuska Derks, *Khmer Women on the Move: Exploring Work and Life in Urban Cambodia*; Neha Jain, "Forced Marriage as a Crime against Humanity"; Peg LeVine, *Love and Dread in Cambodia: Weddings, Births, and Ritual Harm under the Khmer Rouge*; Chan Pranith Phuong, "Forced Marriage to Avoid the Death"; and Heidi Hoefinger, *Sex, Love and Money in Cambodia: Professional Girlfriends and Transactional Relationships*.

2. Susan H. Lee, *"Rice Plus": Widows and Economic Survival in Rural Cambodia*, 23.

3. Ibid., 24–27.

4. Derks, *Khmer Women on the Move*, 12.

5. See, for example, Lee, *"Rice Plus"*; and Hoefinger, *Sex, Love and Money*.

6. Huy, "Khmer Rouge Wedding," 28; Ebihara, "Cambodian Village" 58; Heuveline and Poch, "Do Marriages Forget Their Past?," 102.

7. Huy, "Khmer Rouge Wedding," 27.

8. Jain, "Forced Marriage," 1024.

9. Vickery, *Cambodia, 1975–1982*, 186; Jain, "Forced Marriage," 1025.

10. LeVine, *Love and Dread*, 24, 26; Huy, "Khmer Rouge Wedding," 27.

11. Marx, *Capital*, 1:711.

12. See, for example, Louis Althusser, *On the Reproduction of Capitalism: Ideology and Ideological State Apparatuses*, 48 passim.

13. Engels, *Origin of the Family*, 26; Michèle Barrett, *Women's Oppression Today: The Marxist/Feminist Encounter*, 20; Heather A. Brown, *Marx on Gender and the Family: A Critical Study*, 28.

14. Mandel, *Marxist Economic Theory*, 31.

15. Marx, *Grundrisse*, 158.

16. Barrett, *Women's Oppression Today*, 187.

17. But see, for example, Judy L. Ledgerwood, "Khmer Kinship: The Matriliny/Matriarchy Myth" and "Politics and Gender: Negotiating Changing Cambodian Ideas of the Proper Woman"; and Trudy Jacobsen, *Lost Goddesses: The Denial of Female Power in Cambodian History*.

18. By convention, productive work refers to the provision of food, shelter, and clothing; reproductive work includes those tasks necessary to reproduce people, such as child rearing and socialization.

19. Stuart C. Aitken, *Family Fantasies and Community Space*, 39, 40.

20. Elizabeth Uy Eviota, *The Political Economy of Gender: Women and the Sexual Division of Labor in the Philippines*, 11.

21. Aitken, *Family Fantasies*, 39.

22. Paul Knox, John Agnew, and Linda McCarthy, *The Geography of the World Economy*, 127.

23. Eviota, *Political Economy of Gender*, 12, 13.

24. Peter Saunders and Peter Williams, "The Constitution of the Home: Towards a Research Agenda," 85.

25. Mona Domosh and Joni Seager, *Putting Women in Place: Feminist Geographers Make Sense of the World*, 3–4.

26. Aitken, *Family Fantasies*, 27, 41.

27. Ibid., 46.

28. Domosh and Seager, *Putting Women in Place*, 5.

29. Aitken, *Family Fantasies*, 46.

30. Eviota, *Political Economy of Gender*, 14.

31. Linda McDowell, *Gender, Identity & Place: Understanding Feminist Geographies*, 75.

32. Aitken, *Family Fantasies*, 47.

33. Andrew Sayer and Richard Walker, *The New Social Economy: Reworking the Division of Labor*, 34–36, 43.

34. Wayne D. Myslik, "Renegotiating the Social/Sexual Identities of Places: Gay Communities as Safe Havens or Sites of Resistance?," 159.

35. Domosh and Seager, *Putting Women in Place*, 4.

36. Marx and Engels, *German Ideology*, 48–49.

37. Wendy Z. Goldman, *Women, the State, and Revolution: Soviet Family Policy and Social Life, 1917–1936*, 31.

38. Barrett, *Women's Oppression Today*, 190. See also Richard Weikart, "Marx, Engels, and the Abolition of the Family."

39. Brown, *Marx on Gender*, 42.

40. See, for example, Maria Mies, *Patriarchy and Accumulation on a World Scale: Women in the International Division of Labor*; Leopoldina Fortunai, *The Arcane of Reproduction: Housework, Prostitution, Labor and Capital*; Silvia Federici, *Caliban and the Witch: Women, the Body and Primitive Accumulation*; Lise Vogel, *Marxism and the Oppression of Women: Toward a Unitary Theory*.

41. Lenin, *Essential Works*, 290.

42. Locard, *Pol Pot's Little Red Book*, 269–70; Becker, *When the War Was Over*, 226. An alternative interpretation, having nothing to do with the family, was that aliases were used to promote secrecy. See also Hinton, *Why Did They Kill?* for an extended discussion on the symbolism of proper nouns and forms of address under the Khmer Rouge.

43. Becker, *When the War Was Over*, 226–27.

44. Translated by Sayana Ser, published in *Searching for the Truth* 9 (2000).

45. In practice, top positions were held by men. Here the exceptions prove the rule. Ieng Thirith was minister of social affairs—but she was also the wife of Ieng Sary, the foreign minister and also sister-in-law of Pol Pot. Yun Yat, in charge of culture, education, and propaganda, was the wife of Defense Minister Son Sen.

46. Communist Party of Kampuchea, "Preliminary Explanation," 158.

47. Goldman, *Women, the State, and Revolution*, esp. chap. 6.

48. Hoefinger, *Sex, Love and Money*, 12.

49. Judy L. Ledgerwood, "Changing Khmer Conceptions of Womanhood: Women, Stories and the Social Order," 30–31; Derks, *Khmer Women on the Move*, 171.

50. Nakagawa Kasumi, *Gender-Based Violence during the Khmer Rouge Regime: Stories of Survivors from the Democratic Kampuchea (1975–1979)*, 10; Jacobsen, *Lost Goddesses*.

51. Mam, "Oral History of Family Life," 3.

52. Ibid., 13, 15.

53. This latter concept (social reproduction) has generated substantial debate over the years, including but not limited to the relationship between "productive" work and "nonproductive" work, wage work and domestic work, and the formal and informal labor markets.

54. Marx, *Capital*, 1:275.

55. Rosa Luxemburg, *The Accumulation of Capital*, 6.

56. "Cooperation with the Ministry of Commerce," Document No. D00698, archived at the Documentation Center of Cambodia, Phnom Penh.

57. In attendance were Pol Pot, Nuon Chea, Vorn Vet, Son Sen, and Khieu Samphan; Phouk Chhoy recorded the minutes.

58. "Minutes: Meeting of Standing Committee on May 30, 1976," Document No. D00704, archived at the Documentation Center of Cambodia, Phnom Penh.

59. Luxemburg, *The Accumulation of Capital*, 9 passim. See esp. Marx, *Capital*, vol. 2.

60. Luxemburg, *The Accumulation of Capital*, 10.

61. Ibid., 11.

62. Ibid., 14–15.

63. Marx, *Capital*, 1:1067, 342.

64. Luxemburg, *The Accumulation of Capital*, 43.

65. Indeed, if workers were accused of malingering, they received less rations; if they refused to work, they could be executed.

66. Mam, "Oral History of Family Life"; Jain, "Forced Marriage."

67. Marx, *Capital*, 1:719.

68. Ibid., 381.

69. I am grateful to an anonymous reviewer who raised this key question in an earlier version of this chapter.

7. Dead Labor

1. Interview with Chin Sary, by Phan Sochea, June 15, 2004, archived at the Documentation Center of Cambodia, Phnom Penh.

2. Quoted in Rasy Pheng, "Discovery of the Sre Lieu Mass Grave," 18.

3. See, for example, interview with Chann Eng, by Kan Penhsamnang, September 25, 2010; interview with Hong Khna, by Kimsroy Sokvisal, September 21, 2010; interview with Sao Hoan, by Long Dany, June 16, 2004; and interview with Haom Pheuy, by Pheng Pong-rasy, June 12, 2004, all archived at the Documentation Center of Cambodia, Phnom Penh.

4. Samon Prum, "A Wish to See the Khmer Rouge Tribunal."

5. Quoted in ibid.

6. For an extensive discussion of the memorialization of Cambodia's past violence, see Tyner, *Landscape, Memory, and Post-violence.* For a discussion of the politics and practices of documenting Democratic Kampuchea, see Craig Etcheson, *After the Killing Fields: Lessons from the Cambodian Genocide.*

7. Marx, *Economic and Philosophic Manuscripts,* 71; Don Mitchell, "Dead Labor and the Political Economy of Landscape: California Living, California Dying," 235. See also Don Mitchell, "Dead Labor: The Geography of Workplace Violence in America and Beyond."

8. Scott Kirsch and Don Mitchell, "The Nature of Things: Dead Labor, Nonhuman Actors, and the Persistence of Marxism," 696.

9. Marx, *Capital,* 1:775.

10. Locard, *Pol Pot's Little Red Book,* 227; Communist Party of Kampuchea, "Party's Four-Year Plan," 48.

11. Marx, *Capital,* 1:289, 290.

12. Ibid., 2:434.

13. Wolff, *Democracy at Work,* 100, 101.

Bibliography

Agamben, Giorgio. *State of Exception*. Translated by Kevin Attell. Chicago: Univ. of Chicago Press, 2005.

Aitken, Stuart C. *Family Fantasies and Community Space*. New Brunswick, NJ: Rutgers Univ. Press, 1998.

Albritton, Robert. *Economics Transformed: Discovering the Brilliance of Marx*. Ann Arbor, MI: Pluto, 2007.

———. *Let Them Eat Junk: How Capitalism Creates Hunger and Obesity*. New York: Pluto, 2009.

Althusser, Louis. *On the Reproduction of Capitalism: Ideology and Ideological State Apparatuses*. Translated by G. M. Goshgarian. New York: Verso, 2014.

Angle, Stephen C. "Decent Democratic Centralism." *Political Theory* 33, no. 4 (2005): 518–46.

Barnett, Anthony. "Democratic Kampuchea: A Highly Centralized Dictatorship." In *Revolution and Its Aftermath: Eight Essays*, edited by David P. Chandler and Ben Kiernan, 212–19. New Haven, CT: Yale Univ., Southeast Asia Studies, 1983.

Barrett, Michèle. *Women's Oppression Today: The Marxist/Feminist Encounter*. 3rd ed. Brooklyn: Verso, 2014.

Beachler, Donald W. "Arguing about Cambodia: Genocide and Political Interest." *Holocaust and Genocide Studies* 23, no. 2 (2009): 214–38.

Becker, Elizabeth. *When the War Was Over: Cambodia and the Khmer Rouge Revolution*. New York: Public Affairs, 1998.

Biggs, David. *Quagmire: Nation-Building and Nature in the Mekong Delta*. Seattle: Univ. of Washington Press, 2010.

Bradley, Michael E. "Incentives and Labour Supply on Soviet Collective Farms." *Canadian Journal of Economics* 4, no. 3 (1971): 342–52.

Bray, Francesca. *The Rice Economies: Technology & Development in Asian Societies*. Berkeley: Univ. of California Press, 1986.

Brickell, Katherine. "Gender Relations in the Khmer 'Home': Post-conflict Perspectives." PhD diss., London School of Economics and Political Science, 2007.

Brown, Heather A. *Marx on Gender and the Family: A Critical Study.* Chicago: Haymarket Books, 2013.

Bruton, Henry J. "A Reconsideration of Import Substitution." *Journal of Economic Literature* 36, no. 2 (1998): 903–36.

Buick, Adam, and John Crump. *State Capitalism: The Wages System under New Management.* London: Macmillan, 1986.

Bultmann, Daniel. "Irrigating a Socialist Utopia: Disciplinary Space and Population Control under the Khmer Rouge, 1975–1979." *Transcience* 3, no. 1 (2012): 40–52.

Burke, Roland. "'The Compelling Dialogue of Freedom': Human Rights at the Bandung Conference." *Human Rights Quarterly* 28, no. 4 (2006): 947–65.

Cartwright, Will. "Killing and Letting Die: A Defensible Distinction." *British Medical Bulletin* 52, no. 2 (1996): 354–61.

Chandler, David P. *Brother Number One: A Political Biography of Pol Pot.* Rev. ed. Chiang Mai, Thailand: Silkworm Books, 1999.

———. "From 'Cambodge' to 'Kampuchea': State and Revolution in Cambodia, 1863–1979." *Thesis Eleven* 50, no. 1 (1997): 35–49.

———. *A History of Cambodia.* 3rd ed. Boulder, CO: Westview Press, 2000.

———. "Introduction to Document III." In *Pol Pot Plans the Future: Confidential Leadership Documents from Democratic Kampuchea, 1976–1977*, edited by David Chandler, Ben Kiernan, and Chanta Boua, 36–43. New Haven, CT: Yale Univ., Southeast Asia Studies, 1988.

———. Introduction to *Pol Pot Plans the Future: Confidential Leadership Documents from Democratic Kampuchea, 1976–1977*, edited by David Chandler, Ben Kiernan, and Chanta Boua, 1–2. New Haven, CT: Yale Univ., Southeast Asia Studies, 1988.

———. "Revising the Past in Democratic Kampuchea: When Was the Birthday of the Party?" *Pacific Affairs* 56, no. 2 (1983): 288–300.

———. "Seeing Red: Perceptions of Cambodian History in Democratic Kampuchea." In *Revolution and Its Aftermath: Eight Essays*, edited by David P. Chandler and Ben Kiernan, 34–56. New Haven, CT: Yale Univ., Southeast Asia Studies, 1983.

———. *The Tragedy of Cambodian History: Politics, War, and Revolution since 1945.* New Haven, CT: Yale Univ. Press, 1991.

————. *Voices from S-21: Terror and History in Pol Pot's Secret Prison.* Berkeley: Univ. of California Press, 1999.

Cherne, Leo. "Cambodia—Auschwitz of Asia." *Worldview* 21, nos. 7–8 (1978): 21–25.

Chhor, Siv Leng. "Destruction of Family Foundation in Kampuchea." *Searching for the Truth* 11 (2000): 22–23.

Chomsky, Noam, and Edward S. Herman. *After the Cataclysm: Postwar Indochina and the Reconstruction of Imperial Ideology.* Chicago: Haymarket Books, 2014.

Clegg, Stewart, Miguel Pina e Cunha, and Arménio Rego. "The Theory and Practice of Utopia in a Total Institution: The Pineapple Panopticon." *Organization Studies* 33, no. 12 (2012): 1735–57.

Cliff, Tony. *State Capitalism in Russia.* London: Pluto Press, 1955.

Clymer, Kenton. "Jimmy Carter, Human Rights, and Cambodia." *Diplomatic History* 27, no. 2 (2003): 245–78.

————. *Troubled Relations: The United States and Cambodia since 1870.* DeKalb: Northern Illinois Univ. Press, 2007.

Coates, Karen J. *Cambodia Now: Life in the Wake of War.* Jefferson, NC: McFarland, 2005.

Communist Party of Kampuchea. "Decisions of the Central Committee on a Variety of Questions." In *Pol Pot Plans the Future: Confidential Leadership Documents from Democratic Kampuchea, 1976–1977*, edited by David Chandler, Ben Kiernan, and Chanta Boua, 3–8. New Haven, CT: Yale Univ., Southeast Asia Studies, 1988.

————. "Excerpted Report on the Leading Views of the Comrade Representing the Party Organization at a Zone Assembly." In *Pol Pot Plans the Future: Confidential Leadership Documents from Democratic Kampuchea, 1976–1977*, edited by David Chandler, Ben Kiernan, and Chanta Boua, 13–35. New Haven, CT: Yale Univ., Southeast Asia Studies, 1988.

————. "The Party's Four-Year Plan to Build Socialism in All Fields, 1977–1980." In *Pol Pot Plans the Future: Confidential Leadership Documents from Democratic Kampuchea, 1976–1977*, edited by David Chandler, Ben Kiernan, and Chanta Boua, 45–119. New Haven, CT: Yale Univ., Southeast Asia Studies, 1988.

————. "Preliminary Explanation before Reading the Plan, by the Party Secretary." In *Pol Pot Plans the Future: Confidential Leadership Documents from Democratic Kampuchea, 1976–1977*, edited by David Chandler, Ben

Kiernan, and Chanta Boua, 124–63. New Haven, CT: Yale Univ., Southeast Asia Studies, 1988.

———. "Report of Activities of the Party Center according to the General Political Tasks of 1976." In *Pol Pot Plans the Future: Confidential Leadership Documents from Democratic Kampuchea, 1976–1977*, edited by David Chandler, Ben Kiernan, and Chanta Boua, 182–212. New Haven, CT: Yale Univ., Southeast Asia Studies, 1988.

Cooper, Mark N. "State Capitalism, Class Structure, and Social Transformation in the Third World: The Case of Egypt." *International Journal of Middle East Studies* 15, no. 4 (1983): 451–69.

Creech, Brian. "'The Rising Tide of War': Cambodian Bombings and the Discourses of American Military Power in *Time*." *Communication Review* 16, no. 4 (2013): 189–210.

Cunha, Miguel Pina e, Stewart Clegg, Arménio Rego, and Michele Lancione. "The Organization (Angkar) as a State of Exception: The Case of the S-21 Extermination Camp, Phnom Penh." *Journal of Political Power* 5, no. 2 (2012): 279–99.

D'Amato, Paul. *The Meaning of Marxism*. Chicago: Haymarket Books, 2006.

Deac, Wilfred. *Road to the Killing Fields: The Cambodian War of 1970–1975*. College Station: Texas A&M Univ. Press, 1997.

DeFalco, Randle C. "Accounting for Famine at the Extraordinary Chambers in the Courts of Cambodia: The Crimes against Humanity of Extermination, Inhumane Acts and Persecution." *International Journal of Transitional Justice* 5, no. 1 (2011): 142–58.

———. "Justice and Starvation in Cambodia: The Khmer Rouge Famine." *Cambodia Law and Policy Journal* 2 (2014): 45–84.

Derks, Annuska. *Khmer Women on the Move: Exploring Work and Life in Urban Cambodia*. Honolulu: Univ. of Hawai'i Press, 2008.

Domar, Evsey D. "The Soviet Collective Farm as Producer Cooperative." *American Economic Review* 56, no. 4 (1966): 734–57.

Domosh, Mona, and Joni Seager. *Putting Women in Place: Feminist Geographers Make Sense of the World*. New York: Guilford Press, 2001.

Duiker, William J. *The Communist Road to Power in Vietnam*. 2nd ed. Boulder, CO: Westview Press, 1996.

Ebihara, May. "A Cambodian Village under the Khmer Rouge." In *Genocide and Democracy in Cambodia: The Khmer Rouge, the United Nations and the*

International Community, edited by Ben Kiernan, 51–63. New Haven, CT: Yale Univ., Southeast Asia Studies, 1993.

Edwards, Matthew. "The Rise of the Khmer Rouge in Cambodia: Internal or External Origins?" *Asian Affairs* 35, no. 1 (2004): 56–67.

Em, Sokhym. "Female Patients." *Searching for the Truth* 33 (2002): 25–29.

———. "Rabbit Dropping Medicine." *Searching for the Truth* 30 (2002): 22–23.

———. "Revolutionary Female Medical Staff in Tram Kak District." Pts. 1 and 2. *Searching for the Truth* 34 (2002): 24–27; 35 (2002): 17–19.

Engels, Friedrich. *Anti-Dühring: Herr Eugen Dühring's Revolution in Science.* Moscow: Foreign Languages Publishing House, 1962.

———. *The Origin of the Family, Private Property and the State.* New York: Penguin, 2010.

Etcheson, Craig. *After the Killing Fields: Lessons from the Cambodian Genocide.* Lubbock: Texas Tech Univ. Press, 2005.

———. *The Rise and Demise of Democratic Kampuchea.* Boulder, CO: Westview Press, 1984.

Eviota, Elizabeth Uy. *The Political Economy of Gender: Women and the Sexual Division of Labor in the Philippines.* London: Zed Books, 1992.

Federici, Silvia. *Caliban and the Witch: Women, the Body and Primitive Accumulation.* Brooklyn: Autonomedia, 2004.

Fine, Benjamin, and Alfredo Saad-Filho. *Marx's "Capital."* 5th ed. New York: Pluto, 2010.

Flavin, William. "Planning for Conflict Termination and Post-conflict Success." *Parameters* 33, no. 3 (2003): 95–112.

Fortunai, Leopoldina. *The Arcane of Reproduction: Housework, Prostitution, Labor and Capital.* Translated by Hillary Creek. Brooklyn: Autonomedia, 1995.

Frieson, Kate. "The Political Nature of Democratic Kampuchea." *Pacific Affairs* 61, no. 3 (1988): 405–27.

Galtung, Johan. "Violence, Peace, and Peace Research." *Journal of Peace Research* 6, no. 3 (1969): 167–91.

Goldman, Wendy Z. *Women, the State, and Revolution: Soviet Family Policy and Social Life, 1917–1936.* Cambridge: Cambridge Univ. Press, 1993.

Gupta, Akhil. *Red Tape: Bureaucracy, Structural Violence, and Poverty in India.* Durham, NC: Duke Univ. Press, 2012.

Hamre, John J., and Gordon R. Sullivan. "Toward Postconflict Reconstruction." *Washington Quarterly* 25, no. 4 (2002): 85–96.

Harvey, David. *A Companion to Marx's "Capital."* New York: Verso, 2010.

Hearden, Patrick. *The Tragedy of Vietnam: Causes and Consequences.* 2nd ed. New York: Pearson Longman, 2005.

Heder, Steve. *Cambodian Communism and the Vietnamese Model: Imitation and Independence, 1930–1975.* Bangkok: White Lotus Press, 2004.

Heinrich, Michael. *An Introduction to the Three Volumes of Karl Marx's "Capital."* New York: Monthly Review Press, 2004.

Helmers, Kent. "Rice in the Cambodian Economy: Past and Present." In *Rice Production in Cambodia*, edited by Harry J. Nesbitt, 1–14. Manila: International Rice Research Institute, 1997.

Heuveline, Patrick, and Bunnak Poch. "Do Marriages Forget Their Past? Marital Stability in Post–Khmer Rouge Cambodia." *Demography* 43, no. 1 (2006): 99–125.

High, Holly, James R. Curran, and Gareth Robinson. "Electronic Records of the Air War over Southeast Asia: A Database Analysis." *Journal of Vietnamese Studies* 8, no. 4 (2014): 86–124.

Hinton, Alexander L. *Why Did They Kill? Cambodia in the Shadow of Genocide.* Berkeley: Univ. of California Press, 2005.

Hoefinger, Heidi. *Sex, Love and Money in Cambodia: Professional Girlfriends and Transactional Relationships.* New York: Routledge, 2014.

Horvath, Ron J., and Katherine D. Gibson. "Abstraction in Marx's Method." *Antipode* 16, no. 1 (1984): 12–25.

Huy, Ratana C. "Khmer Rouge Wedding." *Searching for the Truth* 25 (2002): 26–28.

Isaacs, Arnold. *Without Honor: Defeat in Cambodia.* Baltimore: Johns Hopkins Univ. Press, 1983.

Jackson, Karl D. "The Ideology of Total Revolution." In *Cambodia, 1975–1978: Rendezvous with Death*, edited by Karl D. Jackson, 37–78. Princeton, NJ: Princeton Univ. Press, 1989.

———. "Intellectual Origins of the Khmer Rouge." In *Cambodia, 1975–1978: Rendezvous with Death*, edited by Karl D. Jackson, 241–50. Princeton, NJ: Princeton Univ. Press, 1989.

Jacobsen, Trudy. *Lost Goddesses: The Denial of Female Power in Cambodian History.* Copenhagen: Nordic Institute of Asian Studies, 2008.

Jain, Neha. "Forced Marriage as a Crime against Humanity." *Journal of International Criminal Justice* 6, no. 5 (2008): 1013–32.

Javier, E. L. "Rice Ecosystems and Varieties." In *Rice Production in Cambodia*, edited by Harry J. Nesbitt, 39–81. Manila: International Rice Research Institute, 1997.

Jerome, William, and Adam Buick. "Soviet State Capitalism? The History of an Idea." *Survey: A Journal of Soviet and East European Studies* 26 (Jan. 1967): 58–71.

Johnstone, Monty. "Democratic Centralism." In *A Dictionary of Marxist Thought*, edited by Tom Bottomore, 134–37. 2nd ed. Malden, MA: Blackwell, 1991.

Ka-Kui, Tse. "Agricultural Collectivization and Socialist Construction: The Soviet Union and China." *Dialectical Anthropology* 2, no. 3 (1977): 199–221.

Kalecki, Michal. *Essays on Developing Economies*. Hassocks, UK: Harvester Press, 1976.

Kamm, Henry. *Report from a Stricken Land*. New York: Arcade, 1998.

Karkaria, Zal. "Failure through Neglect: The Women's Policies of the Khmer Rouge." Master's thesis, Concordia Univ., 2003.

Kasumi, Nakagawa. *Gender-Based Violence during the Khmer Rouge Regime: Stories of Survivors from the Democratic Kampuchea (1975–1979)*. Phnom Penh: n.p., 2007.

Kiernan, Ben. "The American Bombardment of Kampuchea, 1969–1973." *Vietnam Generation* 1, no. 1 (1989): 4–41.

———. *How Pol Pot Came to Power: A History of Communism in Kampuchea, 1930–1975*. London: Verso, 1985.

———. "Origins of Khmer Communism." *Southeast Asian Affairs* (1981): 161–80.

———. *The Pol Pot Regime: Policies, Race and Genocide in Cambodia under the Khmer Rouge, 1975–1979*. New Haven, CT: Yale Univ. Press, 1996.

Kiernan, Ben, and Taylor Owen. "Making More Enemies than We Kill? Calculating U.S. Bomb Tonnages Dropped on Laos and Cambodia, and Weighing Their Implications." *Asia-Pacific Journal* 13, no. 16 (2015): 1–9.

Kirsch, Scott, and Don Mitchell. "The Nature of Things: Dead Labor, Nonhuman Actors, and the Persistence of Marxism." *Antipode* 36, no. 4 (2004): 687–705.

Knox, Paul, and John Agnew. *The Geography of the World Economy*. 2nd ed. New York: Edward Arnold, 1994.

Knox, Paul, John Agnew, and Linda McCarthy. *The Geography of the World Economy*. 4th ed. New York: Edward Arnold, 2003.

Ledgerwood, Judy L. "Changing Khmer Conceptions of Womanhood: Women, Stories and the Social Order." PhD diss., Cornell Univ., 1990.

————. "Khmer Kinship: The Matriliny/Matriarchy Myth." *Journal of Anthropological Research* 51, no. 3 (1995): 247–62.

————. "Politics and Gender: Negotiating Changing Cambodian Ideas of the Proper Woman." *Asia Pacific Viewpoint* 37, no. 2 (1996): 139–52.

Ledgerwood, Judy L., and John Vijghen. "Decision-Making in Rural Khmer Villages." In *Cambodia Emerges from the Past: Eight Essays*, edited by Judy Ledgerwood, 109–50. DeKalb: Center for Southeast Asian Studies, Northern Illinois Univ., 2002.

Lee, Susan H. *"Rice Plus": Widows and Economic Survival in Rural Cambodia.* New York: Routledge, 2006.

Lefebvre, Henri. *The Production of Space.* London: Blackwell, 1991.

Lenin, Vladimir I. *Essential Works of Lenin: "What Is to Be Done?" and Other Writings.* Edited by Henry M. Christman. New York: Dover, 1987.

LeVine, Peg. *Love and Dread in Cambodia: Weddings, Births, and Ritual Harm under the Khmer Rouge.* Singapore: National Univ. of Singapore Press, 2010.

Li, Tania Murray. "To Make Live or Let Die? Rural Dispossession and the Protection of Surplus Populations." *Antipode* 41, no. s1 (2009): 66–93.

Lin, Canchu, and Yueh-Ting Lee. "The Constitutive Rhetoric of Democratic Centralism: A Thematic Analysis of Mao's Discourse on Democracy." *Journal of Contemporary China* 22, no. 7 (2013): 148–65.

Locard, Henri. *Pol Pot's Little Red Book: The Sayings of Angkar.* Chiang Mai, Thailand: Silkworm Books, 2004.

London, Jonathan. "Viet Nam and the Making of Market-Leninism." *Pacific Review* 22, no. 3 (2009): 375–99.

Louw, Stephen. "In the Shadows of the Pharaohs: The Militarization of Labour Debate and Classical Marxist Theory." *Economy and Society* 29, no. 3 (2009): 239–63.

Luxemburg, Rosa. *The Accumulation of Capital.* Translated by Agnes Schwarzschild. New York: Routledge, 2010.

Mam, Kalyanee. "The Endurance of the Cambodian Family under the Khmer Rouge Regime: An Oral History." In *Genocide and Rwanda: New Perspectives*, edited by Susan E. Cook, 127–71. New Haven, CT: Yale Center for International and Area Studies, 2004.

————. "An Oral History of Family Life under the Khmer Rouge." Working Paper GS10, Yale Center for International and Area Studies Working Paper

Series. New Haven, CT: Yale Center for International and Area Studies, 1999.

Mandel, Ernest. *An Introduction to Marxist Economic Theory.* New York: Pathfinder, 1970.

Marx, Karl. *Capital: A Critique of Political Economy.* Vol. 1. Translated by Ben Fowkes. New York: Penguin, 1990.

———. *Capital: A Critique of Political Economy.* Vol. 2. Translated by David Fernbach. New York: Penguin, 1978.

———. *Capital: A Critique of Political Economy.* Vol. 3. Translated by David Fernbach. New York: Penguin, 1991.

———. *The Class Struggles in France, 1848 to 1850.* Lexington, KY: Aristeau Books, 2012.

———. *A Contribution to the Critique of Political Economy.* Translated by S. W. Ryazanskaya. New York: International, 1970.

———. *Economic and Philosophic Manuscripts of 1844.* Translated by Martin Milligan. Amherst, NY: Prometheus Books, 1988.

———. *Grundrisse: Foundations of the Critique of Political Economy.* Translated by Martin Nicolaus. New York: Penguin, 1993.

———. "The Poverty of Philosophy." In *Karl Marx: Selected Writings*, edited by David McLellan, 219–20. Oxford: Oxford Univ. Press, 2000.

Marx, Karl, and Friedrich Engels. *The Communist Manifesto.* Translated by Samuel Moore. Chicago: Charles H. Kerr, 1945.

———. *The German Ideology: Including Theses on Feuerbach and Introduction to the Critique of Political Economy.* Amherst, NY: Prometheus Books, 1988.

Matar, Linda. "Twilight of 'State Capitalism' in Formerly 'Socialist' Arab States." *Journal of North African Studies* 18, no. 3 (2013): 416–30.

Mbembe, Achille. "Necropolitics." *Public Culture* 15, no. 1 (2003): 11–40.

McDowell, Linda. *Gender, Identity & Place: Understanding Feminist Geographies.* Minneapolis: Univ. of Minnesota Press, 1999.

McIntyre, Kevin. "Geography as Destiny: Cities, Villages and Khmer Rouge Orientalism." *Comparative Studies in Society and History* 38, no. 4 (1996): 730–58.

Meng, Xin, Nancy Qian, and Pierre Yared. "The Institutional Causes of China's Great Famine, 1959–1961." Paper presented at the Centre for Economic Policy Research's Development Economics Symposium. http://www.cepr.org/meets/wkcn/7/780/papers/Qianfinal.pdf.

Mertha, Andrew. *Brothers in Arms: Chinese Aid to the Khmer Rouge, 1975–1979.* Ithaca, NY: Cornell Univ. Press, 2014.

Mies, Maria. *Patriarchy and Accumulation on a World Scale: Women in the International Division of Labor.* London: Zed Books, 1986.

Milios, John. "Marxist Theory and Marxism as Mass Ideology: The Effects of the Collapse of 'Really Existing Socialism' on West European Marxism." *Rethinking Marxism* 8, no. 4 (1995): 61–74.

Ministry of Culture and Fine Arts and the Documentation Center of Cambodia. *The Forced Transfer: The Second Evacuation of People during the Khmer Rouge Regime.* Phnom Penh: Documentation Center of Cambodia, 2014.

Mitchell, Don. "Dead Labor: The Geography of Workplace Violence in America and Beyond." *Environment and Planning A* 32, no. 5 (2000): 761–68.

———. "Dead Labor and the Political Economy of Landscape: California Living, California Dying." In *Handbook of Cultural Geography*, edited by Kay Anderson, Steve Pile, and Nigel Thrift, 233–48. London: Sage, 2003.

Mosyakov, Dmitry. "The Khmer Rouge and the Vietnamese Communists: A History of Their Relations as Told in the Soviet Archive." Available at the Cambodian Genocide Project, Yale Univ. http://www.yale.edu/gsp/Mosyakov.Doc.

Myslik, Wayne D. "Renegotiating the Social/Sexual Identities of Places: Gay Communities as Safe Havens or Sites of Resistance?" In *BodySpace: Destabilizing Geographies of Gender and Sexuality*, edited by Nancy Duncan, 156–69. London: Routledge, 1996.

Neale, Jonathan. *A People's History of the Vietnam War.* New York: New Press, 2003.

Nesbitt, Henry J., and Chan Phaloeun. "Rice-Based Farming Systems." In *Rice Production in Cambodia*, edited by Harry J. Nesbitt, 31–37. Manila: International Rice Research Institute, 1997.

Nhem, Boraden. *The Khmer Rouge: Ideology, Militarism, and the Revolution That Consumed a Generation.* Santa Barbara: Praeger, 2013.

Oesterheld, Christian. "Cambodian-Thai Relations during the Khmer Rouge Regime: Evidence from the East German Diplomatic Archives." *Silpakorn University Journal of Social Sciences, Humanities, and Arts* 14, no. 2 (2014): 161–82.

Office of the Co-Investigating Judges. *Closing Order.* Case File No. 002/19-09-2007-ECCC-OCIJ. http://www.eccc.gov.kh/en.

Office of the Co-Prosecutors. *Co-Prosecutors' Rule 66 Final Submission (Public Redacted Version).* Case File No. 002/19/09/2007-ECCC/OCIJ. http://www.eccc.gov.kh/en.

Ollman, Bertell. *Alienation: Marx's Conception of Man in Capitalist Society.* 2nd ed. New York: Cambridge Univ. Press, 1976.

Ovesen, Jan, and Ing-Britt Trankell. *Cambodians and Their Doctors: A Medical Anthropology of Colonial and Post-colonial Cambodia*. Copenhagen: Nordic Institute of Asian Studies, 2010.

Owen, Taylor, and Ben Kiernan. "Bombs over Cambodia." *Walrus Magazine* (Oct. 2006): 62–69.

Paige, Jeffery M. *Agrarian Revolutions: Social Movements and Export Agriculture in the Underdeveloped World*. New York: Free Press, 1975.

Paolucci, Paul. *Marx's Scientific Dialectics: A Methodological Treatise for a New Century*. Chicago: Haymarket Books, 2007.

Peet, Richard. *Global Capitalism: Theories of Societal Development*. New York: Routledge, 1991.

———. "Materialism, Social Formation, and Socio-spatial Relations: An Essay in Marxist Geography." *Cahiers de Géographie du Québec* 22, no. 56 (1978): 147–57.

Petras, James. "State Capitalism and the Third World." *Development and Change* 8, no. 1 (1977): 1–17.

Pheng, Rasy. "Discovery of the Sre Lieu Mass Grave." *Searching for the Truth* (Second Quarter 2007): 17–19.

Phuong, Chan Pranith. "Forced Marriage to Avoid the Death." *Searching for the Truth* (Third Quarter 2013): 18–19.

Pijpers, Bert. *Kampuchea: Undoing the Legacy of Pol Pot's Water Control System*. Dublin: Trócaire, 1989.

Ponchaud, François. *Cambodia Year Zero*. Translated by Nancy Amphoux. New York: Holt, Rinehart, and Winston, 1978.

Porter, Gareth. "Vietnamese Communist Policy toward Kampuchea, 1930–1970." In *Revolution and Its Aftermath: Eight Essays*, edited by David P. Chandler and Ben Kiernan, 57–98. New Haven, CT: Yale Univ., Southeast Asia Studies, 1983.

Postone, Moishe. *Time, Labor, and Social Domination: A Reinterpretation of Marx's Critical Theory*. New York: Cambridge Univ. Press, 1993.

Potter, Robert B., Tony Binns, Jennifer A. Elliott, and David Smith. *Geographies of Development*. 2nd ed. New York: Pearson/Prentice Hall, 2004.

Prados, John. *Vietnam: The History of an Unwinnable War, 1945–1975*. Lawrence: Univ. Press of Kansas, 2009.

Procknow, Greg. "Human Resource Development in Democratic Kampuchea, 1975–1979." *Human Resource Development Review* 13, no. 3 (2014): 369–88.

Prum, Samon. "A Wish to See the Khmer Rouge Tribunal." *Searching for the Truth* (Third Quarter 2006): 44–47.

Read, Jason. *The Micro-politics of Capital: Marx and the Prehistory of the Present.* Albany: State Univ. Press of New York, 2003.

Resnick, Stephen, and Richard Wolff. "Between State and Private Capitalism: What Was Soviet 'Socialism'?" *Rethinking Marxism* 7, no. 1 (1994): 9–30.

———. *Class Theory and History: Capitalism and Communism in the U.S.S.R.* New York: Routledge, 2002.

———. "State Capitalism in the USSR? A High-Stakes Debate." *Rethinking Marxism* 6, no. 2 (1993): 46–68.

Rostow, Walter W. *The Stages of Growth: A Non-communist Manifesto.* Cambridge: Cambridge Univ. Press, 1960.

Saunders, Peter, and Peter Williams. "The Constitution of the Home: Towards a Research Agenda." *Housing Studies* 3, no. 2 (1988): 81–93.

Sayer, Andrew, and Richard Walker. *The New Social Economy: Reworking the Division of Labor.* Cambridge, MA: Blackwell, 1992.

Schulzinger, Robert D. *A Time for War: The United States and Vietnam, 1941–1975.* New York: Oxford Univ. Press, 1997.

Schurmann, Herbert F. "Organizational Principles of the Chinese Communists." *China Quarterly* 2 (Apr.–June 1960): 47–58.

Seekins, Donald. "Historical Setting." In *Cambodia: A Country Study,* edited by R. R. Ross, 3–71. Washington, DC: US Government Printing Office, 1990.

Seng, Vatey. *The Price We Paid: A Life Experience in the Khmer Rouge Regime, Cambodia.* Lincoln, NE: iUniverse, 2005.

Shawcross, William. *Sideshow: Kissinger, Nixon, and the Destruction of Cambodia.* Rev. ed. New York: Cooper Square Press, 2002.

Sheppard, Eric. "Competition in Space and between Places." In *A Companion to Economic Geography,* edited by Eric Sheppard and Trevor Barnes, 169–86. Malden, MA: Blackwell, 2000.

Short, Philip. *Pol Pot: Anatomy of a Nightmare.* New York: Henry Holt, 2004.

Singham, A. W. "The Fifth Summit Conference of the Non-Aligned Movement." *Black Scholar* 8, no. 3 (1976): 2–9.

Slocomb, Margaret. "The Nature and Role of Ideology in the Modern Cambodian State." *Journal of Southeast Asian Studies* 37, no. 3 (2006): 375–95.

———. *The People's Republic of Kampuchea, 1979–1989: The Revolution after Pol Pot.* Chiang Mai, Thailand: Silkworm Books, 2003.

Smith, Neil. *Uneven Development: Nature, Capital, and the Production of Space*. 3rd ed. Athens: Univ. of Georgia Press, 2008.

Smith, Tony. "The Underdevelopment of Development Literature: The Case of Dependency Theory." *World Politics* 31, no. 2 (1979): 247–88.

Sommerville, John. "Marxist Ethics, Determinism, and Freedom." *Philosophy and Phenomenological Research* 28, no. 1 (1967): 17–23.

Stalin, Joseph. *Dialectical and Historical Materialism*. New York: Prism Key Press, 2013.

Straus, Scott. "Organic Purity and the Role of Anthropology in Cambodia and Rwanda." *Patterns of Prejudice* 35, no. 2 (2001): 47–62.

Tassin, Kristin S. "'Lift Up Your Head, My Brother': Nationalism and the Genesis of the Non-Aligned Movement." *Journal of Third World Studies* 23, no. 1 (2006): 147–68.

Thion, Serge. "The Cambodian Idea of Revolution." In *Revolution and Its Aftermath: Eight Essays*, edited by David P. Chandler and Ben Kiernan, 10–33. New Haven, CT: Yale Univ., Southeast Asia Studies, 1983.

Todaro, Michael P. *Economic Development in the Third World*. 4th ed. New York: Longman, 1989.

Tomlinson, Brian R. "What Was the Third World?" *Journal of Contemporary History* 38, no. 2 (2003): 307–21.

Tully, John. *A Short History of Cambodia: From Empire to Survival*. Crow's Nest, Australia: Allen & Unwin, 2005.

Turok, Ben. "Zambia's System of State Capitalism." *Development and Change* 11, no. 3 (1980): 455–78.

Twining, Charles. "The Economy." In *Cambodia, 1975–1978: Rendezvous with Death*, edited by Karl D. Jackson, 109–50. Princeton, NJ: Princeton Univ. Press, 1989.

Tyner, James A. *America's Strategy in Southeast Asia: From the Cold War to the Terror War*. Boulder, CO: Rowman & Littlefield, 2007.

———. *Genocide and the Geographical Imagination: Life and Death in Germany, China, and Cambodia*. Lanham, MD: Rowman & Littlefield, 2012.

———. *Landscape, Memory, and Post-violence in Cambodia*. London: Rowman & Littlefield International, 2017.

Tyner, James, Samuel Henkin, Savina Sirik, and Sokvisal Kimsroy. "Phnom Penh during the Cambodian Genocide: A Case of Selective Urbicide." *Environment and Planning A* 46, no. 8 (2014): 1873–91.

Tyner, James A., Sokvisal Kimsroy, and Savina Sirik. "Nature, Poetry, and Public Pedagogy: The Poetic Geographies of the Khmer Rouge." *Annals of the Association of American Geographers* 105, no. 6 (2015): 1285–99.

Tyner, James A., and Stian Rice. "Cambodia's Political Economy of Violence: Space, Time, and Genocide under the Khmer Rouge, 1975–79." *Genocide Studies International* 10, no. 1 (2016): 84–94.

Valentino, Benjamin A. *Final Solutions: Mass Killing and Genocide in the 20th Century.* Ithaca, NY: Cornell Univ. Press, 2004.

Vickery, Michael. *Cambodia, 1975–1982.* Chiang Mai, Thailand: Silkworm, 1984.

———. "Democratic Kampuchea: Themes and Variations." In *Revolution and Its Aftermath: Eight Essays,* edited by David P. Chandler and Ben Kiernan, 99–135. New Haven, CT: Yale Univ., Southeast Asia Studies, 1983.

Vilim, Laura. "'Keeping Them Alive, One Gets Nothing; Killing Them, One Loses Nothing': Prosecuting Khmer Rouge Medical Practices as Crimes against Humanity." http://www.dccam.org/Tribunal/Analysis/pdf/Prosecuting_Khmer_Rouge_Medical_Practices_as_Crimes_Against_Humanity.pdf.

Vogel, Lise. *Marxism and the Oppression of Women: Toward a Unitary Theory.* Chicago: Haymarket Books, 2013.

Waller, Michael. *Democratic Centralism: An Historical Commentary.* Manchester: Manchester Univ. Press, 1981.

Warner, Geoffrey. "Leaving Vietnam: Nixon, Kissinger and Ford, 1969–1975. Part One: January 1969–January 1972." *International Affairs* 87, no. 6 (2011): 1485–1506.

Weeks, Kathi. *The Problem with Work: Feminism, Marxism, Antiwork Politics, and Postwork Imaginaries.* Durham, NC: Duke Univ. Press, 2011.

Weikart, Richard. "Marx, Engels, and the Abolition of the Family." *History of European Ideas* 18, no. 5 (1994): 657–72.

Willmott, William W. "Analytical Errors of the Kampuchean Communist Party." *Pacific Affairs* 54 (July 1981): 209–27.

Wolff, Richard. *Democracy at Work: A Cure for Capitalism.* Chicago: Haymarket Books, 2012.

Index

"actually existing socialism," xxi, 19
aerial bombing: in Cambodia, 48–57, 158–59, 193; in Vietnam, 44
Agamben, Giorgio, 36
Aitken, Stuart, 166–69
Albritton, Robert, 138–39, 148
alienation, xiii, 22, 69, 130, 134, 195
Amin, Samir, 3
Angkar, 38, 92, 147, 151, 175
autarky, 3–4, 7

Bandung Conference, 71–72
base people, 80–81, 92, 147, 154–55, 161–62
base-superstructure, 13–17, 148
Becker, Elizabeth, 171
Brown, Heather, 164
"building socialism," 69, 93, 131, 175, 190, 195
Bultmann, Daniel, 131–32

Cambodia: French colonialism in, 29–32; independence, 32–33; pre-colonial, 25–26
Cambodian Civil War, 44–45, 48–57, 59–62, 91, 187
Cambodian genocide, xxi, 1–2, 11, 193

capitalism, 15, 22–23, 110–11, 121, 164–65, 194
Chandler, David, xiii, xvii, 33, 49, 145
China, 5, 8, 33–34, 41, 45, 50, 77, 90, 116, 180, 195
class analysis, xiv, 9–17, 37–38, 194
Cold War, xxi, 71, 156, 193
colonialism, 71–72, 74, 111
commerce, 4–5
commodities, 110–11, 116, 138, 180
communism, xiii, 2–3, 11, 69
Communist Party of Kampuchea (CPK): Central Committee, 80; interpretations of, 1–3, 194–95; and Non-Aligned Movement, 71–77, 96; origins of, 20–21, 34–36, 38–42, 58, 63; postconflict reconstruction and, 62–63; Standing Committee, 4–5, 7–8, 80, 84–85, 89–90, 120, 123, 177
comparative advantage, 113, 115
consciousness: building, 79, 131–32; political, xi, 11, 23, 92, 133, 186; revolutionary, 70
constant capital, 178–80
consumption, 19, 112, 178, 181–84
contradictions, 22
currency, 4–6, 123–24, 182–84

DeFalco, Randle, 4, 157
democratic centralism, 77–80, 89–90
Democratic Kampuchea: administrative structure, 84–89, 115; citizenship, 80–83, 91–92, 154; constitution, 80, 184; cooperatives, 63, 65–67; democratic centralism and, 77–80, 89–90; Four-Year Plan, xv, xx, 11, 107, 110–11, 113, 119, 123–24, 132, 150, 153; governance, 70, 77–91; health care, 142–48, 186; import-substitution industrialization and, 111–12, 185, 193; integrated autonomy, 89; "letting die" in, 151–58; life in, 139–42, 148–51; ministries, 84; nature and, 131–33, 190–91; Non-Aligned Movement and, 71–77, 111, 194; People's Representative Assembly, 83–84; philosophical foundation, 6–7, 70, 78
Democratic Republic of Vietnam (DRV), 28–29, 33, 43, 49
determinism, 12
dialectics, 9, 22, 77, 131, 136
dictatorship of the proletariat, 36–37, 67, 77
disproportionate revenge, 175
division of labor, 12–13, 113, 137, 161
Domosh, Mona, 169

Ebihara, May, 161
Em, Sokhym, 157
Etcheson, Craig, xiii
evacuation of cities, 64–65
expanded reproduction, 178–80
exploitation, 19, 69, 116, 129, 134, 180, 185, 194

family: under capitalism, 166–70; in general, 165–66; under Khmer Rouge, 171–74; Lenin and, 170–71; Marx and, 166–67; in precolonial Cambodia, 160–62
famine, 60–61
Fanon, Frantz, 3
food rations, 116–29, 182–84, 186
forced marriages, 160–63
forces of production, 13
foreign trade, 4–6, 7–8, 112–13, 179–80
Franco-Vietminh War, 28–29, 32, 33
French Indochina, 24–28, 29, 103–4
FUNK (Front Uni National du Kampuchea), 50

gender, 173–74
genocide, xv–xix
geopolitics, 51, 156
"great leap forward," 37, 70
GRUNK (Gouvernement Royal d'Union Nationale du Kampuchéa), 20–21, 50
Gulf of Tonkin Resolution, 43–44
Gupta, Akhil, 154

Harvey, David, xx, 117, 122
Heder, Steve, xiii, 31–32
Hinton, Alex, xvi, 47, 57, 136, 175
Ho Chi Minh, 28–29, 31
"Ho Chi Minh Trail," 39, 43
Hou Yuon, 50, 84
Hu Nim, 50, 84

Ieng Sary, 8, 40, 74–75, 84
Ieng Thirith, 84
imperialism, 24

import-substitution industrialization, 18, 111–12, 185, 193
indifference, 18, 135–37, 148, 159
intentionality, 153–54
international trade, 4–6, 179
irrigation, 106–9
Isaacs, Arnold, 50, 59–60

Jackson, Karl, 3, 6, 11
Jacobsen, Trudy, 174
Johnson, Lyndon B., 43

Kasumi, Nakagawa, 174
Kautsky, Karl, 2
Kennedy, John F., 42–43
Keo Meas, 20–21, 31, 40–41
Keo Moni, 31
Khieu Samphan, 50, 72–73, 83–84, 157
Khmer People's Revolutionary Party (KPRP), 20, 32, 33–35, 38, 40
Khmer Rouge: origins, 20–21; recruitment, 48–57
Khmer Vietminh, 20, 34, 58
Kiernan, Ben, xiii, 35
Koh Sla Dam, 187–89

labor: dead, 189–91, 192; division of, 12–13, 125–26; necessary, 119; nonproductive, 149–50, 173; productive, 149–50, 159; as purposeful activity, 14–15, 132; socially necessary, 120–21, 136, 164
Landscale, Edward, 42–43
Laos, 24, 33
Ledgerwood, Judy, 173–74

Lefebvre, Henri, xiii
Leninism, 2, 10, 18, 23–24, 32, 36–38, 45, 48, 63, 68, 77–78, 84
"letting die," 139, 151–58
LeVine, Peg, 162–63
life, 138, 148–51, 184–85
Locard, Henri, 154–55
Lon Nol, 39, 45–46, 49–51, 60, 91
Lukács, Georg, 2
Luxemburg, Rosa, 2, 176

Mam, Kalyanee, 160, 174–75
Maoism, 2, 10
marriage, 160–63, 169
Marxism, xv–xix, 36–37, 68, 116–29, 130–31
Marxist critique, xix–xxi, 9–17, 163–65, 165–71
mass graves, 189–93
materialism, materialist, xii, 10–11
means of production, 13, 22, 178, 194
medicine, 142–48
Mertha, Andrew, 5–6
Mitchell, Don, 189
mode of production, 9, 13–17, 22–23, 125, 185
money, 3, 110, 116–18, 182–84, 191

National Liberation Front (NLF), 39, 45–46
nature, 18, 129–33
necessary labor. See labor
new people, 80–81, 92, 94–95, 147, 154–55, 161–62
Ngo Dinh Diem, 43
Nhem, Boraden, 2, 4, 84
Nixon, Richard, 48–53, 60

Non-Aligned Movement, 18, 71–77, 96, 194
North Korea, 8, 180
North Vietnam. *See* Democratic Republic of Vietnam
Nuon Chea, 1, 40, 84

Paolucci, Paul, 16
People's Republic of China. *See* China
Phnom Penh, 38, 53, 58, 60, 64–66, 87, 91, 95, 104, 143, 146
Pol Pot, 6–8, 20–21, 35–36, 38, 40–42, 47, 50, 68–69, 84, 177–78, 195
postcolonialism, 7, 193, 195
postconflict reconstruction, 62–63, 66, 93, 96
Pracheachon (People's Group), 20, 34–35
production: for exchange, 118, 130, 134, 137, 165, 175, 178–79, 185, 194; in general, 130; social organization, 10, 129–30

Ramassage du paddy, 46, 106
rape, 174
Read, Jason, 124–25
relations of production, 13, 15
Ren Fung Company, 8
reproduction, 19, 174–84
Republic of Vietnam, 33, 39, 43
Resnick, Stephen, xiv, 11
revolution, xiii, 7, 18, 22–23, 36–38, 67–68, 195; in Vietnam, 27–28, 30–32, 33–34, 39
revolutionary stages, 37, 69
rice: in Cambodia, 98–103; competitive advantage of, 113–14, 191; production under French, 27, 29–30, 103–5;

production under Khmer Rouge, 92, 106–10, 114–16, 117–29, 186; production under Sihanouk regime, 105–6, 114; during revolution, 46, 54, 60, 106
Rostow, Walter, 42

Saloth Sar. *See* Pol Pot
Samlaut rebellion, 46–47
self-reliance, 3, 75–76, 112
sexual violence, 173–74
Shawcross, William, 53–54, 59
Sieu Heng, 31, 34–35, 39
Sihanouk, Norodom, 21, 32, 33–35, 39, 45–46, 49–50, 105, 195
socialism, 194
socially necessary labor. *See* labor
Son Ngoc Minh, 31, 34, 40
Son Sen, 40
So Phim, 31, 40
South Vietnam. *See* Republic of Vietnam
Soviet Union, 6, 11, 30, 33–34, 63, 77
Stalin, Stalinism, 2, 10
Standard Total View (STV), xi, xiv–xv, 62, 65, 106, 137, 141, 145, 156, 157–58, 162, 193
state capitalism, xiii–xiv, 9, 137, 194
State of Vietnam. *See* Republic of Vietnam
subsumption, 124–25, 149, 165
surplus production, 110–16
Sweden, 5, 8

Taiwan, 112
Thailand, 25, 180
Thion, Serge, xiii
Tou Samouth, 31, 35, 40

Trotsky, Leon, 2, 63
Twining, Charles, 3, 128–29

United States of America, 6, 8, 29, 34, 42–45, 48–57, 59–62, 105, 157–59, 195
utopia, 4, 65, 135

value: absolute surplus, 119, 125, 129; exchange, 110–11, 118, 122; indifference to use, 136, 148–50; relative surplus, 116–29; surplus, 117–18, 138, 149, 178–80; use, 110, 122
vanguard, 32, 38, 66, 185, 194

variable capital, 178–80
Vickery, Michael, xiv, 8, 141, 162
Vietnam, 24–29, 33–34, 40–41. *See also* Democratic Republic of Vietnam; Republic of Vietnam
Vietnam War, 42–45
violence, 153–54, 191–92, 195
Vorn Vet, 40, 84

war communism, 63–64
Wolff, Richard, xiv, 10, 11, 194
Workers' Party of Kampuchea, 20, 40

Yugoslavia, 5, 8, 180
Yun Yat, 84

James A. Tyner is a professor in the Department of Geography at Kent State University. A graduate of the University of Southern California, Professor Tyner is the author of several books, including *War, Violence, and Population: Making the Body Count* (2009), winner of the Meridian Book Award from the Association of American Geographers, and *Landscape, Memory, and Post-violence in Cambodia* (2017).